Linking Plant-Based Enterprises and Local Communities to Biodiversity Conservation in Nepal Himalaya

Bhishma Prasad Subedi

ADROIT PUBLISHERS

Published by
ADROIT PUBLISHERS
4675/21, Ganpati Bhawan, Ansari Road,
Daryaganj, New Delhi-110 002
Phones : 011-23266030

Distributors
AKHIL BOOK DISTRIBUTORS
e-mail: akhilbooks@yahoo.com
akhilbooks@hotmail.com

ISBN : 81-87392-70-3

Laser Typeset by
Arpit Printographers
E-mail : arpitprinto@yahoo.com

Printed in India on behalf of
M/s Adroit Publishers by
Arpit Printographers
Ph. : 09350809192, 011-22825424

Preface and Acknowledgment

The present study identifies and analyzes linkages among biodiversity, enterprises and communities in high mountain areas of Nepal. Amidst an increasingly wider endeavor and research towards seeking solutions to conservation problems, the research has attempted to identify strategies and approaches that can be adopted to bring favorable changes in government policies and market structure, and effectively implement conservation programs. This study focuses on understanding the functioning of enterprise-oriented community forest management in high mountains of Nepal in relation to changes in livelihood condition of communities and status of forests and meadows. An analysis is subsequently made regarding the factors that can promote synergy between economic incentives to communities and conservation of forests and meadows from which resources are derived for enterprises.

The study has been presented in eight chapters. The first three chapters define the research agenda, with details in rationale, objectives, methodology, study area, and status of biodiversity, vegetation, and conservation approaches in Nepal. Findings are presented in next four chapters, and the eighth chapter discusses the findings in an integrated way.

I am indebted to a number of persons and organizations who have given their hands for this research. My first and foremost gratitude goes to my guide Prof. Surendra P. Singh, FNA for his inspiration, advice and insightful suggestions throughout the study period. I greatly value his all inputs, feedbacks, guidance during the data collection and help in developing the manuscript. I am thankful to Prof. R. P. Singh for his constant encouragement. Moreover, I would like to express earnest thankfulness to Dr. Jack Croucher, who promoted my interest in enterprise-oriented community forest management and encouraged for undertaking this research. I profoundly express gratitude to Prof. Kailash N. Pyakuryal of Tribhuvan University and Prof. William Burch, Jr. of Yale University for their advice, support and inspiration.

I appreciate the insightful and useful inputs from Surya Binayee, who assisted me during the entire research process. Assistance provided by Sushil Gyawali in collecting and organizing data as well as in generating computer charts is much appreciated. My sincere appreciation also goes to Shova Adhikari for proof reading and editorial support.

I cannot stand without giving thanks to the following ANSAB staff, who contributed to this study in various ways in implementing the interventions and collecting information: Indu Sapkota, Ram Acharya, Sony Baral, Navin Subedi, Ram Hari Subedi, Durga Regmi, Shambhu Charmakar, Bishnu Luintel, Nabaraj Pant, Chandika Amgai, and Gopal Sharma.

I pay honor to the staff of ANSAB partner NGOs and District Forest Offices, who accepted us to work with their programs and assisted with the project activities enthusiastically. Special thanks to Ann Koontz of Enterpriseworks Worldwide for her cooperation, support and involvement in the program. I also owe my gratitude to colleagues working in biodiversity, community forestry and NTFPs in Nepal, during the study period, all of whom contributed enthusiastically to the dialogue during the discussion and provided the necessary cooperation sought. I am grateful to my wife Kabita for her company, patience and support in all aspects of my life during the study period. I am equally thankful to my sons Bhabuk and Anuj. The knowledge and wisdom imparted to me from my late mother, late father (Prithvi Narayan Subedi) and brothers Narayan, Bhawani, Lok, and Bodh to a great extent shaped and sharpen the research idea.

I fondly acknowledge the financial support for the research provided from Biodiversity Conservation Network, Global Conservation Program, Ford Foundation and International Development Research Center. Finally, the people from the participating rural communities were, and will remain, in my mind all the time. If the research is going to help to improve their conditions even in trivial form, that will give me an immense pleasure in my life.

Bhishma P. Subedi

December 2004

CONTENTS

ABBREVIATIONS AND GLOSSARY

AA	Article of Association
ACP	Association of Craft Producers
ANSAB	Asia Network for Sustainable Agriculture and Bioresources
BCN	Biodiversity Conservation Network
BCP	Bhaktapur Craft Printer
BDS	Business Development Services
BPP	Biodiversity Profile Project
BSP	Biodiversity Support Program
CBFE	Community Based Forest Enterprise
CBO	Community Based Organization
CBS	Central Bureau of Statistics
CPFD	Community and Private Forestry Division
CECI	Canadian Center for International Studies and Co-operation
CF	Community Forest
CFUG	Community Forest Users Group
DDC	District Development Committee
DCSI	Department of Cottage and Small Scale Industry
DFO	District Forest Office (r)
DNPWC	Department of National Parks and Wildlife Conservation
DoF	Department of Forests
DPR	Department of Plant Resources
DSCO	District Soil Conservation Office
EFEA	Environment and Forest Enterprise Activity (project of USAID)?
EOCFM	Enterprise-oriented Community Forest Management
EWW	EnterpriseWorks World Wide
FAO	Food and Agriculture Organization
FECOFUN	Federation of Community Forest Users, Nepal
FGD	Focus Group Discussion
FNCCI	Federation of Nepalese Chambers of Commerce and Industry
FORESC	Forest Research and Survey Center
FRISP	Forest Resource Information System Project
FSC	Forest Stewardship Council
GDP	Gross Domestic Product
HDI	Human Development Index
HHs	Households

HMG	His Majesty's Government
HMGN	His Majesty's Government of Nepal
HOPL	Humla Oil Private Limited
HPPCL	Herbs Production and Processing Co. Ltd.
ICDP	Integrated Conservation and Development Project
IDRC	International Development Research Center
INGO	International Non Governmental Organization
IUCN	The World Conservation Union
LFP	Livlihoods and Forestry Programme
LRMP	Land Resources Mapping Project
MAPs	Medicinal and Aromatic Plants
MFSC	Ministry of Forests and Soil Conservation
MHPL	Malika Hand Made Paper Private Limited
MOPE	Ministry of Population and Environment
MoU	Memorandum of Understanding
MPFS	Master Plan for the Forestry Sector, 1988
NACFP	Nepal Australia Community Forestry Project
NCC	Nepal Chamber of Commerce
NFI	National Forest Inventory
NGO	Non Governmental Organization
NPP	Nepal Paper Products
NTFPs	Non-timber Forest Products
NUKCFP	Nepal UK Community Forestry Project
OP	Operational Plan (of CFUG)
PAR	Participatory Action Research
PAS	Protected Area System
SNV	Netherlands Development Organization
SPNP	Shey-phokusundo National Park
SSA	Subsector Analysis
TPC	Trade Promotion Center
UA	Uttaranchal
UAE	United Arab Emirates
UK	United Kingdom
USA	United States of America
VAT	Value Added Tax
VDC	Village Development Committee
VP	Van Panchayat
WHO	World Health Organization
WWF	World Wildlife Fund

Chapter 1

Identification and Rationale of Research Agenda

1.1 Introduction

Conservation of biodiversity along with its sustainable use and equitable benefit sharing is one of the major global concerns today. This particularly applies to Nepal Himalaya, which harbors one of the globally significant biodiversity hotspots and where poverty is acute and dependency of local communities on biodiversity high, with little alternatives for livelihoods. In such a situation the traditional approaches to biodiversity conservation – protected area models, regulatory measures with restrictions and bans, limited property rights and subsistence orientation even in participatory models – are neither practical, nor effective and sustainable. There are promising and nearly untapped opportunities: a) a rich and productive biodiversity from which enough goods, benefits and services of market value can be sustainably harnessed, b) local communities to take effective stewardship of their local biodiversity, and c) biodiversity-linked enterprises to generate meaningful incomes for improving the livelihoods of local communities. But the real scope of these is not known, and there are controversies and differences in opinions among the stakeholders with regard to approaches that link conservation and economic development, since little is known about the potentials of these three, let alone the supporting and restraining forces to achieve the potentials. More importantly, it is unknown whether or not the synergy can be established among the three elements for the conservation of biodiversity and sustainable livelihoods of local communities.

With the goal of contributing to the understanding of biodiversity conservation in the areas where local people are dependent on the use of biodiversity for day-to-day subsistence, this research examines each of these three elements (biodiversity, local communities and enterprises) and their interrelationships in view of local livelihoods and sustainable management (conservation). Our hypothesis is that by developing synergy among local communities, biodiversity and enterprises, it is possible to generate enough economic incentives to local communities for biodiversity conservation.

In the present study investigation process encompassed both a broader understanding of the subject matter and closer examinations of issues and their relationships. Review of literatures, wider interactions with key stakeholders both nationally and internationally (workshops, meetings, seminars, conferences, interviews and dialogues), and observations were used to get a broader understanding of local communities, biodiversity and enterprises in Nepal. Examinations of specific issues and their relationships were done through participatory action research (PAR) and case studies that involved experimentations, observations, interviews and dialogues. To examine the feasibility of enterprise-oriented community forestry, a PAR was done with 37 community forest user groups (CFUGs) in the districts of Humla, Jumla, Dolpa, Bajhang, Darchula and Dolakha. These districts and community groups were characterized by: recognition as global hotspot for biodiversity, acute poverty, very low development index, availability of commercial products, and dependency of local communities on forests and meadows. Additional criteria of habitat connectivity, community's interests to participate, and district level stakeholders priorities were used within the district for selecting the communities. A long-term involvement and deep interest of the researcher in the field of research topic provided the foundation to build on the understanding in the subject.

The thesis is divided in eight chapters. The Introduction chapter briefly presents the context and rationale for the research issue, states the objectives of the research, and finally presents definition of some key terms. The second chapter provides methodological approach, research plan, methods used for each of the study components, and study areas. The third chapter reviews the biodiversity status and conservation approaches. The review elaborates on the factors and components of biological diversity covering types of ecosystems and forest vegetation, species richness and endemism, and approaches of biodiversity conservation in Nepal.

Main findings and analyses are presented in four chapters (Chapter 4 to 7). The first three chapters provide a broad perspective on three components: biodiversity, enterprises and communities in terms of their status, prospects and challenges in relation to conservation and local livelihoods in Nepal. Prospects of biodiversity are examined in terms of community dependence, economic use potentials, changes in vegetation and their likely impact, and threats. The seventh chapter specifically examines the performance of enterprise-oriented community forest management in creating impacts on local livelihoods and biodiversity. The eighth chapter discusses the findings of the study and presents the conclusions.

1.2 Statement of the Problem and Rationale

Nepal is a land-locked, mountainous country, which occupies a large part of the central Himalaya and foothills covering one-third of the entire length of the Himalayan ranges. Its longitudinal range (80° 4' E to 88° 12' E) measures about 885 km, and altitudes range from 90 m in southern low land of Terai well up to the world's highest peak of 8,848 m above the sea level in the north, the Mount Everest. Physiographically, Nepal can be divided into five broad zones: high Himalayas, high mountains, middle hills, Siwaliks and Terai (see Map 1).

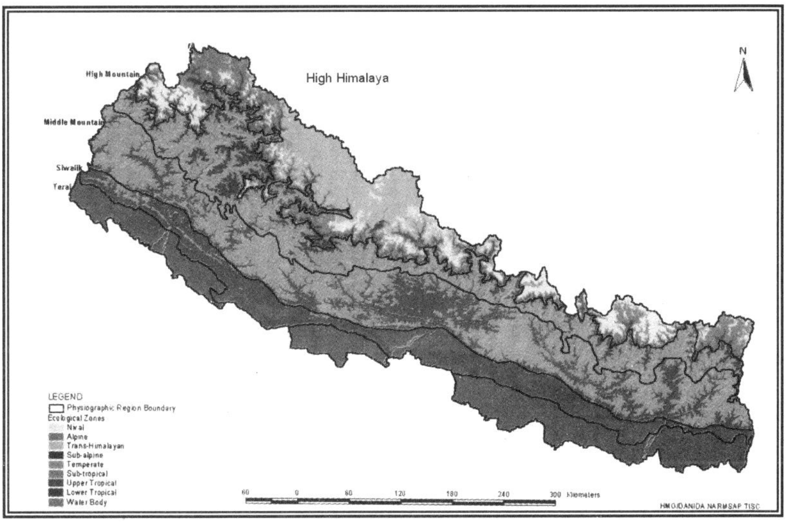

Map 1. Physiographic Zones of Nepal

While small in terms of surface area (1,47,181 square kilometer), Nepal is remarkably rich in species and ecosystem diversity, has high degree of endemism and ecosystem uniqueness, and offers diverse landuse patterns and biodiversity use practices. The diversity of the physiography caused by variations in topography and climate has greatly contributed towards the richness of vegetations in different parts of Nepal which include flora and fauna of tropical, sub-tropical, temperate, sub-alpine and alpine zones. Consequently, Nepal is divisible into 6 phyto-geographical provinces, 11 bioclimatic zones, 35 forest types, 75 vegetation types, and 118 ecosystems (Stainton 1972, Dobremez 1976).

Photo 1. NTFP trading in Humla (left); Ttransportation of sacs of NTFPs from Nepalgunj airport (right).

There has been considerable discussion regarding the economic potentials of forest resources during the last decade or so. Although the comprehensive assessment of economic value of these products (both timber and non-timber) has not yet been made, it is suggested that there is a potential for a multimillion industry from the forest products. For example, Edwards (1996) estimates that 10 to 15 thousand tons of NTFPs are harvested from the Middle and High Mountain belts of Nepal and the value of these NTFPs, which are almost all sold in India, is US$ 8.6 million each year. Kanel (1999) estimates this at US $19 million. The Ministry of Forests and Soil Conservation (MFSC) estimates a lost opportunity of about NRs 42 billion ($567 million) each year from the forest resources of Nepal (MFSC/World Bank draft). According to a survey more than 100 entrepreneurs along the east-west highway traded more than 100 NTFPs generating total sales of 1.5 billion Nepali Rupees (equivalent to US $26 million) in 1995 (Subedi 1997). However, reliable data from any source are lacking because of the secretive nature of transaction, difficult terrain, and porous borders with the neighboring countries. Most of the NTFPs collected in Nepal pass through the Nepal-India border market through a time-tested network of legal as well as illegal routes (Aryal 1993). In addition, about 800 species of NTFPs are used locally to provide medicines, foods, oils, fibers, dyes, incense, building materials, agricultural implements, etc (Edward 1996).

According to an estimate, the value of the most economically important NTFPs in world trade totals about US $11 billion annually (Iqbal 1995). The WHO (2002) estimates that global sales of herbal products in 2000 totalled US $60 billion. Growth in the natural products market is in a range of 3% to 20% (Grunwald 1994), which is on average 3 to 4 times greater than the average national economic growth rate. In future, with more and more emphasis on organic way of living and use of natural products in developed countries, NTFPs are likely to be demanded and diversified further in use and commerce. All these facts indicate that global markets for Nepal's NTFPs is large and demand trend for these products is increasing as more and more people from developed countries are attracted to natural products.

Nepal is equally rich in cultural heritage and diversity. People living in climatically hot areas in the south through the cold areas in the north are diversified into many social, cultural, ethnic and language groups. With at least forty ethnic groups and 92 spoken languages, Nepal's ethnic diversity is also noteworthy. The notable groups include Newars, Magars, Gurungs, Tamangs, Bhotias, Rais, Limbus, Sherpas and Tharus (HMGN 2002). These groups have developed their livelihood strategies, and over the time with the changes in environment and socio-economic conditions they have been adapting their livelihood strategies accordingly. This has given, over a long history of time, a multitude of artifacts and practices contributing to cultural wealth. The depth and richness of knowledge on traditional medical systems including Ayurveda, Amchi, Siddha, Unani, Naturopathy and Homeopathy is reflected by the prevalent practices of both codified and folk systems in Nepal.

The evolution of community forestry in Nepal shows quite promising prospects for the devolution of authority to local communities for the sustainable management and use of forest and meadows. The potential of sustainable management and use of common property resources such as forests and their products for the betterment of the poor and poorest has been recognized and taken into account in the government policies and plans, notably in Master Plan for Forestry Sector, the Tenth Five Year Plan (2002-2007) and Poverty Reduction Strategy Paper prepared on the basis of the Tenth Plan (MFSC 1988; HMGN 2002; HMGN 2003). The outcomes, both realized and potentials, of community forestry policy, program and practices in Nepal are applauded for both environmental and social governance (Gilmour et al. 1991; Jackson et al. 1998; Branny and Yadav 1998; Gautam et al. 2003; LFP 2003; Kanel 2004).

In spite of the enormous biological and cultural wealth, Nepal is one of the world's poorest (per capita GDP estimated at $269) and densely populated nations with average density of 158 people per square kilometer of surface area. Nearly 38% of Nepal's population lives at or below the absolute poverty line (MOPE 1998). The 2001 National Population Census estimates 23,151,423 people as the total population of Nepal (of which slightly over 50% are female) with an annual growth rate of 2.24%. According to the census, the estimated life

Photo 2. Rural people bringing grasses (Dolakha) and firewood (Dolpa) from community forests for their livelihood

expectancy at birth is 59.7 years, adult literacy is estimated at 53.7% (population aged 6 years and over) but only 25.1% among women. And the infant mortality rate is estimated as 64.1 per 1,000 live births (HMGN 2002). The population is unevenly distributed, with fairly high densities in the lower elevations in the south and in valleys in midlands and low densities in the highlands.

A significant portion of rural communities with very little livelihood options relies on the local biodiversity, particularly NTFPs. Collectors of these products generally belong to poorer sections of society and lack viable economic alternatives to uncontrolled collection. For example, in Karnali, a known hotspot for valuable NTFPs, 57% population lives below the poverty line. In spite of the stated goal of reducing the poverty from the government and development agencies, the poverty in these areas is on rise. For the poorest and disadvantaged members of the population in these remotest areas, NTFPs that grow in common property forests and meadows are the only accessible sources of livelihoods. In such a situation, dependency of local communities on biodiversity is very high.

The globally significant, rich biodiversity of Nepal Himalaya faces many kinds of threat. Internally the local people continue to rely on the forest and pasture areas to meet their need of fuel, fodder, timber, and a variety of non-timber forest products (NTFPs). The subsistence demand for these natural resources is increasing along with the population growth. However, the demand from the outside markets for the supply of NTFPs is one of the most serious threats. In most of the areas where collections are done from the resources under unregulated and open access properties, the increased demand from traders result in an increased extraction of natural resources. The demands have resulted in over-harvesting of some species in order to supply the markets of India and the developed world.

Although NTFPs were traditionally used by people from the time immemorial, their importance has been recognized only recently by government officials, professional foresters, researchers, donors, and policy makers. Until recently these products were understudied and neglected resources in Nepal. Several study-reports show that certain NTFP species are being overused and threatened (Edward 1994, 1996; Malla et al. 1995; Hertog 1995; Karki 1996; Sharma 1996; Subedi 1997). NTFPs are in a general state of decline because of the unregulated harvesting from the open access government controlled forests and meadows. In such a situation, the large and diverse resource base for a variety of NTFPs is difficult to conserve. Preliminary indications have shown a decreasing supply of NTFPs from some parts of the country. The challenge is that in many areas it is known, and in other areas suspected, that the diversity, quality, and availability of many species of NTFPs are decreasing.

However, biodiversity management focus is still on protected area system models. Conservation measures taken for both protected areas and outside are heavily focused on regulation, ban and restrictions. In areas where dependence for livelihoods is high on biodiversity, with little alternatives, or where high value commercial products are derived from biodiversity, the approaches of protecting the species through restriction and ban are not only ineffective (Olsen 1997; Olsen and Helles 1997), but also destructive to both nature and society. There is no recognition of enterprise-oriented management of biodiversity and still programs are based on subsistence mode which is capable of neither addressing conservation nor livelihoods and poverty reduction issues.

In this context, the challenges are how to turn the potentials of biodiversity including NTFPs in sustainable economic returns that meaningfully improve the economic conditions of the poor people who are also the stewards of the local biodiversity, and how to conserve biodiversity creating a synergy between the conservation and poverty reduction. Linking biodiversity conservation with enterprises and local communities is a complex social process that requires diverse technical activities (Fig 1.1). For this, an understanding of present and potential processes and functioning of biodiversity, local communities, and natural products based enterprises as well as their interactions are important.

Creating sufficient economic incentives to the communities for sustainable use and conservation of biodiversity and equitable benefit sharing is not straightforward and simple. Even the feasibility of enterprise-oriented, community-based management of biodiversity is not known, let alone the outcomes in terms of productivity, conservation and equity. The nature and characteristics of biodiversity (commercial value, production and production capacity, threats), local communities (property rights, production of goods, benefits and services, and institutional and technical capabilities to manage biological resources and enterprises), and enterprise (market, technology, financial and other business development services) can determine the context. The interrelationships among them may be defined or at least influenced by a number of factors, such as policy and regulatory environment, nature and functioning of markets, local capacities and external supports, practices of resource use and management, available technologies, and enterprise modalities.

These factors may interact among one another to produce desirable or undesirable results in creating economic incentives for conservation. The interplay gives rise to certain issues that need to be addressed to create a favorable environment leading to the desired processes and outcomes.

The outcome of the research would be useful to establish and promote the desired linkages between biodiversity conservation, NTFP enterprises and livelihoods generation of biodiversity dependent communities. The understanding would be useful to national or local governments, non-profit development agencies, private companies and others involved in the long term use, management and conservation of biodiversity together with local communities. With appropriate strategies in place, the interplay could be driven to lead to outcomes that are ecologically sound, financially viable, socially acceptable, and institutionally enforceable. Hence the examination of each of these elements, more particularly their interrelationships with respect to the generation of economic incentives and biodiversity conservation is chosen for the study.

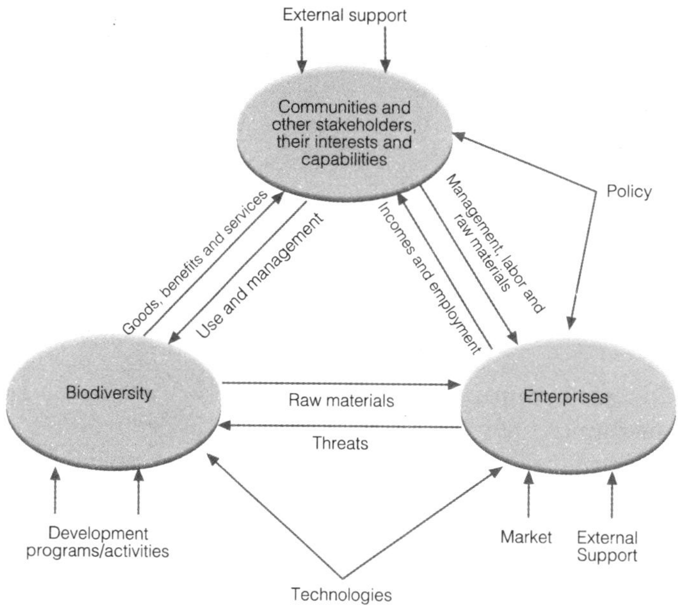

Figure 1.1 Diagrammatic representation of linkages of anthropogenic factors to biodiversity

1.3 Research Objectives

The goal of this research is to contribute to the understanding of biodiversity conservation in areas where local people are dependent on the use of biodiversity for day-to-day subsistence. More specifically, this research will increase our understanding of relationships among local communities, NTFP enterprises and biodiversity in Nepal Himalaya in relation to local livelihoods and biodiversity conservation. The specific objectives of this research are:

1. To understand from broader perspectives the status of biodiversity and conservation approaches in Nepal
2. To assess community dependence, economic use potentials and threats to biodiversity and factors, especially anthropogenic, affecting the threats in Nepal Himalaya
3. To identify key stakeholders and analyze their interdependence, interest and capabilities in non-timber forest products sub-sector in relation to economic incentives to local stewards of biodiversity
4. To assess the status and prospects of community-based forest enterprises, especially in non-timber forest products sub-sector in Nepal
5. To examine the prospects of community based forest management in relation to local livelihoods and conservation in Nepal
6. To analyze the prospects of enterprise-oriented, community-based biodiversity management and factors affecting its performance on generating economic incentives, social equity and conservation in 6 mountain districts of Nepal

The main approach of this study is to look into biodiversity, local communities and NTFP enterprises in an integrated way. This is also reflected in chapterization. For example, the chapter on study areas and method gives an idea of vegetation, anthropogenic influence on biodiversity and conditions of NTFP based enterprises. Similarly, monitoring approaches consider both communities and natural systems in relation to enterprise.

1.4 Definitions of Some Key Terms/Concepts Used

Biodiversity, or biological diversity, is the variety and variability of life. It includes diversity in terms of genes, species, ecosystems, and ecological processes that both support and result from this diversity.

Non-Timber Forest Products (NTFPs) include all goods of biological origin from forest, grassland or any land under similar use, excluding timber. Examples of NTFPs in Nepal include grasses and leaves; fuel wood; bamboo, rattans and canes; nuts, fruits, tubers and berries; barks; plant fibers; medicinal and aromatic products; resins; insect and insect products; and wild animals and birds.

An **enterprise** is defined as an organized economic activity with a motive of earning profits. Organized economic activities may include collection of forest products for sale, processing, trading, transporting, and manufacturing undertaken formally or informally. Community based enterprises are those being operated at rural areas, usually near a resource base that supplies raw materials, and that are planned and operated by local communities or individuals who are also the main stakeholders of local biodiversity, the condition of which will have direct effect on them.

Community Forest User Group (CFUG) means a user group registered for the management and utilization of a Community Forest.

In Nepal, **community forestry** involves the transfer of use rights and management responsibilities of one or more patches of forest, either natural or planted, to the local people who are formed in a specified forest user group (people who have traditionally used the forest and are prepared to take on its management). The term **forest management** encompasses both technical and social arrangements involved in the management of forests, including planting, protection, harvesting, and distribution of forest products.

According to Forest Act, 1993 "A Community Forest is defined as a National Forest handed over to a Users' Group for its development, protection, and utilization for collective benefits."

Equity implies quality of justice and fairness in which males, females, each caste, class or ethnic group of people and those who have been made disadvantaged and have been deprived access in the past have equal opportunity to utilize, conserve, and make benefit from the forest resources. Equity is a measure of how evenly the benefits and burdens of the community forestry activities are distributed among its stakeholders. Community forestry is also concerned with the empowerment of local people, especially those who are socially and economically disadvantaged such as the poor, women, the elderly and children. The goal of ensuring equitable distribution or improving the social structure for equity is one of the distinguishing characteristics of community forestry programs.

Chapter 2

Methodology: Study Framework and Study Area

2.1 General Approach and Strategy

The choice of research strategies and methods was primarily based on the nature of the research issues and theoretical perspectives. The research was essentially of multidisciplinary nature and required flexible strategies. Recognizing the complexity and dynamism of research components (biodiversity, community and enterprises) and their interrelationship, a range of methodologies from both biological and social sciences were applied to focus different dimensions. Methods that use a multiple sources of qualitative and quantitative information were used for this research. The diagrammatic representation of linkages of anthropogenic factors to biodiversity presented in the previous chapter guided the extent of data collection (Figure 1.1). Within the limits of level of efforts, resources and time, the investigation process encompassed both the broader understanding of subject matter and closer examinations of issues and their relationships. This study primary address two scales: a) national scale giving general scenario of Nepal and covering the aspects of biodiversity, enterprises, communities and stakeholders, b) community scale investigations that is based on 37 CFUGs from high mountain areas giving in-depth analysis on the performance of enterprise-oriented community forestry on livelihoods and conservation (Table 2.2).

The methods applied to the research broadly come under participatory action research (PAR), and included biodiversity inventories, participatory resource assessment, participatory mapping, focus group discussions, key informant interviews, informal talks, observations, and a review of secondary sources of information. The data as well as experiences and knowledge generated since 1995 at ANSAB, for which the researcher worked as principal investigator, director, coordinator or team leader, were analyzed. Review of literature, wider interactions with key stakeholders both nationally and internationally (workshops, meetings, seminars, conferences, interviews and dialogues), and observations were used to get a broad understanding of local communities, biodiversity and enterprises in Nepal. Examinations of specific issues and their relationships were done through PAR that included experimentations, observations, interviews and dialogues. An optimal ignorance strategy was applied to avoid irrelevant and unnecessaryinformation. To minimize errors and increase reliability and validity, the information and data were cross-checked by triangulating the sources as well as methods wherever applicable and possible. Each method applied for the research is briefly presented in the section following the selection of the research area.

2.2 Selection of the Research Area

To get broader perspectives on biodiversity, communities and enterprises, general information was collected and analyzed at national level in Nepal with focus on hills and mountains. Enterprise survey covered the road-head traders, processors and manufacturers along the east-west highway. The community and ecosystem level research work was undertaken in six mountain districts of Nepal Himalaya: Humla, Jumla, Dolpa, Bajhang, Darchula and Dolakha (Map 2). A list of the selected districts along with the number of CFUGs and households is given in Table 2.1 below.

Table 2.1
Districts, number of community forest user groups (CFUGs) and households (HHs) selected for the participatory action research

Districts	Number of CFUGs	Number of HHs
Humla	12	1,161
Jumla	5	729
Dolpa	7	771
Bajhang	5	1,165
Darchula	6	730
Dolakha	2	551
Total	37	5,107

The districts and communities were selected using the following criteria.

- Rich in biodiversity regarded as a biodiversity hotspot
- Availability of commercial products
- Acute poverty
- Low development index
- High dependency of local communities on forests and meadows
- For selecting communities: additional criteria of habitat connectivity, willingness of community to participate, and district level stakeholders' priority

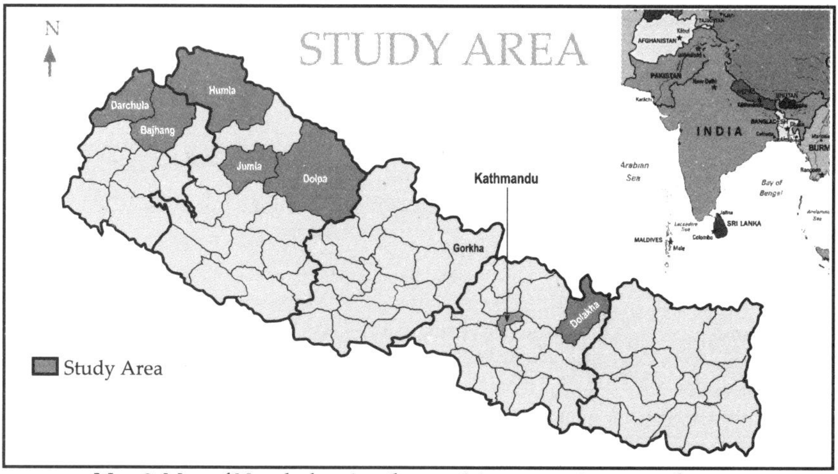

Map 2. Map of Nepal, showing the participatory action research area

The above districts lie within an area, regarded as one of the global hot-spots for biodiversity (Myers 1988; Myers 1990; Mittermeier et al. 1998). The second criterion was the availability of commercially valuable products or services in abundance from which meaningful enterprise activities could be undertaken by local communities in the given context. In our case, we found NTFPs as one of the main group of products with enterprise potentials. The other three criteria were related to the dependency of local communities on forests and meadows. The selected districts are the poverty stricken remote areas with very low development index where communities are heavily dependent on biodiversity for their livelihoods and have very little alternatives. Within the districts additional criteria of habitat connectivity (continuous area of forest and meadows under management), willingness of community to participate, and district level stakeholders' priority were applied in selecting the particular communities and forests. Several communities were deliberately selected to include the cases that may vary in a number of ecological, economic, social/institutional, and technological conditions but inhabits a common set of above criteria.

2.3 Methods of Data Collection

Methods of data collection and levels and units of analysis applied to each of the study components are summarized in Table 2.2 and a short description of the methods used in the research is given below.

Table 2.2
Study components and methods used

Study Components and Major Variables	Methods Used	Level and Units of Analysis
Biodiversity - status (vegetation types, characteristics and distribution, species diversity, ecosystem health and conditions), economic use potentials, community dependence, threats	Review, observations, discussions, resource inventory, transect walk, participatory threat assessment	National, ecosystem, species

Study Components and Major Variables	Methods Used	Level and Units of Analysis
Enterprises - types, distribution, technology, sales, incomes, employment	Enterprise and trade survey, case studies	National, enterprise, groups and households
Communities of stakeholders - institutional capability, technical knowledge, interest, dependency, incomes, employment	Focus group discussion, household survey, key informant survey, workshops, discussions, interviews, literature review	National, districts, category, CFUGs, households
Enterprise-oriented, community-based biodiversity management - community participation in conservation, forest management, harvesting and use, fund mobilization, enterprise contributions	Participatory Action Research - CFUG and enterprise records	37 CFUGs, households, hectares, ecosystem, habitats

2.3.1 Key Informant Interviews

There are always some people in a community who have in-depth knowledge about a specific issue, such as use and management of natural resources, local biodiversity, social issues, community characteristics, and culture. Such key informants were identified and they included traders, enterprise managers and staff, NTFP collectors, raw material suppliers, traditional healers, herders, school teachers, local leaders and concerned staff of facilitating organizations. The key informants were interacted to get in-depth information on various economic, political, ecological, historical and cultural aspects of human-biodiversity dynamics. Community forestry and resource use related information was also collected through interviews and discussions with District Forest Office (DFO) staff, District Soil Conservation Office (DSCO) staff, health workers, Ayurvedic practitioners, local traditional healers (vaidya, amchi, baiji, etc.) and I/NGO field staff. The information was used to assess and monitor human response to biodiversity. Professionals and experts working in Nepal in the field of biodiversity, community forestry, community development and enterprise promotions were also interacted to get their views and opinions regarding the situation, threats, opportunities and challenges.

2.3.2 Focus Group Discussion

Focus group discussion (FGD) is an important method in qualitative research. FGD uncovers in-depth information by tracking a small sample of households carefully. It consists of fostering interactions among an identified group of respondents to identify, assess and understand the perceptions, beliefs, knowledge, attitude, options, problems, power relations, linkages, and other factors. Focus group discussions were conducted with community forest user group (CFUG) members, CFUG committees, enterprise management committees, enterprise beneficiaries such as NTFP harvesters/collectors, women, and *dalits*[1] to identify concerns, perceptions, ideas and options regarding biodiversity, its significance to local livelihoods and sustainable resource management. FGD was also used to capture qualitative information missed in the enterprise and household surveys.

2.3.3 Household Surveys

The household survey measures socio-economic characteristics and the social response to biodiversity. Household data were collected using a survey form, which included questions on demography, economic activities, cattle, agriculture land, crops, private forest, and demand of main forest products. In our action research, the household survey was an integral part of the CFUG formation and forest handover process. Household surveys, which were conducted at the time of CFUG formation or reformation, provided a range of information on perceptions, behaviors and existing human actions in biodiversity, resource policy and access, and several other linkages between communities, enterprises and biodiversity. Information generated from the household survey was important for devising a CFUG's resource management plan.

2.3.4 Enterprise and Trade Survey

NTFP enterprises were assessed through formal and informal surveys. To get the information about NTFPs being traded in and from Nepal and to have the general understanding of the trade and marketing

[1] Dalits are marginalized 'occupational caste' people and engage in traditional occupations such as metal craft (Kami or Lohar), leatherwork (Sarki), and tailoring (Damai), pottery and entertainment (Badi).

practices, a questionnaire survey of NTFP entrepreneurs (producers, processors and traders) operating at road heads and town centers from the eastern borders to the western borders of Nepal was done in 1996 and 2002. The survey was limited to the more accessible areas, and the entrepreneurs operating in inner rural areas could not be covered in this survey. While 112 entrepreneurs were interviewed in 1996, the number increased to 137 in 2002. All the available sources or relevant studies were consulted to verify and triangulate the information on quantity and value of trade for major species. As the comprehensive study on the volume and value of trade itself is a formidable and challenging task in the present context of secretive trade, this was done only to get some idea on the scales of business and its potential contribution to local economy and livelihoods.

To assess the present situation and potentials of community-based forest enterprises (CBFEs), a list was prepared by forest product type. The CBFEs were then categorized according to issues such as ownership structure, scale of operation, property rights regimes (such as private, common and public), management structure/institutional set up, technological sophistication, target market, and seasonality and length of operations. Seventy one enterprises were selected and information was collected using a checklist (Annex 2).

2.3.5 Resource Assessment and Participatory Biodiversity Monitoring

A framework for participatory resource assessment and monitoring system was designed, tested and applied in the participatory action research in the field. The following ecological/biological components were examined:

Biological resource inventory and growing stock: Resource inventory is a method of assessing the vegetations in detail. These inventories were used to document the biological resources (ecosystems, habitats, plant and animal species) and to make estimates of tree resources that produce NTFPs of the study area and more specifically to quantify the current stock of the selected commercially harvested NTFPs. Appropriate sampling as well as observation and measurement techniques were worked out for selected species, and various equipment and tools were used, such as altimeter, clinometer, compass, pedometer, linear tape, topographical sheets and aerial photographs.

Transact walk, a rapid technique was used to assess ecosystem characteristics through observation and measurement of variables visually from a distance. This consisted of moving from one point to another along a specified line, and recording relevant data. The outputs of the resource inventory and participatory mapping included the amount of resources available, condition of forest, regeneration and species composition.

Growth and yield: It is criteria for measuring growth depended on the product to be harvested. For tree and shrub species of which only part was harvested (without destroying the entire individual), we made an attempt to know how much new resource was produced by individuals subsequent to the harvest, while in species where entire individuals were harvested, we made observations of how many new individuals of merchantable size entered the population each year.

Forest regeneration: Regeneration studies were designed along with the sampling of representative forest stands. Data from the inventory and growing stock and close observations of regeneration study plots were used to understand the regeneration pattern of the major species and measure conservation impacts.

2.3.6 Participatory Threat Assessment

Both perceptual and biophysical criteria were used to assess and rank the main threats to biodiversity. Participatory exercises with community groups were done to assess the status of threats with the introduction of action research intervention of enterprise-oriented, community-based biodiversity management. Indicators, such as frequency of fire, area affected by fire, extent and methods of biomass removal (leaves, wood, barks, fruits, flowers, roots etc.), spread of exotic invasive species, and extent and practice of grazing, were used to measure threats to biodiversity. The causes were identified and analyzed based on the dialogues with communities and other stakeholders including experts and professionals working in Nepal.

2.3.7 Observations, Records, Databases and Experiential Learning

Both planned and unplanned observations are important techniques of capturing data, information, and insights. Direct observations were useful in understanding the individual and group behaviors in forestry operations, enterprises and benefit sharing.

Records and databases established and maintained by the research participants as well as other agencies were important sources of information. Chief among them were records of the CFUGs and enterprises involved in the participatory action research, concerned DFOs, community forestry database at Community and Private Forestry Division (CPFD), forest products including NTFPs records at Department of Forests (DOF), database at Trade Promotion Center (TPC) and custom records.

Experiential learning on Nepal's community forestry practices from 1990 through 2003 including author's works during the implementation of ANSAB programs from 1995 through 2003 was instrumental in designing and gathering information. For example, the historical analysis of the forces supporting community based biodiversity conservation was built on the author's previous work (Subedi 1996). Similarly, eighteen case studies commissioned to understand the various aspects of NTFPs covering various ecological zones and longitudinal axis provided the broad understanding of the status of use, management and trade of NTFPs as well as threats to biodiversity conservation. Participation and sharing of research findings at various national and international conferences, meetings, seminars, workshops, and more importantly dialogues with and feed back from the colleagues and scholars working in the subject areas were particularly useful to relate the findings in broader context.

2.3.8 Review of Literature

A literature review went concurrently with the primary research methods starting before the study design and continuing alongside the empirical data collection, analysis and write-up to identify more specific data needs as the research progressed. Over 160 articles, reports, books, proceedings and project documents relevant to the research topic were reviewed. The main areas covered include biodiversity, local communities, enterprises, conservation approaches, local livelihoods, ecology, marketing, community forestry, NTFPs, conservation incentives, land use and changes, social ecology, resource use pattern, and policy provisions and practices.

2.3.9 Participatory Action Research

To see the feasibility and test the performance of enterprise-oriented community-based management of biodiversity, interventions were designed adapting the participatory action research (PAR) methodology (Kolb 1976; Selener 1997; Bawden 2002; Castellanet 2003) and the simplified framework is presented below (Fig 2.1). Combining the top-down and bottom-up

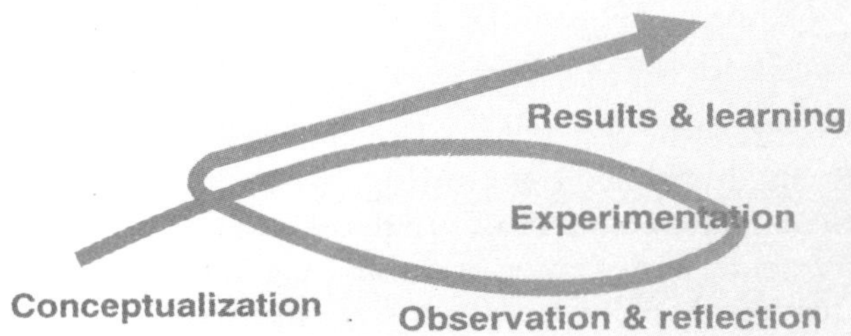

Figure 2.1 Experiential Learning Cycle Applied in Participatory Action Research

approaches, PAR links concept and concrete action (intervention) and evaluates the outcome of an intervention to draw lessons applicable to future intervention (Castellanet 2003). It involved creating experiential collective learning situations and critical learning systems that can encompass plurality of paradigms and methods.

Conceptualization: Building on the past initiatives, experiences and learning of community forestry and biodiversity conservation approaches in Nepal, enterprise-oriented, community-based forest management was conceptualized assuming that when communities are empowered to manage their resource base and provided enterprise options that are linked to biodiversity, it can generate incomes and employment to reduce the poverty while providing incentives to conserve the resources. Although community forestry has been a standard prescription for the hills of Nepal to manage forests for fuelwood, animal fodder, building materials, and grazing areas, its application for high mountains, especially for non-timber forest products (NTFPs) was not in practice until recently. The context and rationale of the new concept is that in Nepal the majority of conservation resources have been allocated to the protected area models and even the participatory models are characterized by regulatory measures with restrictions and bans, limited property rights, and subsistence orientation. But people-centered and economic incentive based resource management strategies were not conceptualized and hence received less attention.

Experimentation: The enterprise-oriented community forest management has been experimented with 37 Community Forest User Groups (CFUGs) in Himalayan and Trans-Himalayan regions of Nepal where Non-timber Forest Products (NTFPs) constitute a valuable group of products for local communities. Building on the existing knowledge base (both indigenous and external) interventions for PAR were designed and implemented in the areas that were identified and prioritized together with local communities. The interventions included sub-sector analysis, threats analysis, strategy development and planning, implementation and reviews. Expanding the property rights of local communities over resources and empowering them with knowledge, information, technologies, and required skills for forest management, institution building and enterprise activities were basic building blocks and core of the experiment. A brief description of the interventions is given below.

Sub-sector analysis (SSA): This involved identifying a sub-sector (a product or a range of products) most potential for creating economic incentives while balancing environmental and social concerns. Reviewing along the value chain (from production to consumption) SSA identified the intervention areas that provide highest leverage both economically and environmentally in the given context (Subedi 1999).

Threats analysis and community forestry planning: With each participating community, participatory analysis of threats to biodiversity, resources assessment, and strategy development in terms of community forests management were undertaken. Considering the variability within and between the communities and forests, the process required adaptation in moving forward with identified communities. As the Community Forest User Group (CFUG) became ready, members assessed resources and analyzed the threats to biodiversity. Communities devised strategies for forest management to optimize the enterprise opportunities and address the threats. The strategies were then translated into their forest management Operational Plan (OP).[2]

Enterprise development planning: Possible options for enterprises were examined and prioritized considering the factors related to policy, resource abundance, market, finance, local skills, technologies, and social issues. A detailed enterprise development plan was developed for the most potential enterprise identified from the feasibility study. While it was unlikely to develop the enterprise plan without external technical assistance by local communities, their role was crucial from the inception since the success depended on community taking ownership and active role in the management.

Implementation: At the interface of activities implementation along with the direct technical facilitation to communities and enterprises, local partnership and networking among the key stakeholders were strengthened.

Observation and Reflection: The observations of the experimentation were made through an approach of multi-stakeholders' perspectives including the involved communities. Regular interactions, dialogues, workshops, meetings and sharing with communities and other stakeholders provided a continuous surveillance of the effectiveness of the interventions. Biological, social, institutional and enterprise performance monitoring were carried out to provide the continuous feedback to the stakeholders.

The observations and experiences of multi-stakeholders were analyzed and reflected in terms of the outcomes and impacts of enterprise-oriented community-based forests management on i) livelihoods and incomes ii) resources management and conservation, and iii) social equity and governance.

---

[2] A community group to formally become a CFUG requires to be registered at the District Forest Office with its Constitution. The Constitution defines the social arrangement and the responsibilities and rights of the group where as the OP specifies how the forest is managed and utilized. To incorporate provisions of managing additional products or expanding the area the OP needs to be revised and approved.

2.4 Analysis

The analysis began with the literature review and continued until the write-up stage. The data, information, knowledge, insights, and wisdoms were not only objectively organized and analyzed but also interpreted in an internally consistent framework. The mode of inquiry, analysis, and synthesis were guided to understand the individual and interdependent capabilities of the three research components in contributing to societal value of conservation and poverty reduction. Given the context and nature of the research, it demanded openness, skepticism, and analytical mind on the part of the researcher. The research process itself was iterative and the understanding of one part influenced the design of the other parts. For example, understanding of the threats to biodiversity and their root causes contributed to designing the research in community based forest enterprise and communities of stakeholders. Similarly, the analysis of stakeholders and conditions and forces of community based biodiversity conservation showed the strong supportive forces and likelihood of continuing support to community based biodiversity conservation, and based on this we designed the participatory action research interventions of enterprise-oriented, community-based forest management.

Analysis of the information from the participatory action research was guided by the analytical framework of the PAR to objectively synthesize the experiential learning of different actors and stakeholders in relation to enterprise-oriented community-based biodiversity management. The analysis integrated the whole process of learning spiral for each issue from conceptualization, design, and action to reflection as indicated in the diagram above (Fig 2.1). The main dependent variables of the research were generation of economic incentives for local communities, social equity, and conservation of natural resources. Two types of independent variables were considered: design and external. The design variables, which can also be characterized as internal to local communities, included the context, communities, biodiversity, enterprises and their relationships. The external variables affecting the dependent variables (often through influencing the design itself and characteristics of design variables) were policy, market, finance, technology, and external support such as technical assistance, information, etc.

Both qualitative and quantitative techniques of analysis were applied depending on the nature and type of information. Qualitative analyses ranged from simple validation, categorization, description, and comparison to the analysis and synthesis of a very complex multivariable, multidimensional relationship that could not be captured by a quantitative technique that requires reduction of a concept into variables that are objectively measurable. Such analysis was mainly guided by the mental process of generalization. Quantitative data were compiled from each site and strata and statistical analyses were done first starting with simple uni-variable (such as frequency, average, and percentage) to multi-variable techniques (such as cross-tabulation and regression).

2.5 Description of the Participatory Action Research Area

2.5.1 Human Population, Land Use and Sources of Livelihood

The study districts, except Dolakha, are among the most remote ones, with the lowest Human Development Index (HDI) in Nepal. Dolakha is accessible by road and relatively developed. All the others have access only by air, as roads are difficult to construct in high mountains with immature and fragile topography and steep slopes. One to two weeks journey from the last road to these places is common. Humla District, the northwest corner of the country, is the most remote. The nearest road to Nepalganj in the Terai is a two-week journey by foot from Simikot, the District Center.

People in these areas are among the poorest in Nepal. Table 2.4 summarizes the population statistics of the districts. Human populations are sparse in these districts with a population density of 4 people per sq km in Dolpa to 92 in Dolakha, and growing at a rate of 0.99 - 1.88% per year. In them the literacy is low, people are poor with very limited access to services and basic infrastructure. The cultivable land is less than 1% in Dolpa and 1% in Humla; the average for the study districts is 4%, far below the national average of 20%. Irrigated land is almost not-existing and most of the farming is rain-fed. In some districts, such as Humla and Dolpa rocky surtace and snow cover combine to account for about 60% of the area, severely restricting opportunities to bring about development.

Because of the limited farming land the population is dependent on livestock, forestry, NTFPs-based trade, and seasonal wage labor. In addition to the subsistence use, the trade of many NTFPs has become the second most important source of cash to local households after wages of seasonal labors that go to Terai and India during the winter. Both Mangolian and Aryan communities are found in the area. Mongolians have more egalitarian social structure and include Lama, Magar, Gurung, etc. Aryans follow hierarchical Hindu caste system and include Brahmin, Thakuri, Chhetri and Dalit groups. They have different patterns of livelihoods as it relates to forest and pasture resources. Main occupations of Mongolian society in the area are trade, livestock raising, and traditional healing services, while those of Aryans are farming and seasonal employment outside the villages well up to India.

Table 2.3
Landuse pattern and livestock population in the study districts (area in ha)

District	Forest Area			Agriculture			Others	Total Area	Livestock Population[1]
	Pasture	Forest	Subtotal	Cultivated	Non-cultivated	Subtotal			
Humla	1,44,450 (24.2)	74,783 (12.8)	2,19,233 (37.0)	6,006 (1.0)	3,731 (0.6)	9,737 (1.6)	3,58,295 (61.4)	5,83,823 (100)	30,870
Jumla	66,225 (26.0)	1,08,571 (44.1)	1,74,796 (67.2)	14,743 (5.8)	9,314 (3.7)	24,057 (9.5)	59,512 (23.4)	2,58,365 (100)	55,143
Dolpa	2,49,730 (31.5)	63,875 (8.1)	3,13,605 (39.5)	6,068 (0.8)	3,333 (0.4)	9,391 (1.2)	4,70,284 (59.3)	7,93,280 (100)	23,108
Bajhang	52,929 (15.2)	1,13,180 (32.6)	1,66,109 (47.8)	27,077 (7.8)	14,638 (4.2)	41,715 (12.0)	1,39,735 (40.2)	3,47,559 (100)	115,874
Darchula	61,215 (26.3)	79,538 (34.1)	1,40,753 (60.4)	16,083 (6.9)	8,911 (3.8)	24,994 (10.7)	67,243 (28.9)	2,32,990 (100)	99,422
Dolakha	34,128 (15.9)	94,478 (44.1)	1,28,606 (60.0)	29,423 (13.7)	15,448 (7.2)	44,871 (20.9)	40,801 (19.0)	2,14,278 (100)	111,976
Study Districts	6,05,677 (25.0)	5,30,425 (21.9)	11,35,102 (46.8)	99,370 (4.1)	54,873 (2.3)	1,54,286 (6.4)	11,35,870 (46.8)	24,26,297 (100)	434,393
National Total	17,57,000 (11.9)	63,05,001 (42.9)	80,63,002 (54.8)	29,68,000 (20.2)	9,86,800 (6.7)	39,54,800 (26.9)	27,29,600 (18.5)	1,47,18,100 (100)	9,660,409

Source : National Research Associates, Nepal. Nepal District Profile 2002
Note : Figures in parenthesis are the percentages of total area.
1. Total livestock population is calculated based on body weight taking 280-300 kg as one livestock unit (LU); thus 1 buffalo =1 LU, 1 cattle = 0.80 LU, and a sheep or goat = 0.1 LU.

Table 2.4
Population and socio-economic characteristics in the study districts in 2001

Districts	Area (km²)	Total Population	Number of HH	Av. HH size	Population Density (person km⁻¹)	Average Annual Growth Rate (%)	HDI	Literacy Rate (%)
Humla	5655	40595	6953	5.8	7	1.66	0.244	27.1
Jumla	2531	69226	12147	5.7	35	1.63	0.218	32.5
Dolpa	7889	22071	4414	5.0	4	1.67	0.218	35.0
Bajhang	3422	167026	28588	5.8	49	1.88	0.201	35.5
Darchula	2322	121996	21029	5.8	53	1.82	0.236	49.5
Dolakha	2191	175912	37292	4.7	95	1.66	0.340	51.1
Study districts total	24040	596826	110423	5.4	24.9	1.71	0.250	38.5
National Total	147,181	23100000	4174374	5.45	157	2.2	0.325	53.7

Source : Population data from HMGN, Central Bureau of Statistics, 2002; HDI data from Nepal Human Development Report, 1998, Nepal South Asia Center, Kathmandu, Nepal, 1998
Note : HH – household; HDI – Human Development Index; Literacy rate 6 years and above

2.5.2 Climate, Geology and Soils

Climate of the region is characterized by the monsoon rainfall pattern, the period from mid-June to late-September accounting for 75-80% of annual precipitation. The three wet months are preceded and followed by drought spells of varying lengths. During the droughts the monthly rainfall generally remains below 10 cm and potential evapo-transpiration is often in excess of precipitation (Singh and Singh 1992). Even in the moist area, dry season water potential for trees often reach -2.5 to -3.0 MPa before dawn, a range that is slightly less than in mid mountain forest, with the summer-long drought in the USA (Zobel and Singh 1997). The annual rainfall in outer ranges generally exceeds 100 cm, but in rain-shadow areas such in Dolpa it is much less, about 50 cm or less.

According to Rao (1981) topographically induced variation in precipitation can be profound. The mean annual temperature in foothills is around 230 C and it declines at lapse rate of 0.440 C per 100 m rise in the altitude (Singh et al. 1994). The difference between the mean temperature of warmest and coldest months range between 100 C and 190 C, this summer-winter difference declines up to 1000 m and then stabilizes at around 100 C in higher ranges (Map 3). In these mountains, generally the sun shine duration decreases towards high altitude due to increased cloudiness, but not in inner mountains. Because temperature and sun shine decline, the effectiveness of precipitation increases with altitude. Consequently, higher mountains particularly in outer ranges remain relatively wet despite lower rainfall. The absolute minimum temperatures at 3600m, corresponding with the upper limit of the forest vegetation, are -150 to -200 C, which are less severe than the temperature reported for continental temperate mountains (Sakai and Mall 1981). In general winters are milder for these altitudes. Around timberline the mean annual temperature is 70 C.

The young and rising Himalayan mountains are unusually vulnerable to landslips and landslides. A highly immature topography is the characteristic feature of the Himalayan ranges. As the Himalaya continues to override Indian sub-continent, it passes through the process of folding and faulting. The high Himalaya where the study sites are located is a zone of about 70 km width and is made up of high grade metamorphic rocks of Precambrian age and intruded by mid-Tertiary granites. In this zone lie most of the snow-clad mountain peaks of Himalaya which feed the glaciers of snow-fed rivers. The deep river gorges provide difficult routes from outer to inner Himalayan ranges. The accumulating stresses within the rock crusts are manifested in recurring earth quakes, and highly shattered and sheared rocks prone to mass movement. The terrain, in general is inhospitable to humans.

Broadly speaking, a majority of forest soils belong to brown earth soil category. In general, soil is thin with the weak podzolization under conifer forests of higher altitudes. Calcium generally dominates the exchangeable bases in most soils, particularly in brown earth type. Color in the surface horizon in forest soils generally varies from dark brown to dark yellowish brown and is generally rich in fine roots, ectomycorrhiza and organic matter. With respect to texture, soils vary from coarse loamy sand to clay loam. Soil pH in high altitudes generally ranges between 5 and 6. The organic content may reach up to 4% in high altitude forests. Generally two to three horizons are identified. Soil depth and drainage are important factors having positive effect on vegetation.

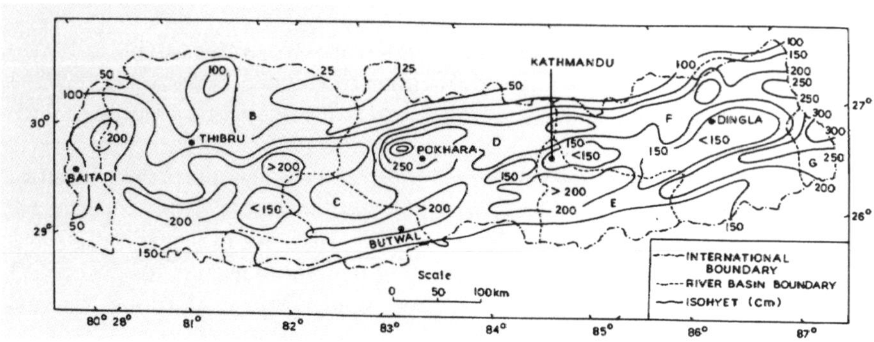

Map 3 Map of Nepal showing the major river basins and distribution of mean annual precipitation (cm) (Singh and Singh 1992). A = Kali river basin; B = Karnali river basin; C = Rapti river basin; D = Gandak river basin; E = Bagmati river basin; F = Koshi river basin; G = Mechi river basin.

2.5.3 Vegetation

Forest types as described in Table 2.5 follow the patterns described for Kumaun Himalaya by Singh and Singh (1992) with some variations. Much of the altitudinal transect is dominated by evergreen species with about one year leaf lifespan. This category includes all oaks as well as chir pine. Deciduous forests occur only in patches around the rivers except in higher mountains where birch is common, particularly in timberline areas. Among the evergreens with several years of leaf lifespan silver fir *(Abies spectabilis)* is the most important. Among the undercanopy species *Rhododendron arboreum* and *Lyonia ovalifolia* are common. *Taxus buccata,* another undercanopy species occurs in higher ranges in upper oak and silver fir forests. Singh *et al.* (1994) and Zobel and Singh (1997) have described major ecosystem properties of these forests as given below.

Both biomass and productivity of these forests remain on the high side of the ranges described for similar forests elsewhere. For example, biomass as high as over 500 t/ha occurs up to 3000 m altitude and productivity does not decline below 15-20 t/ha/year. When these forests are converted into agriculture, the land is able to support only one-fifth of the original productivity.

Even in sub-alpine zone accumulations of litter are more similar to those in tropical forest than to those in temperate forest. Litter production is fairly constant up to an elevation of 3000 m. These forests have residence times for organic matter and nutrients in the forest floor (organic matter 1.9-2.5 years and Nitrogen 1.7-2.4 year) generally closer to those of tropical rainforest (organic matter 0.4 year, N 2 year) than those of temperate forests (organic matter 4-17 years, N 5.5-17.9 years). They have higher proportions of total nutrients of ecosystems in the biomass components compared to temperate forests. Evidently, forest removal would result in a greater proportional loss of ecosystem nutrients in Himalaya than in other temperate regions.

The oak forest of the study area have tree and stand characters intermediate between those of the monsoon evergreen broadleaf forests and evergreen sclerophyllous forest of climate with dry summer, described by Song (1995). Though Box (1995) includes extra-tropical evergreen broadleaf forest among the types considered to describe the pattern of the world's vegetation, generally forests of this type are ignored in the summary and modeling of data. Even some authors do not list the forest of the evergreen broadleaf type separate from the evergreen tropical rainforest (Zobel and Singh 1997).

In the Himalayan evergreen forest with one year leaf lifespan, leaf fall seems to be induced by new leaf formation in the spring. The climate is such that the leaves that maintained relatively high physiological activity round the year have selective advantage over deciduous as well as evergreens with several year leaf lifespan. Winters are relatively mild for the altitude, largely because of the subtropical latitude, high humidity and low wind activity. The massive Himalayan ranges have created a maritime climate in the continental locations.

The upper limit of tree species richness shows a bell-shaped curve along the elevational transact, the values peaking around 1500 m altitudes. However, the upper limit of Shannon-Wiener index remains high over a wider elevational range. It ranges between 0.4 and 3.6 for individual stands and 0.4 and 2.8 as averages for different forest types.

Table 2.5
A Pattern of major vegetation types in relation to altitude (based on Subedi 1999)

I. TEMPERATE ZONE (2001m - 3000m)

1. Lower temperate forests
   a. Chir Pine (*Pinus roxburghii*) forest, quite extensive
   b. Blue Pine (*Pinus wallichiana*) forest, fairly extensive
   c. Lower Oak forest (this includes *Quercus leucotrichophora* forest, Q. *floribunda* forest and their mixture), quite extensive
   d. Mixed broad-leaf deciduous forest (*Juglans, Acer, Populus, Alnus*), occurring in patches
   e. Riverine deciduous forest (*Aesculus indica, Juglans regia*), occurs in patches
2. Upper temperate forests
   a. Upper Oak (*Quercus semecarpifolia*) forest, extensive
   b. Mixed broad-leaf forest (*Acer spp., Rhododendron spp.*), small patches
   c. Mixed Blue Pine - Oak (*Q. semecarpifolia*) forest, small patches
   d. Coniferous forest (*P. wallichiana, Abies spectabilis, Tsuga dumosa, Taxus baccata, Picea smithiana*), fairly well represented
3. On Rocky steep slopes and frequently burned sited grasslands are stabilized

II. SUB-ALPINE ZONE (3001m - 4000m)

1. Sub-alpine forests
   a. Upper Oak (*Q. semecarpifolia*) forest
   b. Silver Fir (*Abies spectabilis*) forest
   c. Birch (*Betula utilis*) forest
   d. Birch-Rhododendron forest
   e. Juniper (*Juniperus spp.*) steppe
2. Sub-alpine scrubs (*Rhododendron and Sorbus microphylla shrubs*)
3. Sub-alpine grasslands

III. ALPINE and NIVAL ZONE (above 4000m)

1. *Rhododendron-Juniperus* scrub
2. Grasslands (Graminae, Cyperaceae)

Alpine meadows: Beyond timberline there occur numerous patches of alpine and subalpine meadows surrounded by forest on lower sides and rocks and snow on upper sides. These meadows are rich in species and have been grazed (chiefly sheep) for millennia by herders migrating from other areas. These meadows and adjoining scrubs are also known for many valuable medicinal and aromatic plants such as *Aconitum* spp, *Delphinium himalayai* (atis), *Neopichrorhiza scrophulariiflora* (kutki), *Nardostachys grandiflora* (jatamansi), *Podophylum hexandrum* (laghupatra), *Rhododendron anthopogan*, and *Ephedra* sp. Use of many of them has been commercialized. Developing enterprises with their sustainable uses and integrating them with the local communities is one of the most challenging tasks having high potential.

A list of plant species that have potential for enterprise activities in the PAR area is given in Table 2.6 and a brief description is given in Annex 3.

Table 2.6

Plant species with enterprise potential in the PAR area

Botanical Name	Vernacular Name	Life-Form	Distribution	Parts Used	Commercial uses
Abies spectabilis	talispatra	T	2400-4400m	L, W	Essential oil, medicine
Acer oblongum	putali phul, phirphire	T	1200-2400m	W	Wooden bowl
Aconitum bisma	bikhma	H	3000-4000m	Rt	Medicine, tonic
Aconitum spicatum	bikh	H	3300-4360m	Tu	Medicine
Acorus calamus	bojho	H	500-2500m	Rt	Medicine, aromatic
Aesculus indica	Pangar	T	1200-3000m	Sd, W	Soap making, medicine
Artemisia vulgaris	titepati	S	300-2400m	St, Rt	Essential oil, medicine
Asparagus racemosus	kurilo, satawari	H	600-2100m	Rt, Ys	Food, medicine
Berberis aristata	chutro	S	1800-3000m	Rt, W, Fr	Medicine, dye
Bergenia ciliata	pakhanved	H	1600-3200m	Rs	Medicine, aromatic
Cinnamomum zeylanicum	dalchini	T	450-2100m	B	Spice
Cinnamomum tamala	tejpat	T	450-2100m	B, L	Spice, aromatic
*Cordyceps sinensis**	yarshagumba	F	3000-5000m	Wp	Medicine, tonic
Cymbopogon jwarancusa	soti ghans	H	1600-3000m	Wp	Essential oil
Daphne bholua	lokta	S	1500-2100m	B	Bast fiber for handmade paper and its products
Daphne papyracea	lokta	S	1500-2100m	B	Bast fiber for handmade paper and its products
Delphinium denudatum	nirbikhi; nirmansi	H	1500-2700m	Rt	Medicine
*Delphinium himalayai**	atis	H	3000-4500m	Rt	Medicine

Botanical Name	Vernacular Name	Life Form	Distribution	Parts Used	Commercial uses
Edgeworthia gardneri	argeli	S	1500-3000m	B	Bast fiber (for paper making)
Ephedra gerardiana	somlata	S	3200-5200m	Tg	Medicine
Eulophia dabia	kaladana	H	2000-3100	Tu	Food, medicine
Gaultheria fragrantissima	dhasingare	T	1500-2700m	L	Essential oil, medicine
Girardinia diversifolia	allo	S	1500-1800	St	Fiber for cloth
Juglans regia	okhar	T	2000-2800m	B, Fr	Root bark for medicine, dye and fruits for food
Juniperus indica	dhupi	T	1800-4100m	W, Fr	Essential oil, incense, medicine
Jurinea dolomiaea	kalthapale, dhupjadi	H	2500-3800m	Rt	Incense and aromatic products
Morchella conica	guchchi chyau	F	2000-3500m	Wpl	Food, tonic
Nardostachys grandiflora	jatamansi	H	3300-4800m	Rz	Essential oil, medicine
Paris polyphylla	satuwa	H	2000-3100m	Tu, Rz	Medicine
Parmelia nepalensis	jhyau	H	1000-3600m	Wp	Medicine, aromatic products
Picrorhiza scrophulariiflora	kutki	H	3000-4200m	Rt	Medicine
Pistacia integerrima	kakarsinghi	T	300-1500m	P	Medicine
Pistacia integerrima	kakarsinghi	T	300-1500m	P	Medicine
Prinsepia utilis	dhatelo	T	2000-2700m	Fr	Edible oil
Pyrus pashia	mayal	T	750-2700m	Fr, L	Food, medicine
Rheum australe Syn. *R. emodi*	padamchal	H	3000-4200m	Rt, St	Medicine, dye
Rhododendron anthopogon	sunpati	S	3000-4800m	Sd	Medicine, essential oil
Rubia cordifolia	majitho	H	1200-3200m	St, Rt	Medicine, dye
Sapindus mukorossi	rittha	T	1000-1600m	Fr	Detergent
Selinum tenuifolium	bhutkesh	H	2500-4800m	Wp	Medicine, aromatic products
Swertia chirayita	chiraito, tite	H	1500-2500m	Wp	Medicine
Taxus baccata subsp. Wallichiana	lauthsalla	T	2100-3400m	L, B	Medicine, anticancer
Valeriana jatamansi	sugandhwal	H	2000-2700m	Rt	Essential oil, medicine
Zanthoxylum armatum	timur	S	1000-2500	Fr	Spice, food flavor, essential oil, medicine

Note: Life Form: T = Tree; S = Shrub; H = Herb; F =Fungi

Parts Used: B = Bark, C = Cone, Fl = Flowers, Fr = Fruits, Fo = Foliage, Inf = Inflorescence; L = Leaves; La = Latex; P = Pod; Re = Resin; Rs = Root Stock; Rt = Root; Rz = Rhizomes; Sa= Sap; Sd = Seeds; St = Stem; Tu = Tubers; Rb = Root bark; Sh =Shoot; Tg =Twig; Sp = Spores/Sporangia; Ys = yearly shoot; Wp = Whole Plant; W = Wood; Hw = heart wood; Sw = Sap Wood

* Banned for export without processing

** Banned for collection

Biological Diversity in Nepal: A Review of Diversity, Distribution, Policy and Regulatory Environment, and Conservation Approaches

3.1 Biological Diversity, Endemism and Products

Nepal's central location with the transitional zone between the eastern and western parts of the Himalaya makes its geographical position unique. It has species of both the Himalayan parts. Both horizontal and vertical variations contribute to the diversity and uniqueness of ecosystem, flora and fauna. In Nepal just within a narrow width of 150-200 km, altitude rises from less than 100 m in the south to 8,848 m in the Himalayan ranges that run east to west across the entire 885 km length. Ten of the world's fourteen peaks exceeding 8,000 m in altitude are found in Nepal. Vertical topographic variations are extreme, with altitude differentials of 6,000 m occurring within a distance of less than 12 kilometers in some places.

Climatic variations from near tropical through temperate, alpine and tundra are found across the country, south to north. The annual rainfall ranges from 250 mm in rain shadow areas to 4500 mm in outer ranges. The precipitation is influenced by monsoon with wet summer and dry winter. Most of the rain occurs during the summer monsoon season from June to September, flowing from the southeastern Bay of Bengal. The dry season runs from October to

May, although precipitation in the form of snow occurs in the High Himal during the winter months. Rainfall is most abundant to the south–eastern parts, decreasing towards the northwest. Because of the orographic effects, a distinct moisture gradient exists, with areas of rain shadow found in the Trans-Himalaya as well as some parts of western Nepal. In terms of topography, Humla, Mugu and Dolpa are the most important areas north of the main Himalayan chain. These are areas of high elevations (3000 m and more) lying in the rain shadow of the Himalaya. They have considerably lower rainfall than the rest of Nepal and are often semi-desert. In the rain shadow area while north aspect may support forests, the dry south aspect generally remains treeless. Most of this zone [trans-Himalayan zone] can be classified as cold semi-desert; it has greater affinities with Tibet than with rest of Nepal (Jackson 1994).

The western region (west of 83°30' E) and eastern region (east of 86° E) show distinct west Himalayan and east Himalayan biotic components, respectively, while the central region represents the biogeographical traffic for both the regions. The Palearctic and the Indo-Malayan biogeographical regions merge in Nepal and the major floristic provinces of Asia (the Sino-Japanese, Indian, western and central Asiatic, Southeast Asiatic and African Indian desert) overlap to create a unique and rich terrestrial biodiversity.

Major rivers form some interesting valleys give riverain and tropical evergreen forests. The country is cut by a number of steep-sided gorges oriented southward from the Tibetan Plateau. One of these, the central Kali Gandaki valley, roughly defines the start of a broad ecozone to the west, dividing moist eastern Nepal (with Oriental biogeography, i.e. with species representative of India and Southeast Asia) from drier western Nepal (with biodiversity more representative of the Holarctic zone, i.e. Central Asia and the Mediterranean). For example, the valley along the Kali Gandaki River starts from the extreme north and covers the narrow gaps of Dhaulagiri and Annapurna. The valley is extremely dry towards its head with reduced flora while towards south it has lush humid tropical forest. Another major north-south river system, the Karnali, flows out of the country's major western watershed which is found within Humla and other districts of the Northwest.

Numerous side ranges and shoulders extend in all directions from the main Himalayan chain, creating a complex mosaic of biologically isolated high altitude ridges and deep valleys, essentially biogeographical islands (Wilson 1992). The complex vertical topography acts to restrict gene flow across the landscape. With this biogeographical isolation and ecosystem diversity ranging from desert and semi-arid areas in the north to tropical monsoon forest in the south, as well as subtropical, montane and alpine forest, tundra, permanent snow and ice, and geothermal hotsprings, the Nepalese landscape fosters a high level of biological diversity.

3.1.1 Forest Vegetations of Nepal

The rich forest vegetation is the major constituent of Nepal's biodiversity, hence warrants an extended account. On the basis of physiography and dominant species, Stainton (1972) classified Nepal's vegetation into 35 forest types. Dobremez (1976) elaborated the

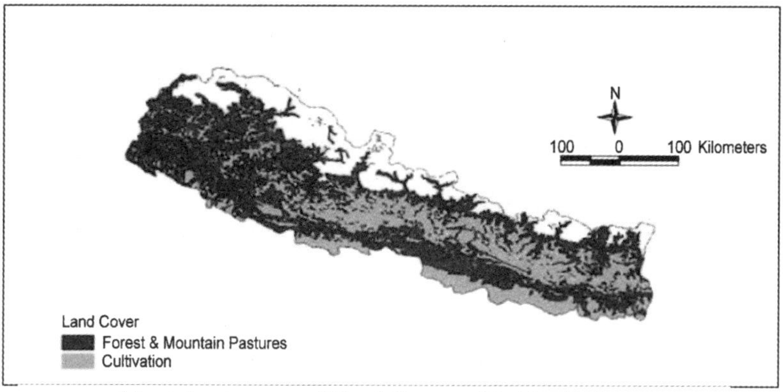

Map 4. Landuse map of Nepal (Karan and Jenkins 1960)

classification into 75 vegetation types. Dobremez and his Nepali colleagues continued to refine the list of forest and vegetation types to come up with 198 types in 1985 (TISC 2002). The small country accommodates dense tropical forests of Terai (wet plains) in the south through subtropical broadleaf and coniferous forests at the middle to temperate, sub-alpine and alpine vegetation in the north in 6 phyto-geographical provinces, 11 bioclimatic zones (Map 4).

The main physiographic zones of Nepal, from north to south, are: the High Himalayas (23% of the total area, comprising alpine meadow, rock and ice between the tree line and the Great Himalaya), High Mountains (20%, extending from the heavily populated hills of the

Photo 3. *Coniferous forest and broadleaf forest*

Middle Hills to the tree line), Middle-Hills (30%, supporting a sub-tropical and temperate zone traditionally most densely populated part of the country), the Siwaliks (13%, representing the first and lowest ridges of the Himalayan system), and the Terai (14%), the northern end of the Gangetic plains (Kenting 1986; MFSC 1988; BPP 1995). There are four main ecological zones of trans-Himalaya, highlands, temperate/subtropical midlands, and tropical lowlands or terai (HMG Nepal/ IUCN 1988).

Much of the non-timber forest products (NTFPs) are derived form forests and the meadows that occur adjacently above the upper limit of the forest zone, generally around 3000 m and above. Both forests and meadows are subject to various extraction activities, such as grazing and biomass collections and harvests. The vegetation is the basis of all NTFPs related activities, and issues relating to the right, control and restriction over this natural resource have always generated contentious debate and policy level controversies. In view of these, it is important to give an idea of forest types, their distribution, their composition and magnitude of diversity. The following summary of forest vegetation is largely based on work carried out by a number of expeditious from Japan and other countries (e.g. Imanishi 1953; Kihara 1955; Kihara 1957; Nakao 1964; Mumata 1975; Mumata 1981; Ohashi 1975) and a comprehensive account of the forest of Nepal by Stainton (1972).

Table 3.1
Forest types of Nepal (derived from Stainton 1972)

A. *Tropical and Subtropical*

Forest Type	Distribution and Related Features
1. Sal forest	Throughout the Nepal in tarai (wet plains), bhabar (dry, tallus land consisting of coarse material) and hills up to 1500 m altitude; tree height declines with altitude from usually 30m to 20m; sal (*Shorea robusta*) is extremely gregarious, with few associated species; epiphytes rare.
2. Tropical deciduous Riverain forest	Occurs along the streams of the bhabhar and dun valley *Bombax malbaricum* most common; others include *Holopetelea integrifolia, Ehretia laevis, Adina cordifolia.*
3. Tropical evergreen forest	Occurs in limited areas as narrow strips (<100 m wide) along water courses or in gulleys in tarai, bhabhar, dun valleys, and outer hills, throughout Nepal. *Michelia champaca* is the tallest tree (>30 m). There are several species of Lauraceae and genus *Eugenia*. Altitude generally below 1000m.
4. Subtropical evergreen forest	Distributed between 800- 1700 m in a few localities of high rainfall in outer hills in extreme east of Nepal, *Ostodes paniculata* and *Eugenia tetragona* abundant, tree height of 15 m.
5. *Terminalia* forest	Occurs in an area of very limited in extent; *Terminalia* species (*T. tomentosa, T. chebula, T. belerica*) generally occur as a component of forests in which sal dominates; only occasionally *Terminalia* species form their own forests; they occur both in the eastern and western parts; trees tall, 30 m or more.
6. *Dalbergia sissoo- Acacia catechu* forest	These deciduous species are widespread along the rivers on new alluvium in bhabar and dun valleys; the extent of the forest is limited by the extent of gravel deposition along rivers and streams, while *D. sissoo* occurs only along rivers, *A. catechue* occurs as a riverain tree as well as the component of deciduous forests.
7. Subtropical deciduous hill forest	In outer foot hills up to 1200m; also penetrates into the midland up the big river valleys which are wide and hence dry; in West Nepal occurs almost exclusively on the southern aspects in outer foothills; species composition very mixed except where *Anogeissus latifolia* predominates; other common species are *Ehretia laevis* and *Terminalia tomentosa.*

Forest Type	Distribution and Related Features
8. Schina – Castanopsis forest	Occurs between 600- 1900 m altitude; common in wet region of Arun and Tamur valleys and lower areas south of Annapurna Himal; it is a major forest type of the E. Nepal and Central Midlands; it prefers mesic aspects (N and W), drier S and E aspects being occupied by sal in lower areas and oaks (*Q. leucotrichophora, Q. lanuginosa*) and *P. roxburghii* in higher areas; extensive between 750-1600 m, particularly in Pokhara area, generally on wet sites when sal is uncommon in the forest; tree height 27 m; on higher side it passes into *Michelia-Laurel-Lithocarpus* mixture, typical of lower temperate mixed broadleaved forest.
9. Subtropical semi-evergreen hill forest	Many species of evergreen forests of both tropical and subtropical common; between 600-1800 m altitudes, particularly in side valleys of upper Arun and Tamur valleys and around Pokhara; surrounded extensively by *Schima Castonopsis* forest; *Padanus furcatus* and *Cyathea spinulosa* (tree fern) typical constituents at the base of big mountains; canopy frequently broken, and tall deciduous trees (*Cedrela toona, Albizzia moliz, Dalbergia tircina*) emerge above smaller evergreens.
10.*Pinus roxburghii* forest (evergreen with about 1 yr leaf life span, e-evergreen)	This long-needled pine occurs from Afghanistan eastward along the Himalayan ranges to Bhutan; in Nepal generally between 900-2000m in midlands; abundance declines from west to east; in east it is scarce, occurring in limited localities in the lower parts of Arun and Tamur valleys; in upper parts this pine merges with oak forests in the west where it is predominant extensively; trees up to 35-40 m of height; it forms almost pure canopy, and climbers; shrubs are almost absent because of frequent fires.

B. *Temperate and Alpine Broadleaved*

Forest Type	Distribution and Related Features
1. ***Quercus leucotrichophora*** (leaf with dentate margin , white underneath)-***Quercus lanuginosa* forest** (large leathery leaf with yellowish underneath) **(both e-evergreen)**	Extensive in the west midlands between 1500-2200 m, but in gulleys it passes down into the pine and sal forests zone, up to 1000 m altitude; in the east midlands it is present in small amounts in the lower Arun and Tamur valleys; highly gregarious trees up to 27 m high; *Rhododendron arboreum, Lyonia ovalifolia* common under-canopy tree species; shrubs many; the tall palm, *Trachycarpus tekel* occur on wet sites; this forest type is uncommon in the adjacent (westward) Indian state, Uttaranchal (UA) where *Q. leucotrichophora* alone in widespread.
2. ***Quercus floribunda* forest** (leaf prickly with green underneath, e-evergreen)	A western Himalayan species occurring from Afghanistan to Nepal; limited to N and W faces where soil is damp, between 1800-2400 m; has a fair representation of *Acer* and other deciduous species (not so common feature in UA), furthermore, and its zone has many patches of *Aesculus-Juglans-Acer* forest; trees tall up to 35 m; occasionally mixes with other oaks; luxuriant epiphytic growth, and lauraceous under canopy in some situations indicating its association with a moist habitat.
3. ***Quercus semecarpifoia* forest** (e-evergreen):	Ranges from Afghanistan to Nepal and Bhutan (prickly leaf with brown underneath) to Manipur above 2200 m; can grow with *Abies*, often dense bamboo undergrowth; epiphytic growth luxuriant on wet sites, common in Humla-Jumla; area often forms a pure top canopy; in west midlands occurs above *Q. leucotrichophora- Q. lamellosa* forest belt, also common in central and east midlands.
4. ***Castanopsis tribuloides- C. hystrix* forest** (close to e-evergreen):	East Himalayan in distribution, but *C. tribuloides* goes up to Kumaun in the west; forms a dark evergreen forest between 1800-2300 m; trees up to 32 m tall; under-canopy trees lauraceous.
5. ***Q. lamellosa* forest** (close to e-evergreen)	East Himalayan forest type, absent from the western Himalaya; dark and gloomy forest, common in Arun and Tamur valleys where rainfall is heavy; trees draped with mosses, ferns and other epiphytes, and under-canopy forms a dense-thickets; 2000-2500m altitudes; in east and central midlands; undercanopy lauraceous (e.g. *Litsea, Machilus, Lindera* and *Ilex*).

Forest Type	Distribution and Related Features
6. ***Lithocarpus pachyphylla* forest** (close to e-evergreen)	East Himalayan type; in Nepal only in the extreme east, including the area between Tamur and Sikkim border between 2300- 3100 m; merges with *Q. lamellosa* forest in its lower part; trees up to 33 m; under-canopy lauraceous.
7. ***Aesculus-Juglans-Acer* forest** (deciduous)	Referred to as Western Himalayan type, it occurs in the west midlands, the Humla-Jumla area, and in some of inner valleys of the western half of Nepal between 1900-2800m; common alongside steams in narrow strips; apart from the common species, namely *Aesculus indica, Acer caesium* and *Juglans regia,* these forests have *Betula alanoides, Alnus nepalensis* (waterside places); trees up to 30 m tall; in eastern Nepal this forest is replaced by the one having *Magnolia campbellii* and *Acer campbellii.*
8. Lower temperate mixed broadleaved forest (close to e-type)	Largely evergreen, this forest occurs in the western parts of Nepal between 1700-2200m, generally on mesic north and west faces of mountains; common in E Nepal; members of family Lauraceae prominent: *Machilus* spp., *Cinnamomum tamala, Phoebe* spp. *Lindera* spp., *Litsea citrate, Meolitsea umbrosa* and others; however, laurels are not confined only to this type, they also occur with several other wetter types, such as forests of *Q. lamellosa* and *Aesculus-Juglans-Acer* forest. In general this is a mixed type of forest. A number of species flower in autumn, e.g., *Michelia kisopa, Symplocos* sp. *Prunus undulata, Cornus oblonga, Eurya acuminata, Alnus nepalensis.*
9. Upper temperate mixed broadleaved forest	Primarily eastern and central in distribution; largely deciduous, includes many maples (*Acer campbellii, A. sterculiaceum, A. pectinatum*), *Magnolia campbellii, Symplocos* spp., *Betula utilis,* but also evergreens like *Ilex* spp., *Rhododendron arboreum*
***10.Rhododendron* forest**	In this rhododendrons form much of the upperstory; other tree species, if present have only a few individuals scattered among them. This forest should be differentiated from those in which rhododendrons are abundant but are present in the undercanopy of *Abies* forest, *Tsuga* forest and *Betula* forest; *R. arboreum* may

Forest Type	Distribution and Related Features
	forest, *Tsuga* forest and *Betula* forest; *R. arboreum* may be up to 12 m tall, but at higher altitudes, above 3000 m the forest is reduced to shrubberies with heights 2-4 m; the absence of tall upperstory trees may occur on steep slopes with thin soil cover resulting from the loss of much of the soil because of the heavy rainfall; it may also result from the felling of trees of taller species, such as of oaks, however, the number of *Rhododendron* species is about 30 in the extreme east and in western Nepal, many of rhododendron are alpine; *Gaultheria* spp., *Vaccinium* spp., and *Lyonia* spp. are some of the common ericaceous plants.
11. *Betula utilis* (birch) **forest**	Ranges from Afghanistan to western China, generally above 3000m; it is widespread in Nepal and dominates tree-line areas, between 3000-3800m; the upper story of birch forest is generally exclusively of birch; trees generally 8-10 m high, with the undercanopy having rhododendrons (*R. companulatum* being the most common), *Acer* spp., *Juniperus recurva, Lyonia villosa, Sorbus foliosa;* in Humla- Jumla, the birch often occurs as a component of conifer forest of *Pinus wallichiana, Picea smithiana* and *A. pindrow;* here the birch forest may occur around 3000 m, but in inner valleys it may go above 4000m.

C. *Temperate and Alpine Conifer*

Forest Type	Distribution and Related Features
1. *Abies spectabilis* (silver fir) **forest**	Occurring throughout the Himalaya from Afghanistan to Bhutan this silver fir is also known as *A. webbiana;* it is quite common in the west midlands of Nepal between 2300- 3400m; it occurs above the low altitude fir *A. pindrow,* and is most extensive in central midlands of Nepal between 3000-3300m on the south side of the main Himalayan ranges; tree height easily 30-35 m; in the eastern parts, particularly from the upper Arun and Tamur valleys it has been replaced by rhododendrons; in the western parts *Q. semecarpifolia* is quite common in a silver fir forest, but in others rhododendrons are abundant (referred to as *Abies- Rhododendron* forest), the common being *R. barbatum, R. companulatum and R. arboreum.*

Forest Type	Distribution and Related Features
2. *Tsuga dumosa* (hemlock) **forest**	It ranges from eastern- most of Kumaun through Nepal, Sikkim, Bhutan to Mishmi hills and upper Burma in the east, between 2200-3500 m; with tree heights generally 25-35m the Himalayan hemlock forest has following species composition in the west midlands: a few trees of *Abies spectabilis, Betula utilis* and *Q. semecarpifolia* in the canopy, and *Acer* spp., *Sorbus, Prunus corunata, Ilex dipyrena, R. arboreum* and *Symplocos theaefolia* in the undercanopy.
3. *Pinus wallichiana* (blue pine) **forest**	Occurs from Afghanistan through the Himalaya to Bhutan and south-east Tibet (does not occur in Sikkim) and it is primarily a forest of dry inner valleys; in Nepal it ranges from 1950 m into timberline areas; less abundant in the midlands than in other parts, away from the full influence of the monsoon(inner valleys); in the midlands it prefers the big river valleys which are drier; an early successional species, susceptible to fire; quite common in the Humla-Jumla area; trees up to 35m of height; many stands are of secondary origin, often pure, but in the Humla-Jumla area it is frequently associated with *Picea smithiana, Abies pindrow* and *Cedrus deodara.*
4. *Picea smithiana* (spruce) **forest**	Called as the western Himalayan spruce, its forest ranges from Afghanistan through NW Himalaya to Nepal; occurs only in areas, at least partly sheltered from the full impact of monsoon rain (inner valleys species); in Nepal abundant in Humla-Jumla area (between 2270-3333m), ascending a long way up dry valleys, absent from midlands; anthropogenic disturbance has favoured blue pine in the Humla-Jumla areas, consequently the spruce is confined to the mesic north aspects; trees tall, up to 45 m and majestic, overtopping its associates viz., *Tsuga dumosa, A. pindrow Populus ciliata, Aesculus indica* and others.
5. *Abies pindrow* (fir) **forest**	This low altitude fir forest generally occurs on mesic north and west faces in the western parts of Nepal, between 2120 -3180 m; grows up to 45m of height(in contrast to A. *spectabilis* which remains below 30 m height); such tall trees occur in damp gulleys where soil is damp; in the west of Karnali it occurs as wide-spaced trees in an otherwise exclusively broadleaved deciduous forest of *Aesculus-Juglans-Acer;* this fir also grows with spruce, closely packed together, both attaining a height

Forest Type	Distribution and Related Features
	of 45 m, and columnar appearance; several broadleave species, such as *Cornus macrophylla, Lyonia ovalifolia,* and *R. arboreum* may occur as the undergrowth, but where the undercanopy is dark, such as in stands having spruce ,undergrowth is poor.
. *Cedrus deodara* (deodar) **forest**	The deodar occurs from Afghanistan through the NW Himalaya to West Nepal; common as a village tree in the Humla-Jumla areas, it does not cover a large area naturally; the altitudinal range is 1970- 2424 m; much of the forest is open and grassy, possibly because of frequent fires; tree height up to 30-35m; occasionally associated with pine and spruce, but generally forms pure canopy.
. *Cupressus torulosa* (noble cypress) **forest:**	The range of noble cypress forest includes Chamba in the NW Himalaya to Nepal's western parts, it is unknown from Sikkim and Bhutan, its presence in Assam is reported on limestone (however, the species identification is doubtful); it is generally associated with the limestone belt, a prominent example being the one running from the Kumaun to Seti Khola; the 40 ha stretch of cypress forest on the south face of China peak at Nainital hill resort is a famous example of its association with the limestone and a very steep slope; the altitudinal range is 2120- 2880 m; trees 30-35m tall, undercanopy tree layer sparse.
. *Larix* **(larch) forest**	A east Himalayan species, the Himalayan larch occurs from the central Nepal eastward through Sikkim and Bhutan into SE Tibet and China (absent from NW Himalaya); the species is most probably *L. griffithiana;* height up to 25 m; altitudinal range, 2878-3636 m; its associates include *A. spetabilis* and *Betula utilis.*

D. Minor Temperate and Alpine Associations

Forest Type	Distribution and Related Features
. *Alnus* (alder) **woods**	Alder (*Alnus nepalensis)* woodland is among the most widely distributed, from Chamba eastwards through the Himalaya to SE Tibet and western China, between 900-2700m altitude; in Nepal or anywhere it occurs as

Forest Type	Distribution and Related Features
	small isolated woods along streams, particularly on landslips, abandoned fields and unstable surface; tree height up to 30 m; in the east and central midlands it occurs in wet places in *Schima–Castanopsis* forest or in temperate deciduous forest; in the west midlands it occurs in *Quercus floribunda* and *Aesculus –Juglans –Acer* forest.
2. *Populs ciliata* (van pipal) **woods**	Its range is wide, from Kashmir through the Himalaya to Bhutan and SE Tibet; in Nepal it occupies drier areas along streams at 2100-3180m altitudes, but can go up to 3630m; probably absent from the central and east midlands; tree height, 25m; it is a common component of *Aesculus- Juglans-Acer* forest in the west midlands; also common in mixed conifer forests in Humla-Jumla areas.
3. *Hippophae* (buckthorn) **scrub**	In Nepal the buckthorn is represented by two species, *H. salicifolia* and *H. thibetana;* the former occurring from Garhwal to Bhutan, and the latter from Garhwal through Himalaya, Tibet and North China; *H. salicifolia* (shrubs to 18m tall trees) occurs between 2120- 3180 m, usually lining the banks of streams, forming pure thickets on newly- laid alluvial gravels or on unstable slopes with water close to surface (like alder) probably confined to the west midlands; *H. thibetana* (a low shrub less than 1m)occurs in the dry inner valleys between 3330-4390m.
4. Moist alpine scrub	It occurs above the tree line, between 3000-4240m moist scrub occur in all wet parts of Nepal: Rhododendrons dominate in them in the east midlands, declining both in dominance and species number towards west; in the east midlands *R. companulatum, R. wallichii, R. campylocarpum, R. weghtii, and R. fulgens* commonly form thickets (1.5-3 m tall), with few trees of birch and fir; of these *R. companulatum* goes up to the highest altitude; in the west and central midlands only three rhododendrons are found in this community (*R. companulatum. R. lepidotumad, R. anthopogon* compared to 9 in the east) and the uppermost alpine forest here often consists of *Betula utilis* with shrubberies of rhododendrons and *Sorbus* spp; in Humla-Jumla *Junipers wallichiana* becomes prominent.

Forest Type	Distribution and Related Features
5. Dry alpine scrub	It occurs in inner valleys, up to 4330 m and more; in this forest type, junipers, viz. *Juniperus recurva,* below 3630m, *J. wallichiana* at 4240 m and *J. squamata* at similar altitudes dominate; in drier conditions *Ephedra gerardiana* occurs on stony riverside terraces and *Myricaria* on riverside gravels; in inner valleys of the west Pinus *excelsa, Betula utilis, Cupressus torulosa* and *Juniperus wallichiana forests* occur instead of the scrub.
6. *Juniperus wallichiana* forest	*J. wallichiana* is the principal species in dry inner valleys throughout Nepal in western and eastern valleys, as well as Humla-Jumla area. *J.* wallichiana occurs both as a shrub and tree, generally 6-9m tall at 2730-4000 m altitudes. *P. excelsa, Betulis* and *C. torulosa* are the principal tree associates. Other junipers include *J. communis* in western parts, generally uncommon, *J. recurva* (occurring both as tree and shrub) in the western and central midlands and *J. squamata* in west of Karnali. *Caragana gerardiana, Spiraea arcuata, Rosa sericea* and species of *Lonicera* and *Berberis, Salix* and *Cotenaster* are common shrubs. An aromatic smell of dry vegetation of pine, cypress, juniper and thyme is conspicuous and different from the forest with monsoon rain.
7. Alpine Steppes	At altitudes 3600 m and above, close to 5000 m altitude some extensive steppes occur, mostly to the north of the Dhaulagiri-Annapurna massif. There the climate is dry as monsoon weakens, more like the Tibet plateau than Nepal. The following description of Stainton (1972) is based on Dolpa district. *Canagana brevifolia* a spring shrub just above 1 m tall with yellow flowers and *Lonicera spinosa,* a spiny plant dominate over many miles. Only along the streams their dominance is broken by the thickets of *Salix* and *Myricaria.*

3.1.2 Distribution of Forests

Summary of distribution across altitudinal gradients with variation along the east-west axis. The tropical (up to 1000m) vegetation is mostly dominated by sal (*Shorea robusta*) in association with *Terminalia* spp, *Phyllanthus emblica, Lagerstroemia parviflora, Cassia fistula, Haldina cordifolia, Syzygium* spp, and big lianas like *Bauhinia vahlii* and *Butea parviflora*. Silky cotton trees (*Ceiba pentandra*) are also common. In eastern Nepal, subtropical forests of true chestnuts, and genus Schima, a member of the tea family, predominates in the subtropical zone (1000-2000m) while in western Nepal, this zone is represented by chir pine (*Pinus roxburghii*). Evergreen oaks (genus *Quercus*) are common in the temperate zone (2000-3000m) in both east and west. Deciduous forests, such as of maples (*Acer* spp) and horse chestnut (*Aesculus indica*), are found at lower elevations in this range, while blue pine (*Pinus excelsa*) predominates at higher elevations in the west. Also found in this altitude range are over 30 species of Rhododendron.

Up to the tree line in sub-alpine zone (3000 m to 3600 m) firs (*Abies* spp), hemlocks (*Tsuga dumosa*) and yews (*genus Taxus*) predominate in the east, while Himalyan birch and silver fir are found throughout this altitude. In wetter areas, dwarf bamboo and rhododendrons are common tree line species, while in dry areas, junipers are found. The plant height gets reduced with the increase in altitudes; the vegetation becomes bushy and dwarf and mat or cushion forming plants prevail. The alpine zone (above 3600m) is characterized by hardy perennials and the annuals. Rhododendron bushes are the dominant shrubs along with the numerous alpine herbs. Above the tree line in meadows numerous species of medicinal and aromatic herbs are found across extensive areas of alpine tundra. Especially in western Nepal, these plants are often characterized by aromatic rhizomes, and include such commercially important species as *Nardostachys grandiflora* (jatamansi) and *Valeriana jatamansi* (sugandhwal), both of the valerian family.

Outer ranges. In the outer ranges of the eastern and western parts common forests are sal, subtropical deciduous and tropical evergreen forests. These include the Siwaliks, foot hills, duns and adjacent plains. *Pinus roxburghii* forest of the western region is replaced in the eastern region by Schima-castnopis forest and the mixed *Quercus leucotrichophora*- Q. *lanuginosa* forest by the one dominated by Q. *lanuginosa* (Table 3.2). Three additional forest types, each dominated by evergreen broadleaved species occur in the eastern region: subtropical evergreen forest, lower temperate mixed broadleaved forest and *Castanopsis forest*. The number of forest community is 8 in the eastern region, compared to 5 in the western region.

However, several local variations in the vegetation described above occur: (i) P. *roxburghii* in western Nepal may descend as low as 600m; (ii) oak may meet sal in a few localities without the intervention of pine; (iii) within the sal zone the recently formed alluvial surface along rivers is occupied by *Acacia catechu* or *Dalbergia sissoo* or their mixed forest; (iv) sal's dominance is also broken by the presence of tropical evergreen riverain forest in shady gulleys; (v) water logged flat areas are often occupied by tall (2m) grasslands, mainly of *Cymbopogon jwarancusa* and *Bothriochola intermedia,* which often establishes even within 18 months of crop field abandonment.

Midlands and Southern sides of the main ranges. The midlands are described as areas lying between the main snow ranges and outer ranges. Most of this densely populated zone is deforested and intensively cultivated. In areas around villages vegetation is generally severely degraded, with heavily lopped trees for the cattle fodder and firewood. In the western part of the country often the only remnants are coppices of oaks among shrubberies of Prinsepia utilis (a shrub the seeds of which have edible oil), Pyrus pashia (a small tree), Rhus spp., Coriaria nepalensis, Jasminum humile, Rhododendron arboreum, Lyonia ovalifolia and Zanthoxylum spp. and several others. In the eastern part of the country the hillsides at village level have often remains of Schima wallichii and Castanopsis spp. among shrubberies having some species common with their western counterparts.

Undisturbed forest. In the west midlands forest vegetation is in similar to that of Kumaun. Both have large areas under Pinus roxburghii forest between 900-2000m, *Quercus leucotrichophora*- Q. *lanuginosa* forest between 1400-2420m and Q. *semecarpifolia* forest about it. The higher ranges, above 2400m have *Abis spectabilis* and *Betula* utilis. However, in adjacent Kumaun Q. *leucotrichophora* forest in generally far more extensive than mixed Q. *leucotrichophora*- Q. *lanuginosa* forest, and Tsuga dumosa forest limited to a few pockets.

In the east midlands (country side roughly between Arun valley in the west and Sikkim border in the east) several of the west midlands forests are either absent or relatively restricted in distribution. These include both the pines (*P. roxburghii* and *P.wallichiana*) and oaks, Q. *leucotrichophora,* Q. *lanuginosa,* and Q. *semecarpifolia*. However, these forests occur in the wide valleys of Arun and Tamur. Over all in the east midlands Fagaceae –Lauraceae content is clearly richer than in the west midlands. Furthermore, *Schima-castanopsis* forest replaces *P. roxburghii* belt, and among the oaks, Q. *lamellosa* is most conspicuous (2000-2450m), above which *Lithocarpus* forest (2400-3000m) is prevalent. *Rhododendron* forest (having several rhododendrons) with little overstorey cover is quite prominent over a wide altitudinal range (2450-4000m). Tree ferns are prominent at the base of big mountains.

In brief, the west Midlands forests resemble those of Kumaun and the east Midlands forests those of Sikkim. In the central Midlands the west Midlands types are prominent on dry south-facing slopes and in wide valleys and the east Midlands types on moist north-facing slopes. However, certain differences from the west Midlands types, as given below are apparent: (i) Q. *floribunda* forest, *Abis pindrow* forest, *Cupressus torulosa* forest, and *Juniperus wallichiana* forest of west-Midlands types are absent in the central Midlands. (ii) The deciduous forest, *Aesculus-Juglans-Acer* forest of west Midlands is replaced by *Acer-Magnolia-Osmanthus- Ilex* forest of upper temperate mixed broadleaved type. (iii) *Populous ciliata* or *Hippophae salicifolia* forest is absent. Differences from the east Midlands type include the following: (i) *Schima-Castanopsis* forest below 1900m and *Michelia-Laurel- Lithocarpus* association type of the lower mixed broadleaved forest between 1600-2100m are very limited in extent and are confined to moist slopes. (ii) Tree ferns, *Padanus* and other species of subtropical semi-evergreen forest type do not form true forest in the central Midlands, they, however, occasionally occur on damp shady faces. (iii) Q. *lamellosa,* though common (2120-2575m), generally occurs mixed with other oaks. (iv) *Castanopsis hystrix* and *Lithocarpus pachyphylla* are generally absent.

The Humla-Jumla area. This area is bounded to the south by the long chain of lekhs, with crestline between 3940-4433m, cutting off much of the monsoon rain which winds carry from the plains. Consequently, the Humla-Jumla area is dry (with less than 50 cm rain) and supports vegetation different from the Midlands. This may be pointed out that the area does not lie north of the main Himalayan ranges, as is the case with the inner valleys.

Snow fall is quite frequent, but is never massive because the scarce moisture, and snow does not last long because of the clear sky and sun. That is why cultivation continues up to 3180m (rice cultivation up to 2720m), compared to the usual limit at 2420m in the Midlands where sunshine is much lower due to the heavy monsoon effect. The land is not deeply eroded as in the wetter parts, and gently sloping valleys, and absence of large snow mountains gives an open appearance. A mixed conifer forest of *Pinus wallichiana* and *Picea smithiana* is the characteristic forest of the Himla-Jumla area. Being a good colonizer, the pine has taken advantage of the human disturbance. A pure spruce forest is confined to mesic north and west aspects. *Tsuga dumosa* occurs only as a minor component of the pine-spruce forest. *Cedrus deodara* and *Cupressus torulosa* are grown as village trees.

Inner Valleys. Valleys lying north of the main Himalayan ranges, deep into the mountains hardly receive rain during the monsoon period. Here water-worn outline typical of mountain areas of the heavy monsoon is missing, and valley floors are broad and flat. P. *wallichiana* is the most widespread, followed by *Cupressus torulosa* particularly in the upper Bheri valley. Q. *semecarpifolia* which is widespread in many parts of Nepal high up to timberline, is scarce here, and absent from the valley heads, largely because of the dryness. Presence of Picea smithiana even in limited areas is rather surprising, as it generally grows at damp sites. *Tsuga dumosa* and Abies pindrow are absent, but Cedrus deodara is known to occur in a belt in the Bheri valley. Among the broadleaved Aesculus-Juglans –*Acer* forest at low altitudes, *Betula* forest at high altitudes, and *Ulmus, Populus, Prunus* and *Euonymus* on riverside flats are common. *Juniperus wallichiana* (the black juniper) can go up to 4500m. At such altitudes *Myricaria* spp. are common on riverside gravels, Ephedra gerardiana on strong terraces, and *Hippophae thibetana, Lonicera myrtillus* and *Caragana* spp. on the valley floor.

Dolpa, Mustang and Manang represent the arid zone, where in continuous sunshine cultivation of barley can be seen upto 4400m. Sheltered from most of the influence of the monsoon by the Dhaulagiri range to the south, Dolpa is a country of rolling hills, often smooth and round in outline. The higher parts of Dolpa, is largely treeless, only on the north-facing slopes forest patches, generally of *Pinus wallichiana* and *Betula utilis* occur. The treeless steppes have the domination of the shrubs, *Caragana brevifolia* and *Lonicera spinosa*. In the southern parts where moisture is not that scarce several rhododendrons *(R. anthopogon, R. lepidotum, R. nivale), Juniperus wallichiana, J. squamata* and *Berberis* spp. occur.

Both the Humla-Jumla and inner valleys are known for their meadows and steppes where several medicinal plants grow and their collection is a major activity.

Table 3.2
A comparison of forest types of the western and eastern Nepal (derived from Stainton 1972)

Forest type	Western Nepal	Eastern Nepal	Altitude(m)
Sal	Present	Present	300-900
Subtropical deciduous hills	Present	Present	300-1300
Pinus roxburghii	Present	*Schima-Castanopsis*	600-1820
Tropical evergreen	Present	Present	300-900
Subtropical evergreen	Absent	Present	900-1650
Q.leucotrichophora-Q.lanuginosa	Present	*Q.lanuginosa*	1300-1820
Lower temperate mixed broadleaved	Absent	Present	1650-2120
Castanopsis	Absent	Present	1870-2170

3.1.3 Species Richness and Endemism

Nearly 7,000 species of higher plants are found in Nepal, of which about 5% are endemic to Nepal (Table 3.3). Out of an estimated 9,000 species found in the eastern Himalaya as a whole, 39% are endemic to this mountain range (Myers 1988; Myers 1990; Bajracharya et al. 1998; IUCN 2000). For example, over 30 species of *Rhododendron* are endemic to the Himalaya, including the national flower of Nepal, *Rhododendron arboreum*, the only tree species of the genus (grows up to 18 m tall).

Photo 4. *Rhododendron flowers and rhodendron tree with flowers*

Faunal diversity is also impressive, it consists of 181 species of mammals, 850 species of birds, 100 species of reptiles and 635 species of butterflies (Table 3.3). Wild animals used for direct economic returns either from recreation hunting or use of their products includes deer, blue-sheep, musk deer, porcupine, honey bees, and lac insects. The other species such as tiger, wild elephant, one horned rhinoceros and snow leopard offer economic value through ecotourism in Nepal.

Table 3.3

Recorded species richness and endemism of major groups of organisms in Nepal

Group	Number of species recorded	Reference	Number of endemic species	Reference
Plant				
Angiosperms	5856	Koba *et al.* 1994; Akiyama *et al.* 1998	246	Shrestha and Joshi 1996
Gymnosperms	28	Koba *et al.* 1994	2	
Fungi	1822	Adhikari 1999	16	Joshi & Joshi 1991
Lichen	465	Sharma 1995	39	Sharma 1995
Algae	687	Baral 1996 compiled from Kattel and Adhikari 1992	3	Joshi & Joshi 1991
Liverworts and Mossess (Bryophytes)	853	Mizutani *et al.* 1995; Furuki & Higuchi 1995	30	Joshi & Joshi 1991
Fern and Allies (Pteridophytes)	380	Iwatsuki 1988	8	Joshi & Joshi 1991
Total	10063		342	

Group	Number of species recorded	Reference	Number of endemic species	Reference
Animal				
Mammals	181	Suwal & Verheugt 1995	1	Suwal & Verheugt 1995
Birds	852	Grimmet et al. 2000	2	Shah 1995
Reptiles	100	Shah 1995	2	Shah 1995
Amphibians	43	Shah 1995	9	Shah 1995
Fishes	182	Shrestha 2001	8	Shrestha 1995
Butterflies	640	Smith 1994, 1997	*29	Smith 1994, 1997
Moths	2253	Smith 1997 (pers. com.) in MFSC 2002		Smith 1997 (pers. com.)
Spiders	144	Thapa 1995	108	Thapa 1995
Total	3755		160	

Note: (* Possible endemic taxa).

Oberonia nepalensis is a recently reported endemic species of angiosperm (Shakya & Chaudhary 1999)

Akiyama *et al.* added 49 new species of Angiosperm and 1 Gymnosperm to the list of Koba *et al.* (1994)

On a world scale of plant species richness Nepal is placed 31st (Caldecot *et al.*1994). In Asia, Nepal is ranked the tenth richest countries in flowering plant diversity (BPP 1995). While small in terms of surface area (147,181 sq km), Nepal is remarkably diverse in flora and fauna due to its climatic and topographical variation (Map 1). Representing only 0.1% of the earth's land area, Nepal is home to more than 2.6% of all the flowering plants, 5.1% of gymnosperm, 9.3% of all birds, and 4.5% of all mammals. It is noteworthy that almost 50% or 203 out of about 410 angiosperm families in the world are represented in Nepal. Families with large numbers of species are the daisies (Asteraceae or Compositae, about 400 species), grasses (Poaceae or Gramineae, over 350 species), orchid (Orchidaceae, over 300 species), peas (Fabaceae or Leguminosae, 300 species), rose (Rosaceae, 180 species), sedge (Cyperacace, over 170 species), crowfoot or buttercup (Ranunculaceae, 150 species), mustard (Cruciferae, 90 species), and pink or carnation (Caryophyllaceae, 80 species). Nepal is also a home for a number of globally important rare and endangered species of plants and animals. CITES lists 136 species of animals from Nepal including 60 mammals, 61 birds, 12 reptiles, 1 amphibian and 2 butterfly species. IUCN lists 88 species of animals under their conservation status categories. Similarly, Shrestha and Joshi (1996) listed 60 species of plants under various categories of threats using the IUCN threat categories. Of these 22 are listed under rare, 12 under endangered and 11 under venerable category.

Nepal is known for its long history of mycological exploration, which started way back in 1850s. The region is rich in mushrooms. Already 1250 species of mushrooms have been described, of which about 50 are of genus Russula alone (Adhikari 2000). Many of them are mychorrhizal that help numerous species of trees to derive nutrients from infertile soils. Similarly, hundreds of lichen species grow on trunks, branches and twigs of many tree species, particularly of oaks and many of them are exported to the major cities and towns.

Ohsawa (1983) made a summary of tree species richness in the forest of eastern Nepal. He sampled 45 plots, generally ranging between 300-600m2 area. In six of the 45 plots, distributed from 145m to 3470m altitude, the tree species richness was 20 or more; of these three were located below 1000 m altitude, two between 1000-2000m and one between 2000-3000m. The highest species richness, 29 occurred at 2670m altitude on a north-facing slope. Plots having 10 or more species occurred up to 3000m altitude. Carpenter and Zoomer (1996) showed that the tree species richness is generally higher on the mesic north-aspect than drier south aspect. For example, in a lower altitudinal belt (< 1000m) they found 17 and 6 species in 20 x 20m plot, respectively at north and south aspect.

Nepal also has a large number of wild relatives of cultivated plants and domesticated animals and many trees, medicinal herbs, and ornamental plants (Shrestha 1999).

3.2 Relevant Policies and Regulatory Environment

Policy environment consists of policy formulation (policy statements, legislation and regulatory provisions), implementation and enforcement, and processes and mechanisms of policy development (stakeholder participation, mechanisms of negotiation, etc.). The prevailing policy and regulatory environment is assessed in terms of these elements identifying key issues that have implications on biodiversity conservation, enterprise promotion and sustainable community development in Nepal.

3.2.1 Existing Policies and Legislation

Nepal's forestry policy and legislative framework is generally innovative and does provide several opportunities. However, the regulatory environment is a challenge for sustainable, efficient, equitable management and use of resources. Several polices, plans, acts and laws interact to regulate and set the context in which forestry resources are managed and utilized for subsistence and commerce.

The most relevant policy and legislation include:

- Master Plan for the Forestry Sector (MPFS) 1988
- National Conservation Strategy 1988
- The Ninth (Five-Year) Plan (1997 – 2002)
- The Tenth (Five-Year) Plan (2002 – 2007)
- Nepal Biodiversity Strategies, 2002
- Nepal Environmental Policy and Action Plan 1993
- EIA Guidelines for the Forestry Sector, 1995

- Forest Act 2049 (1993), Forest Regulations 2051 (1995) and their Amendments
- Local Self-Governance Act (LSGA) 1998
- Decentralization Act 1982
- National Parks and Wildlife Conservation Act 1973
- Environment Protection Act 1996 and Environmental Protection Regulation 1997
- Soil and Watershed Conservation Act 1982
- Pasture Land Nationalization Act 1974
- Aquatic Life Protection Act, 1961
- New Industrial Policy 1992
- Trade and Transit Agreement (with India) 1992
- Import and Export (Control) Act, 1957
- New Trade Policy 1982
- Custom Act, 1963
- Plant Protection Act, 1972
- Land (Survey and Measurement) Act 1961

According to the stated policy of the HMGN, community forestry through User Groups is seen as a high priority for meeting the basic needs of the rural population for forestry products. The HMGN has also placed a high priority on environmental objectives, especially in the prevention of land degradation and the rehabilitation of eroded or degraded lands. In the present political context, transfer of decision making directly to User Groups for the management and use of local forest resources is of major importance.

The details of HMGN's forestry sector policy and programs are incorporated in the Master Plan for the Forestry Sector (MPFS), which was published in the December of 1989 (MFSC 1989). The MPFS has the long-term goal of meeting the basic needs of rural Nepalese for fuel, fodder and timber. Its long term objectives are to improve farming systems, conserve the soil and water ecological balance, conserve genetic resources and eco-systems, and develop and manage the forests for income and employment opportunities. Its medium term objectives are to achieve people's participation in forest development, management and conservation by decentralizing authority, to develop a legal framework to involve people in forest management, and to build the institutional capability of forestry institutions to perform their job effectively.

Community and private forestry is the main focus in the MPFS, receiving 47% of funding for the 20-year period of the Plan. The focus for activities has until recently been in the middle-hills, where the forest cover is small and the condition of which is degraded.

The MPFS discusses development aims and objectives for seven groups of NTFPs: medicinal and aromatic plants, *Daphne* paper, pine resin, *katha* from *Acacia catechu*, sabai grass, and canes and bamboo.

The policy document has recognized the participation of the people in managing their resources around their locality and also emphasized the principle of decentralization to be implemented in community forestry program. Policy also favors the poor and marginalized people by explaining that people below the poverty line, small farmers and entrepreneurs based on forest resource will manage the surplus forest area (after fulfilling the needs of local people) on the basis of priority (MFSC 1989).

The ninth five-year Plan has targeted the forestry sector development "to initiate the private sector and adopt the free market system for the long term development of forest sector". The Plan has sought

Photo 5. *Women at a community forest meeting in Dolpa*

women's carrier development through the forestry sector, as they are the main users and managers of the resource. It has further explained that forest resources will be mobilized for the individual, poor and oppressed class.

The Plan has further mentioned that "as women are mainly involved in collection of timber, firewood, fodder, animal bedding and so on, necessary arrangements will be made to compulsorily include them in the forest users committee".

The Government of Nepal is a signatory to the Convention on International Trade in Endangered Species of Wild Fauna and Flora (CITES). This established lists of endangered species in which international trade is either prohibited or strictly regulated. The Forest Act (1993) and National Parks and Wildlife Act (1973), amended in 1995, ban the collection or hunting of many endangered species of plants or animals.

Nepal has ratified the Convention on Biological Diversity (CBD) emanated at the UN Conference on Environment and Development in 1992. Most of the regulations listed above were passed previously and do not match the objectives and provisions of CBD.

3.2.2 Property Rights and Access to Resources

The Forest Act of 1993 and several amendments, the Forest Regulations of 1995 and the Community Forest Directives of 1995 provide a framework for the ownership/tenure and structure of community forests in Nepal. Community forestry involves the transfer of user rights and management responsibilities for one or more patches of forest to the local people formed into a specified forest user group (CFUG). The Act states that the "District Forest Officer (DFO) may hand over part of a national forest to a user group in the form of a community forest, entitling the group to develop, conserve, use and manage the forest, and sell and distribute the forest products by independently fixing their prices according to an operational plan[3]."

The legislation recognizes CFUGs as self-governing and autonomous entities and entrusts them with the management, control, utilization

[3] An Operational Plan (OP) is the legal document signed by a CFUG and the District Forest Office for the management, utilization and conservation of forest resources.

and sale of community forest resources in a planned way. The CFUG has the rights to exclude others from using the forest. However, forestland ownership is not transferred to the user groups but remains with the government under state control.

Once the forest is handed over there is not a time limit for retaining the use rights. These remain with the CFUG for an indefinite period of time. The DFO can cancel the CFUG's registration and resume the community forest in cases where the CFUG fails to implement their operational plan, observe overall provisions of the Forest Act, or undertakes any actions that have significant negative effects on the environment.

With supporting policy and legislation in place, the community forestry program creates good opportunities to manage forest products including non-timber forest products (NTFP) in a common property system. But in contrary to the policies outlined here, very little has been translated into practice. In current community forestry practices in Nepal, NTFPs are generally excluded in the plans with very few exceptions. The size of CF is inadequate in most cases.

Even private land represents a very small source of these products. Most of the commercial NTFPs still come from wild collection, usually from extensive areas of the government-controlled national forest and grasslands. Whether these resources are in government controlled national forests or community forests (where NTFPs are not formally included in the OP), they are in a state of open access property. This means collectors have an incentive to harvest as much as possible before someone else does. In such circumstances, there is no incentive to conserve or manage the resource base.

Confusion over property rights also comes from the contradiction and inconsistency between forestry legislation and other laws, such as LSGA. Sometimes private companies/organizations are given exclusive collection rights for certain products, even in community forests. This creates confusion on the use rights of products between the CFUG and the private licensee.

Even with a good policy framework and legislation for clearly delineating and enforcing rights and responsibilities, the prevalent *de-facto* property rights situation is defective. The confused property rights issue results in an environment that is unable to improve production efficiency, conservation and social equity.

3.2.3 Product Regulation on Local Use and Commerce

The existing acts and regulations are still restrictive in nature and the role of government agencies is perceived to be as controlling authorities rather than agencies that help local environments.

The Forest Act (1993) restricts NTFP use by a) imposing a licensing system for product removal, sale, transportation and export; b) a royalty system; c) a controlling authority at the local district forest office; and d) severe punishments for product collection.

The Forest Rules (1995) further describes the regulations. Some noteworthy provisions in relation to NTFPs include:

- A collector must submit a detailed application to the DFO for collection in national forests. The DFO shall check the quantities to be collected and issue a release order. The right to collect, sell and distribute may be auctioned to the highest bidder.
- NTFPs from community forests may only be transported after informing the DFO.
- Species not mentioned in the legislation cannot be traded until sanctioned by the government.
- The government may impose a ban on the collection, use, sale, distribution and export of any forest product without justification.

In a recent change in regulation the complete ban on Yarshagumba (*Cordyceps sinensis*) is lifted but still royalty is prohibitively high. The ban of *Panchaule* (*Dactylorhiza hatagirea*) remains. *Kutki* (*Picrorhiza scrophulariiflora*), a very important medicinal plant, and the bark of the walnut are added to the complete ban list. These three species are now completely banned for collection, use, sale, distribution and export.

Similarly, an additional eight species are banned for export in their unprocessed form. These are *Nardostachys grandiflora, Valeriana jatamansii, Cinnamomum glaucescens, Taxus baccata, Abies spectabilis, Rawolfia serpentina, Permelia* spp and *silajit* (a mineral). Confusion surrounds the vague definition and interpretation of "processing". For some very high value products such as *Cordyceps* the processing would only reduce the value.

Photo 6. *Yarshagumba, panchaule, and kutki*

Regulatory agencies in the forestry sector include DFOs, Wardens of National Parks at local level and the Department of Plant Resources. As for forest based enterprise development, Cottage and Small Industries Development Board, the Office of the company registrar and Custom Offices also form an important part of the regulatory institutions.

DFOs have large areas of national forests in which to monitor, manage and control destructive human actions. In practice, no DFOs have any plans for the management of national forests except handing over some of them as community forests. DFOs in all the districts have limited capacity to properly regulate the timber and non-timber forest products. Besides, they have limited local accountability to local institutions and communities, and this is manifested in their emphasis on royalty rather than local incomes from NTFPs.

For unrestricted products, any national individual or organization can apply for the collection of NTFPs, by stating the types, area, quantity and purpose of collection. But in practice, the DFO issues collection licenses to traders, not harvesters, who produce an income tax certificate. Traders holding these licenses can strongly influence prices if they collude together, since harvesters can only sell these plants to one of them. The CFUGs can also provide collection licenses to collect from its community forest, if it is mentioned in the operational plan.

In and around some national parks, e.g. Shey-Phoksundo National Park (SPNP), communities are allowed to collect medicinal and aromatic plants for subsistence use only, under the permission of the park authorities. Issues are often raised by concerned stakeholders and conservation and development organizations to innovate appropriate institutional arrangements that allow communities to use and conserve the local resources. This issue needs to be dealt with both locally as well as nationally as a policy agenda. A number of buffer zones have been established or are being established around several national parks. Local institutions believe the establishment of buffer zones around the parks creates more problems than opportunities for communities, particularly in terms of extending park control over communal as well as privately owned natural resources.

Inconsistencies and contradictions found within and between the Forest Act, Regulations, Executive Orders and Circulars also complicate the situation. Consequently, this law is frequently circumvented. Most NTFP trade occurs in the informal sector. Regulations regarding ban or restrictions are distorted in practice. *Yarshagumba,* which had long been banned for collection and trade till very recently has always been in trade.

Another important regulatory issue on NTFP trade is related to multiple taxation. Different agencies such as VDCs, DDCs and even local clubs impose tax on the NTFPs trade. For example, DDC taxes NRs 500 per litre of *Jatamansi* oil produced by distillation plants installed by the communities of Jumla. An additional financial burden of the NTFP sub-sector is the forced payments to rent-seekers all along the transport route – road heads, airports, check posts, etc.

Producing and selling forest products including NTFPs is considered a difficult and illegal business. With all these hassles, the entrepreneurs and traders have little incentive to grow and market forest products even in privately controlled land. The restrictive regulations are apparently by-passed, generally not enforced and grant power to the regulating authorities to extract rents (Olsen and Helles 1997; Subedi 1998; Kanel 1999). There is a lack of policies to facilitate commerce, institutional support and provision for public services (such as information, research, technology, infrastructure and finance) to private and community enterprises. Under such conditions only the resourceful and influential big traders are able to manage the business tactfully at good profit.

3.3 Approaches of Biodiversity Conservation

All forests, excluding private forests, are called national forest in Nepal. The national forest, which also includes grassland, can be divided into several management options: protected forest (within the protected area system), government-managed forest, community forest, leasehold forest and religious forest.

The land under the protected area system (PAS) is controlled by the Department of National Parks and Wildlife Conservation (DNPWC), which includes the national parks, wildlife reserves, hunting reserves, and conservation areas. All national forests outside of the PAS are under the jurisdiction of the Department of Forest (DOF). About 61% of the total national forest within the DOF, is considered to be the potential community forest, of which more than 55% is forested and the rest is non-forested.

Conservation of biodiversity along with its sustainable use and equitable sharing of benefits are one of the major global concerns in forestry today. All over the world a number of organizations and individuals are directly or indirectly involved in conservation programs with a variety of approaches. A variety of the interventions are currently taking place to address internal and external threats to the biodiversity of the particular area with various assumptions. Some of these also consider biodiversity enhancing activities. These can be grouped into the following four major approaches.

3.3.1 Protected Area Approach

In this approach the areas considered for biodiversity importance are reserved, kept back or withheld for conservation. The assumption is the government agency and/or project team establish a protected area to stop both internal and external threats to the biodiversity of the area. Primary stakeholders of biodiversity in this approach include conservationist, government and international community, and often local communities are seen as the problem.

The designation of protected area system is the most common model for biodiversity conservation throughout the world. In Nepal, the government enacted the Private Forest Nationalization Act, 1956 to protect, manage, and conserve the forests for the benefit of the entire country (Nepal Gazette 1957). Nepal began emphasizing the conservation of biodiversity in protected areas and related endangered wildlife in the 1970s with the enactment of National Park and Wildlife Conservation Act, 1973. Nepal does have a fairly extensive Protected Areas network. A total of 26,696 sq km is occupied by 8 national parks and 4 wildlife reserves, 1 hunting reserve and 3 conservation areas in Nepal. This represents nearly 18.1% of total land area (DNPWC, 2002).

In a fairly extensive Protected Areas network of Nepal regions of the terai and central and eastern High Himal are well-represented. The "Conservation Area" concept of Protected Area management in the central Annapurna and eastern Makalu-Barun regions, encompassing Trans-Himalaya, High Himal and Midhills regions is remarkable. Even with the extensive Protected Areas network, Nepal's natural resources are being exploited above their sustainable capacity in order to meet the increasing needs of a rising human population that is predominantly agrarian and subsistence in nature (IUCN 1992; WCMC 1992; Yonzen 1993). There is no protected area in Middle Hills. In several mountain districts like Humla, biodiversity is threatened not only by dependence of people on fuelwood, fodder and grazing land, but also by over exploitation of medicinal and aromatic plant populations, primarily for use in Ayurvedic medicinal preparations in India. Traditionally these areas have been only suppliers of raw materials for processors in other countries, forcing collectors to extract growing amounts of material to increase their revenue while returning little of the final value of the product to the local economy.

Internally the local population continues to rely on the forest and pasture area of this region for fuel, fodder, timber, and a variety of non-timber forest products (NTFPs). The subsistence demand for these natural resources is increasing along with the population. At the same time demand from the outside markets for NTFPs without an internal system of sustainable harvesting has induced a serious threat. Additionally, there is a vast amount of biodiversity rich area of global significance outside the protected area system. In a situation where the conservation benefits are seen to serve individuals living outside of the area while local people pay the costs of the conservation actions, it is unlikely that the conservation project will be successful in meeting its goals (Murphree 1991).

3.3.2 Communities and Biodiversity

The increasing realization that the conservation faces greatest challenges when local communities are not involved led to the evolution of participatory approaches of involving local communities for the conservation. A critical review by Wells, Brandon, and Hannah (1992) defines Integrated Conservation and Development Projects (ICDPs) to include: "activities in buffer zones, biosphere reserves, small-scale rural development projects on park boundaries, and protected areas included in regional development plans." These projects aim to enhance the conservation of biodiversity in protected areas by focusing on the social and economic needs of people living in nearby communities. In each instance, ICDPs represent a shift away from traditional approaches to park management, which emphasize patrols and penalties for illegal use, to increased emphasis on promoting the participation of local resource users in conservation activities. These integrated conservation and development projects (ICDPs) place particular emphasis on promoting participation of local people in conserving natural resources (Heinen 1988, Upreti 1990). Funding for some of these activities comes from ecotourism, which is intensive in the central Annapurna and eastern Sagarmatha (Mt. Everest) conservation areas.

Community forestry and buffer zone management concepts are popular in Nepal. Most Nepalese people are bounded to the natural resources for their daily subsistence needs. This leads to the isolation and fragmentation of the species habitats causing the loss of the species. To reduce the human impact upon the natural resources of the protected areas of Nepal, five buffer zone areas have been established and it is likely to have more buffer zone areas.

This approach is also recognized and applied in India in the form Joint Forest Management (JFM). A more interesting reference for Nepal would be of Uttaranchal (UA). The 2001 Van Panchayat (VP) forest rules and JFM rules in UA made a provision that part of civil Soyam land or even reserve forest can be transferred to villagers as VP forest or JFM forest, although the procedure of getting reserve forest is too stringent and policy and regulation are too restrictive showing little trust in practice to local communities. There are good examples of protection of forest and distribution of forest products within the community such as grasses in many of 6700 VP forest in Uttaranchal.

In both Nepal and India, the indigenous and traditional system of managing their forest and pasture shows that they are interested and capable of managing their forest both technically and socially.

However, merely "repairing the subsistence living" by enabling people to have access to fodder, firewood, and leaf litter is not enough for a long-term sustainable development. It is particularly unattractive to young people, exposed to the fruits of open economy based on consumerism.

3.3.3 Enterprise and Biodiversity

Programs in the name of poverty alleviation or reduction are getting more popular. Some of these are also linked to biodiversity with the reasoning that one of the prime factors leading to the loss of biodiversity is poverty. They are focusing on the programs that address poverty by creating alternative sources of income. The assumption is that the promotion of an economic activity will substitute the damaging activities by the local stakeholders. But there are many cases of failure than successes. Most of the conservation organizations either do not have enterprise perspective and capability to provide useful services for enterprise development or assume it is too simple, or it can happen easily even if they do not know. From this approach, there are few examples, if any, of successes in generation of economic opportunities, let alone the synergy of income generation and conservation.

Furthermore, the programs of generating more incomes may contribute to reduce the pressure on biodiversity use, but it does not automatically lead to conservation. Just having more income that does not have any linkage or interdependency may actually lead to over use of biodiversity, and there are examples of resource degradation with the economic prosperity indicating that economic prosperity or linkages to market does not automatically lead to conservation.

3.3.4 Communities, Enterprises and Biodiversity

To date, the majority of conservation resources have been allocated to protected area system models while innovative people-centered, economic incentive-based resource management strategies have received less attention. Balancing economic, social, and environmental concerns is a difficult task that many conservation groups still view with skepticism. Moreover, community-based organizations and government agencies have few, if any, examples to follow in adopting a balanced approach. A number of authors, such as McNeely (1988), Silverstein (1993) and Subedi and Binayee (2000), have made attempts to establish that economic and ecological objectives do not contradict, but tend to merge in the long run. Development initiatives are also underway to scrutinize the integrity and correlation across level of economic incentives generated out of biodiversity use and status of biodiversity. But economic growth may not promote conservation on its own; therefore there is a need to explore all positive linkages between economic growth and conservation.

The approach of promoting local communities and enterprise that are directly linked to biodiversity is relatively new. The assumption is that the enterprise provides benefits to a community of stakeholders who have incentive and capacity to take initiatives for biodiversity enhancing activities and counter the threats to the biodiversity. Biodiversity Conservation Network tested this approach in seven countries across Asia and the Pacific in thirty nine sites spending 20 million US dollar in seven years (Salafsky et al. 1999; BCN 1997). Their conclusions are that "An enterprise strategy can lead to conservation, but only under limited conditions ... and never on its own. An enterprise strategy can be subsidized and yet still create a net gain for conservation. And to determine how to optimally use an enterprise strategy, you need to use adaptive management at both project and program levels."

Economic incentives approach addresses the question of how human activities are affected to promote biodiversity conservation by increasing the expected benefits of biodiversity-enhancing activities. There are a number of issues that arise from two interrelated questions. First, does economic incentives approach work for conservation? And if yes, in what conditions? Second, how to create sustainable economic incentives to conserve biodiversity?

Chapter 4

Economic Use and Enterprise Potentials of Biodiversity, Particularly NTFPs in Nepal

The literature review and analysis presented in Chapter 3 and our experiential learning show that Nepal is very rich in biodiversity with many valuable plant species. A large number of diverse forest and grassland communities contain many species of valuable plants, some in large amounts. In this chapter, we explored distribution, availability and enterprise use potentials of wild plant species vis-à-vis community-based forest enterprises and market and market value of Nepal's NTFPs.

4.1 Availability and Uses of Economically Useful Plants

4.1.1 Resource Base, Species Richness and Use Diversity

Of the total forest area, according to the 1994 National Forest Inventory (FRISP 1999), about 52% is classified as reachable forest area (with less than 100% slope). In addition, grassland and non-cultivated inclusions have good potential for the improved management and sustainable use of biological resources. The forests (29%), shrub lands (10.6%), meadows (grass lands) and non-cultivated inclusions, covering over 50% of the total geographical area of the country constitute the biological resource base including Non-Timber Forest Products (NTFPs) of Nepal.

Although in many areas of the world, especially developing countries, NTFPs have been used since time immemorial, only recently there is some thinking and realization that substantial economic benefits can be derived from biodiversity, and more particularly from NTFP enterprises. Even in developed countries recreational mushroom hunting and commercialization of wild mushrooms have been in practice for quite long. The people of several ethnic groups living in Nepal have been making use of many NTFPs in many ways since time immemorial. In a way, NTFPs represent a hidden harvesting, but of great value to poor people.

Earlier studies of several investigators reveal that 1000 species of plants, comprising over 14% of the known vascular plant species of the country, are recorded for economic use (Table 4.1). Current estimates show that the number is still greater in Nepal. People estimate many additional number of plant species are used in Nepal. Among these over 700 species are used for medicinal purpose, 440 species for wild food, 30 species for spices, 71 species for fiber, 50 species for fish-poisoning, and over 100 species for fodder. Our investigation shows more than 161 wild plant species are used to harvest NTFPs for commercial purpose; the list is given in Annex 3. In Mountains and other Himalayan areas of Nepal, forest and other natural vegetation have been used extensively for timber, fodder, firewood, leaf litter, medicines, foods, spices, fibers, tannins, gums, resins, fatty oils, dyes, incense, cosmetics, building materials, and agricultural implements.

Table 4.1

Number of plant species recorded by economic uses in Nepal

Economic Uses	Number of species
Medicine	700
Wild food	440
Essential oils	238
Fodder	100
Fiber	71
Fish-poisoning	50
Spices	30
Total	1000

Source: Malla and Shakya 1984; Malla and Shakya 1995; HMGN 1982; HMGN 1984.
Note: As many of the species have multiple uses, the total is 1000 though the sum is 1629.

Besides these economic uses, many plants have also been used for cultural purpose, such as parts of plants (leaves, flowers, fruits, roots and rhizomes) or standing trees in rituals and worships. For many of the uses, the local demand requires only a small amount, but many of the species are used for more than one purpose and are in high demand even at local level. For example, some commercially traded plants are also used for local medicine and incense making. The most notable products in our study area are insect galls on Pistacia integerima and roots and rhizomes of *Neopicrorhiza scrophulariflora* and *Nardostachys grandiflora*.

4.1.2 Distribution of Commercially Valuable NTFPs

In Figure 4.1 an attempt has been made to show the distribution of life forms and prime parts used for commercial purpose. It also gives an idea of these plants in terms of 161 commercial NTFPs species of Nepal by ecological zones and along east-west axis. Many of the commercial species are found in more than one altitudinal range, but only 2% are found in all three major land form zones of high mountains, middle hills and wet plains (terai). Being the transitional zone, mid-hills harbor 71% of commercial species, the highest of all. High mountains and terai each contain 48% of the commercial species. But 17% of the species are found only in high mountains as compared to 12% in terai and 6% in mid-hills, indicating importance of high mountains as a centre of NTFPs. Major wild plant species producing commercial products that are harvested and traded in significant volumes or that are of high values from different altitudinal zones are given in Table 4.2. The altitudinal range for each of the commercially used species is given in Annex 3. While there are a considerable number of NTFPs in tropical and mid-hill regions, and some of which are also produced in sizable volumes, the Himalayan and trans-Himalayan regions are rich in high value NTFPs.

Along the east-west axis, western Nepal is richer in commercially harvested species than the eastern part. With regard to growth term, the commercial NTFPs are as following: herbs 36% followed by trees 30% and shrubs 22%. The numbers of the fungi, orchids and climbers that are used commercially are relatively small but many of them are playing important role in trade because of their high prices in the market.

Fig 4.1 Distribution of plant species of Nepal used for commercial NTFPs (based on 161 species)

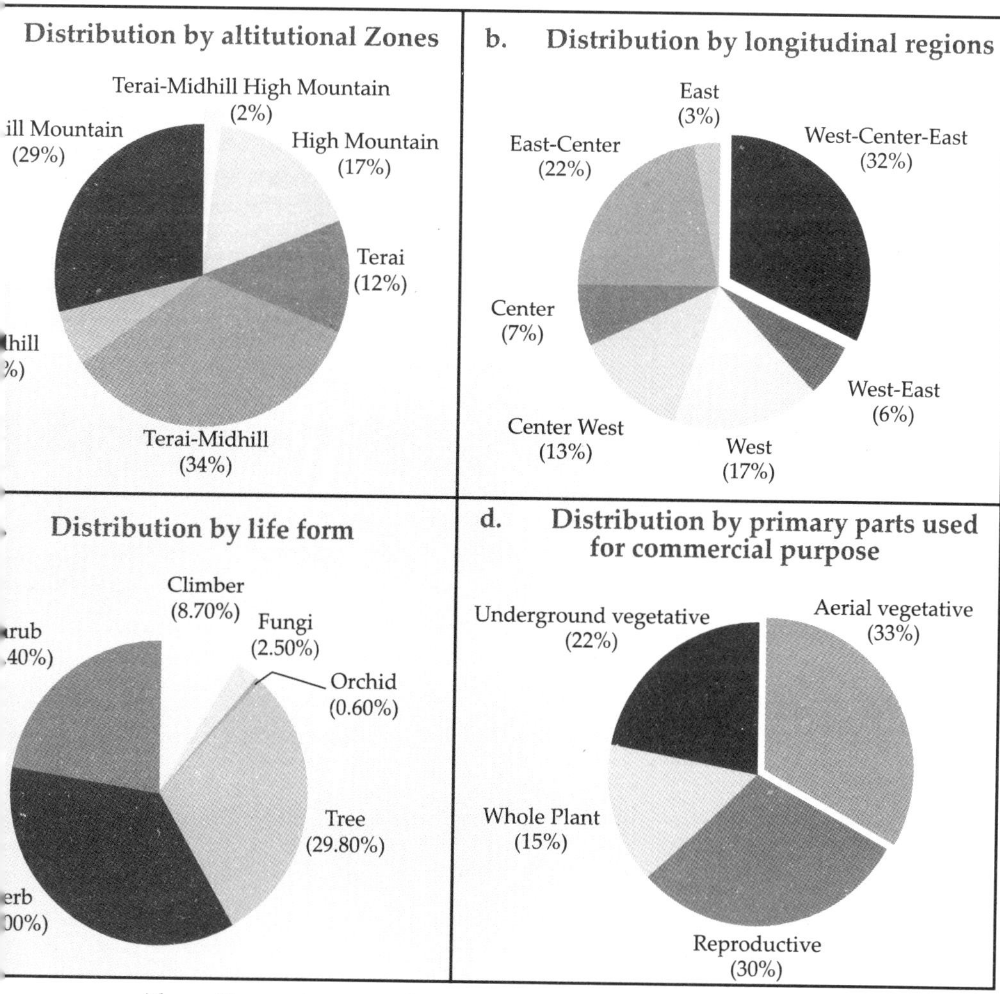

Along the east-west axis, western Nepal is richer in commercially harvested species than the eastern part. With regard to growth term, the commercial NTFPs are as following: herbs 36% followed by trees 30% and shrubs 22%. The numbers of the fungi, orchids and climbers that are used commercially are relatively small but many of them are playing important role in trade because of their high prices in the market.

Table 4.2
Notable commercially valuable, indigenous NTFPs of Nepal by altitudinal zones

Altitudinal zone	NTFPs species
1. Tropical (up to 1000 m)	Neem (*Azadirachta indica),* haldu (*Adina cardifolia), Artocarpus heterophyllus,* babul *(Acacia nilotica),* harro (*Terminalia chebula*), barro (*Terminalia bellirica*), amaltus *(Cassia fistula),* amala (*Phyllanthus emblica*), sikakai (*Acacia guguta*), wild asparagus (*Asparagus racemosus*), tendu (*Diospyros sp.*), sarpagandha (*Rauwolfia serpentina*), tulsi *(Ocimum sanctum sp.),* khaer *(Acacia catechu),* Bel *(Marmelos),* and Neem (*Azadirachta indica*)
2. Subtropical (1000- 2000 m)	Lokta (*Daphne spp*), argeli, wintergreen (*Gaultheria fragrantissima*), pipla (*Piper longum*), timur, Shila pushpa *(Didymo carpus redicellata), Zanthoxylum armatum,* tejpat, dalchini, rudraksha, ritha, majitho, gurjo, bhyakur, bajradanti, sugandhwal (*Valeriana jatamansi*), sugadhkokila, chiraito (*Swertia chirayita*), and wild asparagus (*Asparagus racemosus*), Vasa *(Adhatoda vasica)*
3. Himalayan and trans-Himalayan	
a. Temperate (2000-3000 m)	Atis (*Delphinium himalayai*), sugandhwal (*Valeriana jatamansi*), chiraito (*Swertia chirayita*), and nirmasi (*Parnassia nubicola*), *Berberis aristata,* tilpushpi *(Digitalis purpurea)*
b. Sub-alpine (3000-4000 m)	Chiraito (*Swertia chirayita*), morels (*Morchella spp.*), padamchal (*Rheum australe*), satuwa (*Paris polyphylla*), sunpati, juniper, lichens, laghupatra (*Podophyllum hexandrum),* lauthsalla (*Taxus sp.*), and panchaunle (*Dactylorhiza hatagirea*)
c. Alpine (above 4000 m)	Kutki (*Neopicrorhiza scrophulariiflora*), jatamansi (*Nardostachys grandiflora*), and yarshagumba (*Cordyceps sinensis*)

The plant species are likely to be severely impacted from unmanaged harvest, as many of the commercial products are derived from whole plants (15%) and underground parts (22%). Aerial vegetative parts are used as the primary parts for commercial purpose from 33% of the species. Of these, several species are used for their bark.

4.2 Community-Based Enterprises and Commercially Valuable Products

From our surveys, observations, and reviews, we found 161 plant species are harvested for commercial NTFPs in Nepal (Annex 3). Similarly, there are at least 137 entrepreneurs and 71 community-based forest enterprises (CBFEs) in Nepal. The CBFEs existed in various modalities, which can be outlined in aspects of geographic distribution, ownership and management structure, product types, linkages to sources of raw materials (wild crafted vs. cultivated, geographical areas, stewards of resources), technology, target markets, seasonality of operation, and similar characteristics (Subedi *et al.* 2002).

4.2.1 Types of Commercial Product, Plant Species and Sources

Our analysis based on the 161 commercial NTFPs species of Nepal shows that many of the species are used for more than one purpose. Figure 4.2 shows the distribution of the plant species by primary use category. Over 50% of plants are used primarily for medicinal purpose, which is followed by those for food (17%), essential oil (7%), plant fiber (6%) woods and crafts (5%), spice and flavor (4%), and dye (4%). The rest 7% are used for tonic, gum and resin, edible oil, broom, incense, soap making, etc.

ig 4.2 distribution of plant species by primary, commercial use (Total number of species=161)

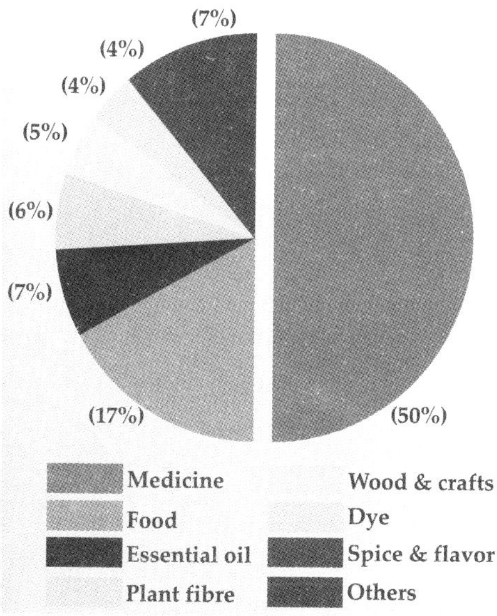

Most of the enterprises were involved in trade of dried, unprocessed products such as medicinal and aromatic products, mushrooms and health foods, and spices and flavors; some were involved in value-added processing such as essential oils, plant fibers, handmade papers, edible oils, gums and resins, herbal dyes; and few others were producing final consumer products such as Ayurvedic preparations, handmade paper products, wild fiber cloths, personal care products, herbal teas, handicrafts (Table 4.3).

Table 4.3
Types of product produced by community enterprises using NTFPs in Nepal

Products	Examples of Plant Species Used
A. Raw Plant Products	
Medicinal and aromatic	Kutki, chiraito, louth sallo, yarshagumba, panchaunle, pakhanved, harro, barro, amala, neem, silajit and many more
Spices and flavors	Cinnamon, timur, amala, juniper, large cardamom, also many of the aromatic plants
Wild mushrooms and health foods	Morels, kurilo
Dyes and tans	Padamchal, chutro, majitho, louthsallo, banjh, thingre sallo, okhar
Plant Fibers	Lokta, allo, argeli, hemp, bhimal, lefuke
Gums and resins	Chirpine, blue pine, sal
Handicrafts (leaves, woods, sticks)	Sal, pipal, bhorla, firfire, bamboo, nigalo, rattan
B. Products after value-added processing	
Lokta Handmade paper	Lokta
Argeli whiteskin	Argeli
Other plant fibers (threads, ropes, fabric)	Allo, hemp, bhimal, bhorla, argeli, sabai grass, lefuke
Fats and oils	Chiuri
Essential oils and extracts	Jatamansi, sugandhawal, titepati, sunpati, juniper, wintergreen, sugandhakokila, abies, deodar, lauth salla
C. Finished Products	
Ayurvedic preparations (medicines, tonic, nutrient supplements)	Kutki, chiraito, lauth sallo, yarshagumba, panchaunle, pakhanved, barro, barro, amala, neem, silajit and many more (Annex 3)
Traditional medicines	Kutki, chiraito, louth sallo, yershagumba, panchaunle, pakhanved, harro, barro, amala, neem, silajit and many more (Annex 3)
Handmade paper products	Lokta, argeli
Wild fiber cloth	Allo, hemp
Incense	Jatamansi, juniper, sunpati, mahuwa
Herbal teas	Thyme, gurjo, gandhaino, tulsi, mint, cinnamon, and a number of medicinal and aromatic plants
Herbal drinks, juices	Bel, rhododendron, seabuckthorn
Brooms (amriso, sabai grass)	Amriso, sabai grass
Bamboo and rattan products	Bamboo, nigalo, rattan
Wood handicrafts (Phuru)	Firfire
Leaf products (sal leaf plates, handicrafts)	Sal, pipal, bhorla
Edible fats and oils	Dhatelo, chiuri, khamu, walnut
Rosin, turpentine and gums	Chirpine, blue pine, sal
Personal care products (soaps, shampoo, creams)	Pangar, chiuri, ritha, amala, sikakai, naru, aromatic plants

In terms of sources of raw materials, most of the commercially important NTFPs come from the collection in wild, except some species in small areas such as *Zanthoxylum armatum, Sapindus mukorossi, Ammomum subulatum,* and recently *Swertia chirayita*. These NTFPs are collected from extensive areas of the government controlled forests and meadows including those in national parks and conservation areas, except some which are harvested from community forest and private land. Since in most of the cases, including community forests, the use and management provision is not incorporated into the management plans, these resources are governed under open-access property system. Although not primarily meant to benefit the NTFPs in the forest, indigenous protection systems for some forests are in place. It is found that species cultivated on private land are better managed than the same species on public access land indicating some management knowledge certainly exists and tenure is an important factor for making investment.

4.2.2 Geographic Distribution

Geographically the forest based enterprises cover all three major ecological zones: terai, Hills and Mountains as well as east, central and western regions of Nepal (Annex 2). However the production of NTFPs is a more important activity in mountains and hills. Although the availability of tradable raw materials is the necessary condition for an enterprise, we found that it did not automatically lead to an enterprise. Knowledge, technology and market demand were found to be the primary driving forces for the establishment of a new enterprise. Depending on the availability of the natural sources of raw materials, enterprise initiatives begin from the more accessible areas to the market centers, and then moved to new locations. A case of handmade paper production enterprises illustrate this pattern. Handmade paper production enterprises for outside sales were initially concentrated in Dolakha, Parbat, Kaski, and Baglung, but now have expanded to more remote locations such as Bajhang and Bajura.

4.2.3 Seasonality of Operation

The current practice of NTFP utilization involves only harvesting during certain period that is convenient to the collectors. There is mismatch in the biological maturity and harvesting period for several NTFPs that people practice. For example, *Swertia chirayita* propagates only from seed which get matured and is shed during October-November but because of high competition and cash need during Dashain collectors usually harvest this plant during July -August, before its biological maturity.

Enterprises also differ in terms of seasonality of operation. Those that collect NTFPs and sell to traders in crude form have a limited season of operation, mostly confined to a few winter months. Papermaking enterprises are done generally during summer or on other periods with sunny days, provided the raw material is in plenty. The comparison of harvesting seasons with the enterprise-oriented community based forest management is given in Chapter 7.

4.2.4 Ownership and Management Structure

There are four legal options available for enterprise registration: sole proprietorship (1 shareholder), private limited (1 - 50 shareholders), public limited (at least 51 shareholders) and cooperative (at least 25 members). Three different acts govern these registration options: Private Firm Registration Act, 2014 BS (1957) governs sole proprietorship firms; registration process for private limited and public limited is under the jurisdiction of Companies Act, 2053 BS (1997); and Cooperative Act, 2048 BS (1992) is responsible for cooperative registration and operation.

Sole proprietorship firm is registered with Department of Cottage and Small Scale Industry (DCSI) or its district offices. Registration process is simple that can be done using predetermined format. In practice, the firm does not need to produce its balance sheet for tax assessment and clearance. However, the firm cannot issue share, debenture, and owner's liability is unlimited. The firm is subject to income tax and value added tax, depending on the turnover.

As per the Companies Act, 1997, minimum 1 and maximum 50 shareholders can register private limited company, and 7 shareholders at the time of incorporation can register public limited company, but the number of shareholders should exceed 51. Office of the Company Registrar registers the companies incorporated under this Act. For the registration of the company, shareholders must produce Memorandum of Understanding (MoU) and Article of Association (AA) during incorporation process. Firm incorporated under this act enjoy a various benefits. It can issue and allocate different types of shares (Preference, Ordinary and Bonus), debenture, and the liability of the shareholder is limited. Similarly, provisions for making private limited into public limited and vice-versa, is clearly stipulated in the act. The company is subject to income tax and value-added tax, depending on their total turnover, and need to produce audited balance sheet for tax assessment and clearance. In addition, any enterprises intended to undertake trading business also need to register with Department of Commerce.

A minimum of 25 members can register a cooperative. It can issue and allocate share and debentures. Cooperative is also authorized to operate limited banking transactions, including saving and borrowing schemes for their members. However, authorization from the Nepal Rastra Bank - the central bank of Nepal - is required. Cooperative can distribute net profit to its member after keeping aside one quarter of the profit. However, dividend amount cannot exceed 15% of the paid-up capital per share. A cooperative is exempted from local taxes, full or partial waiver on import of agricultural machineries, industrial plants, raw materials, office supplies, etc.

From the point of view of ownership structures, we investigated seven types of enterprises operating within the aforementioned legal options. The ownership structures investigated make up the primary ownership options in Nepal and include:

1) Individual or family enterprises: The enterprises primarily owned and managed, with or without formal registration, by an individual or a family fall in this category. Many of the household based enterprises are limited to collection and sale of NTFPs from community or national forests; some produce handicrafts using traditional skills; and very few are involved in small scale value added processing enterprises such as handmade paper making.

2) Community based organization (CBO) enterprises: These include individual CFUGs, buffer zone management groups, leasehold groups, mothers' club or other community groups managing or with access to forests as a common property resource and producing, selling or distributing forest products. They are engaged in economic activity with a legal provision within their own constitution, but as they grow or want to focus more on enterprising activity they get registered either as a cooperative or private company. One example of such private company is Malika Handmade paper making. The company is registered under the Kailash Pimidanda CFUG's name, but through its internal arrangement the group has distributed all shares among its all 235 member households based on their contribution (mostly in the form of labor). Thus, the individual collectors, who are shareholders, receive dividends on their shares according to the net profits at the end of the year. This gives an insight on how a group can be innovative to accommodate national law and local requirements.

3) A network of CFUGs: This includes two or more CFUGs working together for the collective production and marketing of forest products. The experience of few CFUG consortiums in Nepal illustrates a method of using locally established institutions in order to introduce relatively capital intensive technology to improve products and achieve economies of scale and thereby to achieve more efficient marketing. Once the CFUG members agree to work together for a processing or marketing enterprise, the CFUG network has a choice of registration as a cooperative or private company. Several processing enterprises established and owned by more than one CFUGs are found registered as a private limited company, while a few are operating as a cooperative (Box 4.1). Private limited companies are corporate entities registered as per prevailing company legislation in Nepal which at present allows a maximum of 50 shareholders. A cooperative is network of individuals and groups registered under the Cooperative Act with at least 25 members.

Box 4.1 Private limited companies vs cooperatives

There are some differences of private limited companies from the cooperatives. Shareholders can receive benefits as in the case of a cooperative. But, they do not need to have any other savings fund, unless the company and shareholders decide so to be useful. The board representatives can be selected in order to ensure equity and participation of all stakeholders.

The challenge for shareholding companies is that the most disadvantaged may not be able to afford the shares. In addition, influential members of the community can try to acquire a majority of the shares, and thereby end up as important decision-makers, since they are the ones with the most capital at risk. In a private limited company, there is no guaranteed dividend. However, a co-operative is required by the Act to actually put some of its profits aside for this purpose.

A private limited company can be set up with any number of shareholders from 1 to 50 but a cooperative needs at least 25 members.

4) Networks of groups and individuals: In this combination, a number of community-based organizations, such as CFUG, and individuals become the shareholders. The majorities of the NTFP enterprises of this type are operating as private limited company, but it can be operated as a cooperative as well. With the understanding of the multiple roles and expertise required for an enterprise activity, this model has some advantages. As described above, CFUGs are becoming an important source for the sustainable supply of NTFPs. Association and good partnership among such groups and individuals would consolidate the supply, and improve their selling price. Similarly, the ownership and management of professional entrepreneurs can be helpful in product development and marketing.

5) Network of individuals: There are various options to register an enterprise when more than one individual are interested to work together. If only few of them are working closely under the leadership of one individual then a sole proprietorship company can be registered. But to give a flexibility people opted to register the enterprise as a private limited company. If there are 25 or more members they have opted for a cooperative. The main purposes of the network, mainly in the form of cooperative, were for procuring inputs; sourcing financing; providing savings and credit services; supporting marketing functions such as collection of information and bargaining with buyers; technological inputs; or acting as a broker on behalf of the producers by buying their product and reselling it.

6) Government parastatals: This category includes companies with all or majority of shares owned and controlled by the government. Herbs Production and Processing Co. Ltd. (HPPCL), Singha Durbar Vaidyakhana Vikas Samiti, Rosin and Turpentine Company and Timber Corporation of Nepal are the examples of this type. They have the options to register either as private limited or as public limited company.

7) Promoters and Public Shareholders: All the companies established by private investors such as Dabur Nepal, Bhaktapur Craft Printer (BCP), Nepal Paper Products (NPP) are registered as private limited company. There is no enterprise in this sector promoted by private investors with public shareholders to date. This indicates that practically NTFPs sub-sector is still not seen as viable enterprise.

4.2.5 Processing Technology

From a technological point of view, many enterprises use simple and locally available technologies. For value-added processing a range of technologies are in practice in Nepal: drying, grading, packaging, distillation of essential oils, debarking, papermaking, rope making, stitching, and so on (Table 4.4).

Although a wide range of Ayurvedic preparations is already produced, only a small percentage of NTFPs collected are processed within Nepal by a few processing industries (producing resins, turpentine, kattha, paper, essential oils, etc.) or cottage industries (using fibers and wood materials). Most of these were established only recently. Some weaving of allo (*Girardiana diversifolia*) and hemp (*Cannabis sativa*) cloths and other fibers is going on but is not rewarding, with market being not so remunerative. The weaving of bamboo and nigalo (*Arundinaria falcata*) for baskets, mats and other goods for daily, seasonal, and ceremonial use is common in hills and plains. Other small-scale cottage industries practiced in Nepal include hand-made paper making, production of herbal teas, juices from wild fruits and flowers, cold creams, soap, shampoo and other personal care products, herbal dye making, honey production from bees, incense making, chiuri (*Aesandra butyracea*) butter production, and *Bhutun* production (a sour juice concentrate locally made from the plant, *Pyrus pashia*).

Table 4.4
Technologies in practice by CBFEs in Nepal for value added processing and product development

Technology	Examples of Applications
Drying: mainly traditional sun and fire drying, but some practices of using solar dryer, hybrid solar dryer and solar cooker	All medicinal and aromatic products except wintergreen, mushrooms including morels, spices, etc.
Distillation: a range of steam distillation	Essential oils from wintergreen, jatamansi, sugandhwal, zanthoxylum, anthopogon, seabuckthorn, and a range of aromatic products
Solvent extraction	Fixed oils and fats from cinnamon, caster, jatropha, sugandhkokila as well as harro, barro for leather tanning
Extraction of active ingredients	*Taxus*, *Podophylum*
Sapogenin extraction	Ritha and other soap bearing plants

Technology	Examples of Applications
Extraction of juice	Seabuckthorn, bel, rhododendron
Grinding (grain mill), mixing	Herbal teas, ayurvedic medicines
Debarking	Argeli
Paper-making (handmade)	Argeli and lokta
Detoxification	Removal of saponin from chiuri ghee
Oil expeller: various types	Dhatelo oil, chiuri, jatropha
Fiber extraction	Ketuke
Rope maker: pedal operated	Babiyo
Weaving: shuttle loom (instead of backstap loom) and pedal operated spinning (Charkha)	Allo cloth
Compacting: pressing to reduce volume	Chiraito
Packaging: bulk	All raw NTFPs, value added products and finished products
Leaf plate stitching, pressing and drying	Sal leaf, bhorla
Soap making	Ritha, pangar, chiuri butter

Through the technological interventions there is a scope to improve the quality, reduce the loss, increase the efficiency of operation and thereby reduce the cost. Technological improvement can also be made building on the traditional and existing technologies to match the current market requirements.

4.3 Market and Market Value of NTFPs

Global markets for Nepal's NTFPs have been large and the trend for these products is increasing as more and more people from developed countries are attracted to natural products. The custom records and information from Trade Promotion Center (TPC) shows that Nepal's NTFPs are exported to over 30 countries in Asia, Europe and America. The countries include India, Pakistan, Hong Kong, Singapore, Japan, South Korea, UAE as well as France, Germany, Italy, Sweden, Switzerland, the Netherlands, the UK, the USA and Canada.

Many of the enterprises focus on domestic markets as their targets. High value low volume products, such as essential oils, and unique or specialty natural products, such as Lokta handmade paper products, have their markets outside the country well up to Europe and Americas. The bulk of NTFPs are exported, mostly to India, in raw form, making Nepal the leading supplier of medicinal plants to the Indian sub-continent. Several processors and manufacturers (such as HPPCL, Singha Durbar Vaidyakhana, Dabur Nepal, NPP, and Gorkha Ayurveda) were producing a number of items with international markets (HPPCL 1999). Many of these products are moved through several hands (Chhetri and Pokhrel 2000) before they eventually sold to Europe and Americas.

NTFPs harvested for commercial purpose are carried away from the villages and district headquarters and are sold to the traders and middlemen in bigger markets like Nepalgunj. Local harvesters bring products harvested from nearby forests and pastures to village level traders and/or district level traders who stockpile the products and resell them to terai wholesalers. The wholesalers often place orders for specific products with the local/district traders or come to the areas directly to arrange the purchase of the products. The terai wholesalers then supply the products to markets of India. Many of the Indian buyers of Nepal's unprocessed NTFPs are commission agents.

The main demand for medicinal plants comes from big Indian companies and pharmaceutical concerns. These firms generally buy from traders or middlemen of India or Nepal. Indian wholesalers come from time to time to trading towns and road heads - the major collection points in the hills. They have agreements with shopkeepers who, in turn, are in touch with a network of village based traders and collectors throughout the less accessible parts of the country. Several NTFPs wholesalers are also based in Kathmandu and use the same network of middlemen to buy the products. They also sell on the materials to their contacts in India.

In international markets, many of Nepal's NTFPs except fiber and handicraft products are traded under the "Herbs and Spices" category and they follow the same trade structure and distribution channels of herbs and spices. Very few dealers and brokers deal exclusively with medicinal herbs. In recent years direct trade between producers/exporters in developing countries (mainly medium and large scale) and processors in consuming countries is increasing.

Of the 161 NTFP species that are traded in and from the country, only few products are exported after some value-added processing and

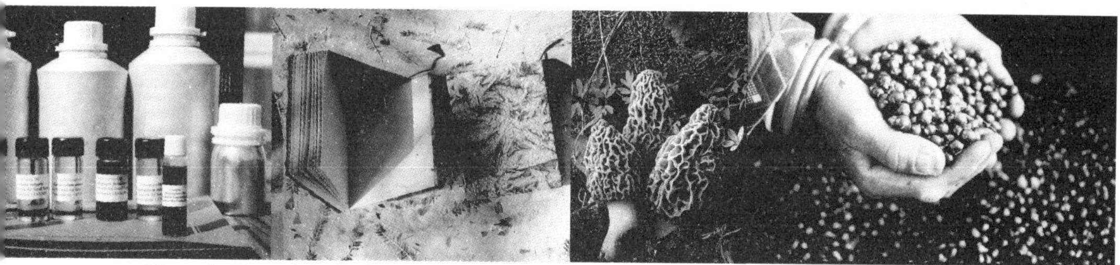

Photo 7. Essential oils, handmade paper products from lokta, morels and juniper berry

most products without much processing except cleaning, drying and in very few cases grading. The total value of these products based on the selling price at two major cities of Nepal (Nepalgunj and Kathmandu) is estimated to be about NRs 2.5 billion (equivalent to nearly US $35 million) every year (Table 4.5). Of these, some notable products found in the hills and mountains include yarshagumba (*Cordyceps sinensis*, an Ascomycete fungus, grown on the head of a moth larva), dried morels (Morchella spp. - members of Ascomycete), handmade paper and products from lokta (*Daphne spp*), Dactylorhiza hatagirea, Podophyllum hexandrum, Taxus leaves, chiraita (*Swertia chirayita*), timur (*Zanthoxylum armatum*), jatamansi (*Nardostachys grandiflora*), sugandhwal (*Valeriana jatamansi*), atis (*Delphinium himalayai*), dhupi (*Juniperus indica*) and kutki (*Neopicrorhiza scrophulariiflora*).

Table 4.5

Export quantity and value of major NTFPs of Nepal in 2001/2002

Products	Value in '000 Rs	Volume in MT
NTFPs in crude form (43 major species)	892,519 (35)	5009
Large cardamom	1,160,000 (46)	5800
Lokta handmade papers and its products	275,375 (11)	-
Pine resin	108,000 (4)	6000
Essential oils	50,559 (2)	23
Allo and hemp products	43,675 (2)	-
Incense	16,503 (1)	-
Total	2,546,631 (100)	

Source: Primary survey 1999-2004

Note: Figure in parenthesis shows the percentage of the total

There was less interest in natural products from late 1960s to the early 1980s with the new possibilities in biotechnology and the synthetic drugs. But by the mid-1980s, the interest in natural products increased with the growing health consciousness and with a recognition that technology alone could not solve the pressing health care needs of the world's population (Tempesta and King 1994). According to an estimate, the value of the most economically important NTFPs in world trade totals about US $11 billion annually (Iqbal 1995). The WHO (2002) estimates that global sales of herbal products totalled US $60 billion in 2000, which is estimated to grow to US $5 trillion by 2050.

Growth in the natural products market is in a range of 3% to 20% (Grunwald 1994), which is on average 3 to 4 times average national economic growth rates. Similarly, with more research and product development new uses of natural products are developing. In future, with more and more emphasis on organic way of living and use of natural products in developed countries (World Bank 1996), Nepal's NTFPs are likely to be demanded and diversified further in use and commerce.

4.4 Challenges for NTFP Enterprises

From the more in-depth interviews, discussions and dialogues in meetings, workshops and interactions with existing, new and potential traders, processors and exporters it was found that there are barriers and challenges in marketing. These can be grouped into the following categories:

- Imperfect wholesale market for NTFPs created by the following conditions: a) limited number of wholesalers, b) controlled price information, and c) government the major buyers for some products;
- Less developed market for many products and high price fluctuations;
- Many producers with small quantities of products -- receive only a small portion of the total income;

- Role and services of brokers and middlemen -- myths and reality (exploitation by middlemen versus their services: cash advances, transport, storage, risk-taking, etc.);
- Lack of market information: current marketing channels, amount of each products, price variation as well as future supply and demand of the products, processed product, development and future price projection;
- Most of the traders with an inadequate marketing knowledge and skills;
- Limited access to availability of information and technology for product development;
- Lack of marketing infrastructure – storage, transportation, quality testing laboratory facilities, etc.;
- Approaching the international buyers (branding and standards for Nepali products, certifications – especially to ensure that the product is produced organically and the practice is socially fair and environmentally sustainable);
- Difficulties in matching market requirements by suppliers (including the quality and quantity assurance) due to several uncertainties such as production fluctuation, decreased collection due to early snow fall, inconsistent quality of products coming from many sources, lack of quality checking facilities, and guaranty of collection permits.
- Inherent limitations with regard to quality centre- e.g., regulation is poor because not so many persons can identify NTFPs species, consumers particularly in Indian subcontinent are not concerned about ascertaining the purity of material, therefore they are unlikely to help premium for high quality products.

List of challenges as perceived by entrepreneurs with the frequency of response in 1995 and 2002 is given in Table 4.6. It is important to note that the entrepreneurs represent the established traders or businessmen, who are also doing NTFPs business.

Table 4.6

Challenges perceived by NTFP entrepreneurs in 1995 and 2002 in Nepal (number of respondents in 1995: 111 and in 2002: 137)

Challenges	Frequency (%)	
	1995	2002
Regulatory hassles in transport, sale and export -- both formal and informal	58.6	51.4
Impractical government bans and restrictions	52.3	48.3
Illogical royalty rates and multiple taxation	49.6	60.6
Lack of clear and specified policy and regulation on NTFPs collection, transport and sale	46.0	87.3
Sustainable supply of products – no programs on conservation of sustainable production of NTFPs	15.3	45.8
Lack of or difficult access to finance	5.4	0.7
Lack of business development services	3.6	4.2
Lack of marketing information	2.7	4.2
No organized market and difficult to access markets	1.8	3.5
Lack of infrastructure (transportation, storage)	0.9	2.1

Source: ANSAB survey 1996 and 2003

Lack of clear and specific policy was a serious challenge perceived by the entrepreneurs and percentage of such persons increased conspicuously from 1995 to 2002. In 1995, regulatory hassles were a challenge for a majority (59%). Three other challenges perceived by the majority were related to policy provisions: impractical government bans and restrictions for 52%, illogical royalty rates and multiple taxation for 50%, and lack of clear and specified policy provisions in relation to collection, transport and sale for 46%. Many of these traders complained that the governments' policies in regulating NTFPs are not realistic with the current trend of business. They also complain that the government is not giving enough support for the enterprise and trade. Only few (15%) realized the problem of sustainable supply. Access to finance, business development services, market, marketing information and infrastructure were not problems for most of the entrepreneurs.

But in 2002, majority (87%) reported the lack of policy provisions a challenge for them. Percentage of entrepreneurs finding impractical bans, restrictions, and hassles a problem decreased slightly but the percentage of those finding illogical royalty and taxes increased in 2002. Because of increased interest in the sub-sector, the policy issues seem to be blown out seriously. Traders' concern was found to be increased towards sustainable supply. Probable cause might be increased understanding of higher threat to sustainable supply of raw material and their business. Challenge of technology was not perceived as serious as previous. Traders might be more prepared for technology challenges if the major challenges of policy were reduced. Realization of need of business development service is still underestimated, though it is in increasing trend. As majority of the entrepreneurs are already established in the business and there are limited opportunities for investment, challenge of accessing finance was not taken as serious as previously.

While policy related problems are common for different types of entrepreneurs, although they may be impacted in different ways, new entrepreneurs may face different types of challenges. Since many high-value NTFPs are located in very remote areas, the processing and marketing costs are generally high. The support services available for processing and marketing of NTFPs are not adequate for small fair trade businesses and in some cases these are favorable for illegal transactions. Most of the local traders do not have easy access to the capital required for processing and marketing of NTFPs. Similarly, most of the exporters to India reported that hassles and trade barriers in India for Nepali products, especially unpredicted and frequent imposing of restrictions, are a serious bottleneck.

Many of the stakeholders feel that one of the reasons why the policy provisions are not practical is due to the improper policy formation process. Entrepreneurs complain the way new policy decisions are made, for example while fixing or revising royalties or imposing bans on certain species no relevant stakeholders are consulted.

Chapter 5

Proximate Threats to Biodiversity and Underlying Causes

5.1 Change in Vegetation and Its Likely Impacts

5.1.1 Ecosystem Health

Detailed account of ecosystem health is not available for all areas and many inaccessible parts, north of terai and the Middle Hills remain poorly known. Nevertheless, it is evident that uncontrolled exploitation of forests for fodder, fuelwood, timber, grazing, and the conversion of land for agriculture, exacerbated by the mass migration of people from the Middle Hills following the eradication of malaria in the lowlands, continue to reduce forest cover throughout Nepal.

The comparison of 1994 National Forest Inventory (NFI) results (FRISP 1999) with that of 1978/79 Land Resources Mapping Project (LRMP 1978) shows that the forest cover of Nepal decreased from 38% to 29% whereas the shrub cover increased from 4.7% to 10.6% (Table 2.2). The net loss of forest and shrub land combined is 0.5% per year and the loss of forest is at the rate of 1.7% per year. In plain land (terai), the forest area has decreased at the rate of 1.3% per year; the most of it was converted to other land use such as agriculture. In the hills forest decreased at the rate of 2.3% per annum, most of it turning into shrublands; the net loss of the forest was only 0.2% per annum.

What has been changing is the decline in quality of the forest, as measured by its crown cover. The available estimates show there is less than 20% of the forest with more than 70% crown cover which was more than 40% in 1960s (WECS 1986). Theoretically all forestland is capable of supporting a full crown cover, therefore forest areas with less than 70% crown cover are considered to be over-used and degraded. Both the coverage and the quality of forest in Nepal have been declining over the past decades, even where forestland has not been cleared for agriculture. However, in the hills some positive signs are now in place with the increased number of trees on private lands and improvement in conditions of community forests (Jackson *et al.* 1994).

In contrast to the decreased crown-cover reported in the above study (WECS 1986), Nepal's aggregate figures regarding the growing stock, show that there are positive changes in terms of both mean stem volume and number of stems per hectare from 1960 to 1994 (Table 5.1). It shows that the forest stands have become more stocked during the period. The biggest increase has occurred in the diameter class 10-20 cm and in over 50 cm, whereas the class 20-50 cm has remained almost the same. From these studies it can be concluded that there is loss of forest cover, and most of which is converted into shrubland; but on the whole the remaining forest stands are getting overstocked indicating the scope for sustainable management and harvesting of the forest stands.

Table 5.1
Change in forest conditions in Nepal

Category	1960	1978/79 (LRMP)*	1994 (NFI)**
Forest area in million ha (as % of the total land area)		5.59 (38%)	4.27 (29%)
Shrubland area (in % of the total land area)		4.7%	10.6%
Forest and shrubland combined (in % of the total land area)		42.7%	39.6%
Mean stem volume (dbh>10cm) (m^3/ha)	85		131
Total stem (dbh>10cm) density (number of stems/ha)	313		408
Stem (dbh 10-20 cm) density (number of stems/ha)	159		244
Stem (dbh 20-50 cm) density (number of stems/ha)	141		143
Stem (dbh>50cm) density (number of stems/ha)	13		21

Source: * LRMP 1978; ** FRISP 1999.
Note on methods: A national level inventory of commercial forest was carried out in 1960s based on the clusters located in a systematic grid of 3.2 km by 16.1 km. Each clusters located in a systematic grid of size of 810 m^2.

As for the maximum dbh (diameter at breast height) of trees along the altitudinal gradients, Ohsawa (1983) undertook a study taking a sample of 45 forest plots of size ranging between 300-600m^2 area in eastern Nepal, and found that 12 plots had trees with values above 100 cm dbh, of which 10 occurred between 2000-3000m altitude, and one each between 1000-2000 m and below 1000 m. Very high dbh values were recorded in the plots located at 2580m (187 cm), 2670 m (176 cm), and 2850 m altitude (146 cm). These high dbh values at the plots above 2500 m may simply indicate that the human disturbance is lower in high altitudinal areas than in lower parts (Ohsawa 1983). Much of the forests of lower altitudes are secondary, while in higher parts the remnant trees of old growths forests are still present. Only in 7 plots the maximum tree height was 30 m or more (up to 47 m), of which three were below 2000 m and four between 2000-3000 m altitude. The two plots with over 40 m tree height were located at 2580 m (47 m tree height) and 2890m (41 m tree height). These exceptional tree heights were of *Tsuga*. Similarly, Carpenter and Zoomer (1996) recorded a total tree basal areas of 125 m^2 ha^{-1} in a plot located around 2500 m altitude, and values as high as 45.7-65.2 m^2 ha^{-1} in sub-alpine belt.

5.1.2 Deforestation and its Likely Climatic Impact

The Himalayan region has lost a substantial amount of forest cover during the last three decades. Almost nothing is known about sustainable use of species and monitoring of biodiversity to achieve sustainability. This has affected the people living in mountains, depending on forest and biodiversity for sustaining their subsistence. Large scale changes in vegetal cover, particularly resulting from deforestation can directly raise temperature which for certain areas could be greater than the global warming (Foley *et al.* 2003). Several model-based studies suggest that deforestation in tropics will probably cause a substantial increase in surface temperature and a decrease in precipitation (Costa and Foley 2000). The reduction in precipitation in a cleared area is largely a result of changes in energy and water balance. Both the reduction in absorbed solar radiation and increase in albedo lead to a decrease in radiative heating of the land surface leaving a smaller amount of energy to drive atmospheric circulation. The eventual effect of this includes the cooling of upper atmosphere, followed by subsidense or shrinking of air, and reduced precipitation. Further with the loss of forest, leaf area, surface run off and root depth decline, which in turn results in a reduced evapo-transpiration. This means reduction in the amount of water that could be pumped out into atmosphere, thereby resulting in a lesser rainfall. The forest depletion coupled with inherently unsuitable geology, immature topography, steep slopes, and the monsoon rainfall pattern, result directly in accelerating soil erosion, increasing sedimentation, declining soil fertility and crop productivity, and indirectly in loss of capital and life.

5.2 Proximate Threats to Biodiversity

Anthropogenic pressures on natural resources are beginning to be reflected in terms of their exploitation above their sustainable levels. The extensive spread of *Eupaturium odoratum*, a heliophyous herb and of the shrub, *Lantana camara* clearly indicates that the human pressure on the forest has been severe and persistent for quite some time. The presence of invasive exotic species can be seen right from the sal zone to close to 1500-7000m. *Shorea robusta* is among the most preferred timber tree; therefore its stands have been felled almost in all accessible areas. Sal forest stands seem to have recovered since the establishment of forest user groups. As *Schima wallichii* is one of the preferred species of villagers for making tools, its stands have been severely disturbed in village areas. The open forest patches have been invaded by several early successional species. The human activities have been high in the *Castanopsis* and *Quercus* zones since time immemorial, as they broadly overlap with human settlements in the Midlands. Much of them have been converted into crop-fields and pastures. These species, however, have been able to survive through their great ability to coppice after tree cutting.

Our observation shows that human use of the resources has converted formerly diverse vegetation into homogenous strongholds of a few resilient species indicating the degradation and loss of biological diversity, especially close to human settlements. Degraded areas in Humla, Dolpa, Jumla, Bajhang, and Darchula are often taken over by resilient species such as *Urtica dioica, Girardinia diversifolia, Salvia moorcroftiana, Chenopodium album, Prinsepia utilis, Artemisia sieversiana,*

Rumex nepalensis, Berberis asiatica and *B. aristata*. Some of them such as *Urtica dioica*, in fact, owe their existence to the deposition of household wastes. In Humla, side valleys still harbor stands of native coniferous forest (*Abies pindrow and Picea smithiana*), but in areas near human settlements *Pinus wallichiana*, an early successional conifer is replacing them.

While working with the local communities, which were later organized into community forest user groups (CFUGs) in the districts of Humla, Jumla, Bajhang, Dolpa, Darchula and Dolakha, the top threats to biological diversity were identified and ranked by the CFUG members and the Project staff at the beginning of the joint planning activities. The threats to the biodiversity were linked to human activities such as uncontrolled harvesting (over harvesting, inappropriate timing, and methods of harvest), over grazing, burning, shifting cultivation, poaching, and other activities that lead to deforestation and habitat loss. Three distinct categories of forest and meadow areas were found for the identification and ranking of threats in the study areas. These are: upland meadows (28 CFUGs); forests and shrublands near human settlements (19 CFUGs); and outlying forests and shrublands (20 CFUGs).

Tables 5.2, 5.3 and 5.4 present the list of threats by their ranking. Ranking of these threats was done using the following four criteria: the size of the affected area; the intensity of the damage; the urgency to counter the threat; and the feasibility of countering the threat by communities. Each category is ranked on a scale of 1 to n, where n equals the number of threats ranked and represents the highest threat among others or the higher the number the severer is the threat. To get the overall rank for all the CFUGs, the ranking scores from the individual CFUGs were added for each criterion for each threat, and again ranked on a scale of 1 to n. As can be noted from the Tables 5.2, 5.3 and 5.4 equal weight was given to all four criteria, and overall ranking was based on the total score from all four criteria for the threat. A brief explanation of these threats as found at the start of the enterprise-oriented community forestry intervention is given below.

Table 5.2
Ranking of major threats to the biodiversity – upland meadows in the study area

Threats	Area Ranking	Intensity Ranking	Urgency Ranking	Feasibility Ranking	Total Score	Rank
Burning of forest/pastures	2	4	4	3	13	1
Unmanaged harvesting of NTFPs	3	3	2	4	12	2
Over grazing	4	2	1	1	8	3
Poaching of wild animals	1	1	3	2	7	4

Table 5.3
Ranking of major threats to the biodiversity – forests and shrublands near human settlements in the study area

Threats	Area Ranking	Intensity Ranking	Urgency Ranking	Feasibility Ranking	Total Score	Rank
Burning of forest/pastures	4	5	5	4	18	2
Unmanaged harvesting of NTFPs	5	2	2	6	15	3
Encroachment	3	7	7	3	20	1
Slash and burn farming	2	6	1	5	14	4
Unmanaged harvesting of timber, fodder & firewood	6	4	6	2	18	2
Over grazing	7	3	4	1	15	3
Poaching of wild animals	1	1	3	7	12	5

Table 5.4
Ranking of major threats to the biodiversity – outlying forests and shrublands in the study area

Threats	Area Ranking	Intensity Ranking	Urgency Ranking	Feasibility Ranking	Total Score	Rank
Burning of forest/pastures	4	4	5	3	16	1
Unmanaged harvesting of NTFPs	3	3	3	4	13	1
Slash and burn farming	2	5	2	2	11	2
Over grazing	5	2	4	1	12	4
Poaching of wild animals	1	1	1	5	8	5

Uncontrolled Burning of Pasture and Forest

In upland meadows and outlying forests and shrublands, uncontrolled burning was the number one in the ranking exercises on threats while it ranked second with a tie with unmanaged harvesting of NTFPs in forests and shrublands near human settlements. Man-made surface fires were common in the area and they destroyed tree regeneration and other fire sensitive species. People set fires for a number of reasons. In some cases, it was for bringing up the new shoots of grasses for grazing, in other cases, it was for slash and burn farming (*Kurilla halne*), and still in other cases, for honey collection or hunting. Sometimes it also occurred without any obvious reason. Generally, fires were highly patchy, mild but frequent. It has been found that fires destroy some portion of the forests every year and threaten the biodiversity of the area.

Unmanaged Harvesting of NTFPs

Unmanaged harvesting includes the over harvesting as well as inappropriate timing and methods of harvesting. This tied for number one with burning in the threat ranking exercise in outlying forests and shrublands while it was second in upland meadows and third in forest and shrublands near settlements. The communities of the study areas have been harvesting a large number of plant products from the government controlled national forest and grasslands. Although there was little pressure on species that were collected for local use on a subsistence basis, the pressure on some of the commercial species has already resulted in over harvesting, and in some cases, immature and unscientific harvesting leading to the threat of extinction.

The indigenous knowledge and traditional skills of a few individuals on harvesting NTFPs at a subsistence use level were not enough or enforceable to apply to the harvesting of commercially demanded species. The same was true of production management, post harvest operations, processing, and marketing.

Slash and Burn Farming

Slash-and-burn agriculture, locally called *Kurilla Halne,* is the process of burning the forest trees and the shrubs in which the crown fire is set and small patch of the forest is cleared for the cultivation of cereals and potatoes. Though the first year's production is comparable to "regular agricultural areas", the production gradually goes down year after year and the people finally abandon the land. These lands then become susceptible to soil erosion and landslides. This ultimately leads to the loss of vegetation and disturbs the ecosystem thereby threatening the biodiversity of the area. Kurilla Halne was ranked as the second major threat to biodiversity in outlying forests and shrublands, and fourth in forests and shrublands near human settlements.

Unmanaged Harvesting of Timber, Fodder and Firewood

Harvesting of timber, fodder, and firewood for subsistence purpose has exceeded sustainable yields, especially in areas near the human settlements. Timber is required for the construction of houses as well as cattle sheds. Firewood is almost the sole source of energy for cooking and heating. Common trees used for fodder are *Quercus semecarpifolia, Thinke, Acer acuminatum, Betula utilis,* and *Sorbus microphylla.* Construction of goths (temporary huts for farmers during herding season) in the forest during the grazing season has also accelerated the deforestation rate in the area. Mature trees of birch and fir are cut down to construct a *goth.* The people staying at goths also require a lot of fire-wood for cooking and heating purposes. Thus, the areas around the goths were found degraded with an abundance of disturbance-induced species such as Hale (*Rumex nepalensis*) and Bijauri Phool (*Senecio chrysanthemoides*). This category was ranked second among the seven categories of threats in forests and shrublands near human settlements, but it was not a threat in other areas.

Overgrazing

Overgrazing ranked third in upland meadows as well as forest and shrublands near human settlements, but fourth in outlying forest and shrublands. From the point of view of the size of the affected area, overgrazing is a top most threat in all three zones, but communities found this also the most difficult to address given the socio-economic conditions. Many households keep large herds of sheep, goats, cattle, mules, and horses. Transhumance (migratory herding system) was still in practice in many areas. During the summer season (May to October) the farmers keep their cattle around a goth and graze the cattle in the forest. Grazing is done generally in the land close to the homestead as well as the alpine pasture located as high as 4500m. The grazing animals include *Jhumas* (Yak hybrid), horses, goats and sheep. There is pressure from both overgrazing and lopping of trees for fodder. While leaves of some medicinal plants such as *Jurinea dolomaea, Megacarpa polyphylla,* and *Rheum australe* are grazed by most of the animals and severely affected, leaves of other plants, such as *Jatamansi,* are only grazed by sheep and goats and appear to be less severely affected. Secondary effects of grazing, such as trampling, compaction, destruction of rootstock, and soil erosion adversely affect the biodiversity.

Poaching of Wild Animals

This was ranked least among all the threats in all zones and most communities rated this as the most feasible to address as well. A traditional practice of hunting of wild animals, although it is illegal in most cases, poses a threat to the species being hunted, such as musk deer (*Moschus moschiferous*) and Himalayan black beer (*Selenarctos thibetanus*). Musk deer and Himalayan black bear are among the most commonly hunted species, and they are hunted for their valuable musk and bile respectively. The musk is found only in the male animal. Both musk and bile are important ingredients of the traditional medical system. These products have good demand from abroad and are sometimes illegally traded to international markets. Musk deer is one of the endangered wildlife species confined to the shrubland of the sub-alpine zone. Himalayan black bear resides in oak and spruce forests. Most time of the year musk deer live in high altitude shrubland, but during the winter when the area is covered with snow these animals come to the lower altitudes.

5.3 Underlying Causes of Threats to Biodiversity

The reasons for the above threats are complex. The threats arise from endogenous as well as exogenous variables, and more importantly these variables interact with each other and the combined effects become more damaging than the sum of their individual effects. There are both natural and anthropogenic forces affecting biodiversity, but anthropogenic factors are posing the greatest threats in the areas. All these human activities linked to the threats to biodiversity were the results of several socioeconomic factors such as poverty, immediate cash needs of local people, lack of alternative income generating opportunities, defective property rights, lack of incentive for conservation, limited knowledge on conservation particularly silvicultural practice, and increasing market demand for these products. From participatory analyses with local communities, our observations and interactions with concerned stakeholders, we found the following root causes:

a) Poverty, dependency on biodiversity for subsistence and lack of alternative income generating opportunities (immediate cash needs of local people)

b) A poor ecosystem generally does not get enough respite to recover, because humans are always there, collecting fodder, firewood, litter and NTFPs. On a given day removal of biomass is inconspicuous, and its damaging effect keeps on accumulating, and biomass extraction never stops. No attention is paid to. For example, regeneration of species. Consequently, forests may degrade even when biomass extraction is well within the carrying capacity of productivity. Almost no training in proper silvicultural practices was given to people

c) Property systems (the pattern of the distribution of rights and responsibilities, sanctions, and legitimacy) - both exogenous as reflected in government policy provisions and their implementation practices (government action and law enforcement), and endogenous as reflected in local customary norms, rules and practices

d) External market demand

e) Knowledge, skills and capacity to manage and earn

f) Education and conservation awareness

5.3.1 Poverty, Dependency and Alternatives

Biodiversity, particularly forest resources are an integral part of the livelihood support system in Nepal, where about 80% of 23 million people live in the interface between forestry and agriculture. About 86% of the population still lives in rural areas. Agriculture (farming of crop, livestock, fisheries, horticulture and forestry) is the mainstay of the economy, providing a livelihood for over 80% of the population and accounting for about one-half of the GDP. The cultivated land is only 20.2%, non-cultivated agricultural land is about 7%, and forests, shrubs and grasslands cover nearly 55% of the Nepal's total area 147,181 km^2.

About 6% of the GDP is contributed from industry sector, of which about 30% comes from cottage industries. Industrial activity is limited, mainly involving the processing of agricultural products such as sugarcane and tobacco in plains. The agro-based and forest-based industries account for more than 80% of the manufacturing enterprises. More than 40% of the population is thought to be undernourished and large food deficit areas exist in the high mountain areas. Since 1991, although the government of Nepal has been moving forward with economic reforms, particularly those that encourage trade and foreign investment, progress has been slow due to the small size of the economy, low level of technology, remoteness of resources, and susceptibility to natural disaster due to the climate and geology of the Himalaya. Food security, which is a situation when all people, at all times, have physical and economic access to sufficient, safe and nutritious food to meet their dietary needs food preferences for an active and healthy life (FAO's definition) is weak in high mountain areas.

The country's economic stagnation in the past decade has actually increased the forest-dependency of its population. The demand for forest products (both timber and non-timber) continues to increase. With very few alternatives, most of the poor people living in hills and mountains are dependent on the forest and forest products that are mostly under open access. For many of the communities of high mountains, NTFPs are the only source of cash income, while in some other cases these are more important source of income than timber. It is also interesting to note that there is a strong association between the availability of high value NTFPs and poverty. The area from which vast majority of NTFPs are harvested from wild and sold in the market include remotest mountains (Karnali and other mountainous area and in these areas 57% live below poverty line.

Thus, ecological zones rich in biodiversity have also some of the world's poorest peoples. They depend on natural resources around them for both production and extractive purposes, and the issues of environmental sustainability are of immediate relevance to poor people as they directly depend on the viability of the resource base for their day-to-day living.

The communities in biologically rich areas unfortunately manifest abject poverty, such as in terms of isolation, limited livelihood options, economic insecurity, and low cash incomes. The communities are poor producers of farm crops in areas with little or no non-farm jobs. Extractive forest industry activities were done at varying levels but with little benefit to the local communities and often with great harm to the biodiversity. Securing basic livelihoods happens to be an overriding activity for the communities: they cannot be expected to worrying for biodiversity until they have proven options of livelihoods. A community member is forced to collect NTFPs in a manner that gives maximum benefits for the time being with no consideration of sustainability of the resource base. Lack of economic opportunities and alternatives to destructive subsistence activities fueled the threats. Several categories of people urge their conflicting interests. In Nepal, the issues are more intense, because for many villagers, the struggle is for survival. Growing populations clear forest land for agriculture; villagers cut fuelwood and fodder for cooking and heating and to feed livestock; they cut timber for construction; grazing animals prevent new trees from growing; and soil erosion and landslides remove fertile soils and trees. The disturbance is chronic, in which human presence in forest never stops. Though on a given day the biomass removal is inconspicuous, the chronic form of disturbance is not less destructive than the acute form of disturbance.

5.3.2 Property System

Most of the NTFPs of Nepal come from the collection in wild. Sometimes they are over-harvested because of an uncontrolled system of harvesting from the government owned and controlled forests. These areas often have limited enforcement mechanism to control over harvesting. There are discrepancies between the formal stated rules and observed behaviors regarding the rights, responsibilities and sanctions pertinent to forest and forest products.

The DOF is the government agency for the control and management of forests including NTFPs. However, its function is limited to giving permission and issuing license for collection. Practically, there is no supervision or control in collection, nor is any rational basis for allotting plots for NTFPs harvesting. The bigger traders or their agents usually get the collection permits for large-scale collection of NTFPs, for which the government receives royalty. The DFO rangers have difficulties correctly identifying NTFPs because there are many species and some of them are often referred to by various local names. In some cases, the same name is used for different species, and in others a species has different names.

Photo 8. Harveting of timber and NTFPs in mountain districts in Nepal

Lack of clear tenure rights for local communities and lax enforcement of extraction permits obtained by outsiders were the main contributing factors that allowed the threats to run unchecked. Overharvesting and unscientific collection triggered by the *de-facto* property right arrangement and other economic conditions led to the depletion of these resources even from the protected areas like national parks. Since the forests and grasslands where forest products (both timber and non-timber) are collected are considered to be under the government property regime and not under the control of the communities, there was an incentive to harvest as much as possible before someone else gets to it. All these factors related to property rights combined with the poverty and dependency were, thus, found to be responsible to a large extent for inappropriate harvesting, ultimately destroying the regeneration potential of the species being harvested.

5.3.3 External Market Demand

As we have assessed and analyzed the external market demand, it is high and growing but the present buying practices are mostly exploitative to both the people who harvest and supply the products and the nature from which they are produced. The big companies employ the agents whose main job is to get the products as cheapest rate as possible, and they do not see how their buying practices are leading to the depletion of resources. The products move through several hands from Nepal to India and ultimately some of them to the U.S. and European markets without any recognition of their origin. These practices on one hand provide only little income to local communities and the other hand uncertain quality supply to industry. As a result, there are low incentives to collectors, traders and industry for conservation and threats to biodiversity, livelihoods and sustainable supply.

5.3.4 Knowledge, Skills and Capacity to Manage and Earn

Current practices or level of skills for NTFP extraction/harvest, production management, and post-harvest operations are not satisfactory. Unlike agricultural crops and timber producing trees, the management knowledge and techniques for NTFPs are not well developed. The species specific information required for *in-situ* as well as *ex-situ* management is generally lacking for most of the species. The continuous inappropriate harvesting of biological resources throws new challenges of biodiversity conservation, particularly when not much is known about the ecosystem dynamics and biology of species from which they are obtained.

The indigenous knowledge and traditional skills of limited individuals on harvesting NTFPs at a subsistence use level are not enough or enforceable to apply to the harvesting of commercially demanded species. At the same time, there was little or no awareness of the biodiversity conservation coupled with lack of alternative income generating opportunities that would change the unsustainable practices. As most of the commercially used plant products are derived from whole plant, bark, stem or root, they are likely to be severely impacted from unmanaged harvest.

Chapter 6

Communities: Key Stakeholders and Stewardship in Relation to Biodiversity Use and Management

6.1 Key Stakeholders in NTFP Sub-sector: Dependency, Interest and Capabilities

Biodiversity involves stakeholders who might be positively or negatively affected by the resource related activities and/or have influenced on these at varying degrees of scale, power and interest. In our study we found the following groups of key stakeholders that are linked through a value chain involving the flow of products (originating from natural resource base) and the money (originating from the end users): local harvesters, community forest user groups (CFUGs), village level traders, local NTFP cooperatives, local level processors, road-head/airport traders, regional traders, exporters, large-scale processors, manufacturers and retailers. Their characteristics, business functions and scale is summarized in Table 6.1 and more elaborate description is found thereafter.

Photo 9. CFUG workshop in Humla

There are also other stakeholders in the sub-sector that facilitate or regulate the business functions in thc value chain and that include the government line agencies, non-profits development and conservation organizations. Table 6.2 provides such functions and organizations involved for that. Their characteristics are not analyzed here, but their roles in the sub-sector development were found important, and that is taken into consideration in analyzing the factors affecting the sub-sector in various sections.

Table 6.

Socio-economic characteristics and business functions of the main stakeholders in the NTFP value chain

Stakeholder	Principal Socio-Economic Characteristics (needs and interests)	Business Functions
Local Harvesters	Represent poorer groups of community including children, women, elderly, and other disadvantaged people; obtain seasonal employment and incomes to meet critical livelihoods requirements; have limited knowledge of and exposure to marketing and entrepreneurship.	Harvesting mainly from wild, preliminary cleaning, drying, storage and transportation; scale of business ranges between Rs 10,000 and Rs 50,000.
Community Forest User Groups (CFUGs)	Recognized as a self-governed local institution for forest resources management; mostly heterogeneous (economically and politically) social groups living in various settlements; members have diverse needs and expectations from the forests; common and formal rules may ignore the interests of specific NTFP interest groups; generally the entire group lacks business orientation at present.	May undertake business functions including harvesting, trading, resource management, regulations, and local processing.
Village Traders	Represent relatively well-offs within village community, also include leaders and teachers, however, poorer in the national context; obtain products in credit from harvesters and also provide advance payments (received from regional traders); generally work in a low profit margin; have some exposure to the market as well as knowledge about resources.	Storing, preliminary packaging and drying, and providing skills and techniques (such as harvesting, drying, and storage) to CFUGs and local harvesters; business scale up to Rs 50,000 to Rs 100,000.
Local Processors	Represent collectors, CFUGs and local traders; generally use easily accessible technologies that generally aiming at reduce weight, volume and cost of handling and transportation.	Simple processing such as drying, fiber extraction, handmade paper making and sometimes distillation; business scale up to Rs 1,500,000.

Stakeholder	Principal Socio-Economic Characteristics (needs and interests)	Business Functions
Local Cooperatives	Represent organized groups of local harvesters (generally formed through outside interventions); usually registered and eligible for certain state subsidies but not encouraged to do export business.	Various, including harvesting, processing and trading; scale of business up to Rs 100,000.
Road-head and Airport Traders	Represent wealthy, educated and local elites (political leaders, service holders and businessmen); have ability to work in a complex administrative environment; positioned at points where bulk transportation is possible; have good exposure and knowledge of national NTFP markets; operate in strong horizontal competitions.	Mainly storing, transport and trade; scale of business up to Rs 500,000.
Regional Traders	Often represent traditional business groups with high investment capacity; have supply linkages with road-head traders and also village traders and local harvesters; have high political influence and smooth access to business services/inputs; often form cartels to safeguard their interests.	Packaging, storing and trading; business scale up to Rs 20 million.
Exporters	Represent a few educated and professional traders having international market access; have international exposure on market trends and export and import regulations; have specific market linkage; heavy use of electronic media in business communication.	Grading, cleaning, drying, packaging, export complying with certification and trade regulation; business scale may be around Rs 25 million.
Big Processors and Manufacturers	Represent national level companies, both public and private; have legal backing; unnecessary political interference to public companies to make business decisions; private represent a mixed group of professionally managed as well as those controlled by strong and influential groups; most face internal (management) and external (marketing) challenges.	Large-scale processing and manufacturing of limited number of products, research and development; scale of business is very high up to Rs 500 million.
Retailers	Vary from small business persons exclusively dealing with herbal medicines, wild vegetables, spices, etc. to large business houses dealing with finished goods, partly or wholly composed of NTFPs, in large cities.	Retailing; scale of business vary from very small to over a million rupees.

Source: Primary survey 1996-2004

Local Harvesters. Local harvesters live within communities near natural resources areas. In high mountain areas traditional NTFP trade is often the only source of cash for poor communities. They represent poor and medium classes and include children, women, elderly, and other disadvantaged people. They meet a significant portion of the household incomes from NTFP collection. This seasonal employment generates about 30-50% of their total household incomes (that supports 3-6 months requirement of food, festival expenses and the two basic food items to be purchased - salt and cooking oil).

Local harvesters collect NTFP from forests, alpine pastures and rocky areas. They often walk 2-5 days passing the nights in caves, climbing steep slopes and coping with extreme cold with insufficient clothing. Customary laws prevail and are enforced by the communities to protect the consequences of human activities that will have direct impacts on the sustainability of the species being harvested, where there is little outside interventions. Sometimes customary laws do not allow lower caste groups to collect natural products in specific locations (such as Malika area in Bajhang). Lower caste groups undertake cleaning, drying and storage of collected products in the houses in a traditional way.

Scale of business goes up to an annual sales turn over of Rs 50,000. Several risks that surround the business include chances of accidents (wildlife attacks, fall down, calamities), damages and loss (due to decaying, wastage and leakage), price reductions and failure to sale.

Community Forest User Groups (CFUGs). CFUGs are recognized as and projected to be the stewards of forest resources in all accessible forests and meadows, and the concept of forest user is used as being the defining feature for membership of a local forest management organization (Hobley 1996). The Department of Forest database shows that presently (as of July 2004) there are 13,397 community forest user groups across Nepal, who represent a third of Nepal's population covering 1,509,023 households. About 40% of these CFUGs harvest one or more NTFPs commercially. CFUGs are self-governed local institutions and recognized as a legitimate user and manager of community forests. They earn money from NTFP trade as taxes as well as revenues, and spend the money in a variety of community services. Economically and politically heterogeneous members within CFUGs have diverse needs and expectations. The common and often formal rules hardly favor the interests of specific NTFP interest groups, which include harvesters, small traders and local healers.

Most CFUGs have yet to incorporate NTFP provisions into the forest management operational plans (OP), and hence have practically no control of such commercial products. In such cases, outside traders get local harvesters to extract the products from community forests under DFO permissions. The Forest Act, 1993 provides authority to CFUGs to develop, conserve, use and manage the forest and sell and distribute the forest products independently by fixing their prices as per the provisions made in OP. Most CFUGs lack enterprise orientation at present, but with the proper enterprise-oriented management, they are likely to take some business functions including harvesting, trading and local processing (see Chapter 7).

Village Traders. Village traders are relatively well-off members of the communities, who have stronger social capital in terms of linkages with downstream traders. They also have some exposure to NTFP marketing channels within the country. The prime economic objective of trade for village traders is to meet requirements for cloth, children's education, and household necessities. Village traders are partly higher up on the need hierarchy compared to the local harvesters. But, they also fall into the poor and deprived group in the national context.

They generally do not invest money of their own, and they operate like agents of road-head and regional traders. They often provide some advance payments and also obtain products in credit from harvesters. They have relationships with particular groups of local harvesters as well as road-head or airport traders, and sometimes with regional traders. Usually, they provide skills and techniques (such as harvesting, drying and storage) to local harvesters. Overall, local communities have mixed impressions of these traders, in some cases as cheaters and in other cases as contributors in marketing of NTFPs. They operate in low profit margin and the business scale is generally a working capital of Rs 50,000 to Rs 100,000.

Local Processors. A very few CFUGs, village traders and community-based enterprises are doing local processing. CFUG and village trader cases have already been mentioned. The conservation and social implications depend on how enterprises employ people, source raw materials through collectors, to whom they sell the products, and to whom they compete with in terms of raw materials procurement as well as product sales. Business scale varies depending on the value of products and technologies. In our study cases, it ranges from Rs. 100, 000 to Rs 1,500,000.

Local NTFP Cooperatives. This structure represents organized groups of collectors (generally formed through outside interventions); usually registered and eligible for certain government subsidies but not generally encouraged to do export business. They also represent poorer community groups. Examples of this group include Praja NTFP Cooperative in Chitwan and Allo Cloth Production Club in Sankhuwasabha. Their main business functions include collection, processing and trading. The business has generally a scale of up to Rs 100,000.

Road-head and Airport Traders. This category represents wealthy, educated and local elites (political leaders, service holders, shopkeepers, and other businessman) who have the ability to work in complex administrative environments. They have a good exposure and knowledge of NTFP markets, and often operate in strong horizontal competitions. They are positioned at points where bulk transportation is possible. Their scale of business goes up to Rs 500,000.

Regional Traders. They represent traders with a higher investment capacity and often are members of traditional business groups. They often combine NTFPs with their other regular trading business. They often have multiple supply linkages with local harvesters, village traders and road-head traders. They can exercise high political influence and have smooth access to business services/inputs. They often formed cartels to safeguard their interests. Their main business functions include consolidating the supply, packaging and selling out to manufacturers and Indian traders. They may also directly export to overseas. Their business scale is as high as Rs 20 million.

Exporters. This group includes a few educated and professional traders having international market access. These traders have exposure on some international markets. They also have knowledge and skills on requirements, regulations, and handling business in relation to export and import. They often have specific market linkages. Their transactions and communications are sophisticated and involve the use of electronic media. They often have a good business culture and professionalism, and this gives them a competitive advantage to deal with international buyers. They undertake grading, cleaning, drying and packaging before exporting the products. Their business scale is around Rs 25 million, but many of them do not need up front investment as they get payment from buyers before the shipment and manage to get materials on credits from sellers.

Big Processors and Manufacturers. Processing and manufacturing is still in its infancy in Nepal. They represent national companies, both public and private. These include Herbs Production and Processing Co. Ltd. (HPPCL) – mainly produces essential oils and related products, Nepal Paper Product (NPP) and Bhaktapur Crafts Products (BCP) – produces products from Nepali hand-made paper, Gorkha Ayurveda, Singha Durbar VaidyaKhana (SDVK), and Dabur Nepal – produce and market Ayurvedic preparations. They have strong legal backing but most of them are facing internal (management) and external (marketing) challenges. With the growing international markets for Nepali products, they have a good scope of providing employment and developing new natural products that can fetch better prices in international markets.

Retailers. Retailers vary from small businesspeople exclusively dealing with herbal medicines and spices to large business houses dealing with finished goods, partly or wholly composed of NTFPs, in large cities. Examples include Ayurvedic medicine shops, arts and crafts stores including handmade paper products, groceries containing tea, herbal dyes, bamboo and rattan products retailers, sal leaf plate retailers around temples and marketplaces, and others. As the consumer products from NTFPs are limited, the presence of these stakeholders is also low in Nepal. The scale of business may vary from a few thousand to a million rupees.

Table 6.2
Organizations involved in regulatory and supportive functions in NTFP subsector in Nepal (as of December 2003)

Enterprise Function/Activity	Organizations
Company Registration	Office of Company Registrar, Department of Cottage and Small Industries, Department of Commerce
Collection Permit/License	District Forest Officer (DFO) and Forest User Group (CFUG)
Royalty Payment	DFO, CFUG
Checking and Verification of Quantity	DFO, Range Post or CFUG
Release Order or Transit Permit	DFO
Local Taxes	District Development Committee, Municipality
Checking and Endorsement	Forest Check-post
Export Recommendation	DFO (recommends the concern to the Customs Office)
Product Verification and Export Permission for Selected Natural Products	Department of Plant Resources (DPR) (Permission to export processed natural products that are prohibited from export in crude form.)
Certificate of Origin	Federation of Nepalese Chambers of Commerce and Industry (FNCCI), Nepal Chamber of Commerce (NCC)
Export Permission and Duty	Customs Office of exporting country
Import Permission and Duty	Customs Office of importing country
Taxes	Department of VAT, Department of Income Taxes, Department of Customs
Market Information	Trade Promotion Center (TPC), FNCCI, NCC, NGOs
Financial Support	Agriculture Development Bank, commercial banks
Processing Technology	Department of Industries, Department of Cottage and Small Industries, Private companies, NGOs
Resource Management and Research	DPR, DFO, CFUGs, NGOs

6.2 Community Forestry: Progress and Forces Influencing Community Based Biodiversity Management

From the analysis of the key stakeholders in NTFP subsector and community based forest enterprises in the previous section and Chapter 4, it became clear that among all the stakeholders, CFUGs are at the cornerstone for taking legitimate stake not only for use but also conserve the biodiversity. Therefore, we now turn to make an in-depth analysis of its potential for the management of biodiversity. The Forest Act, 1993 classifies the forest into five categories: government managed forests, protected forests, community forests, leasehold forests, and religious forests (HMGN 1995). In Nepal, the Government officially owns almost all forested land except private forest. With the exception of few small tree farms and trees on agricultural farms, virtually there is no forest under private ownership. National forests[4] outside the Protected Area System (PAS) are owned, protected, and maintained by the government through its Department of Forests (DOF). Community forestry that was formally initiated in 1978 has evolved as common property resources governance system with many promises.

Several forces were found to be responsible for determining the extent and degree of power devolution. The power devolution and emphasis on community forestry is a radical change in the direction of forestry development in Nepal, and resulted from the combination of several factors. On the basis of historical analysis and our experiential learning from the participatory actions with community groups, meetings, workshops, conferences and interactions with relevant stakeholders, we observed certain factors contributing to the evolution of community forestry in Nepal which are also likely to influence community based biodiversity management in the future. There are both supportive and restraining factors. The supportive factors are grouped into two categories: a) exogenous factors (included those factors that are external to CF system, are related to but outside and above the CF system) and b) endogenous factors (includes those factors internal to CF and its subsystems).

6.2.1 Exogenous Factors Supporting Community Forestry

While a great deal of change in thinking on development took place in the past five decades, the decentralization remained the incessant theme of the government and development agencies in Nepal. People began to question not only on the outcomes of the development but on its process as a whole. So was the thinking on environmental conservation. In many cases, the decentralization has been limited to only delegation of some administrative authority to lower hierarchies, mainly assigning them some selective functions. In case of forestry, this shift has also created forces for devolution of authority towards community-based resources management. The following factors were found to exert some influence to favor the community

[4] Legally, the national forest, which includes grassland, is divided into several management options: protected forest (within the protected area system), government-managed forest, community forest, leasehold forest, and religious forest.

based forest management in Nepal:

- Since the second half of the 1970s, increasing attention has been given to the multiple relations between forestry and rural development. A shift in the development philosophy took place in the ideological world of international development, from 'trickle down' theory, and urban industrial development to a 'basic need' approach, equity, and popular participation. Especially FAO and the World Bank did much to draw attention to these formerly neglected aspects of forest management, as did the discussions at the 8th World Forestry Congress in Jakarta held in 1978 which had as its theme "Forests for People". In such a way, forestry as a discipline has evolved over time, reflecting new challenges and the need to incorporate the needs and practices of local communities (Wiersum 1999; Sapkota 2000).
- It was also a time especially during 1970s, international attention was drawn to the floods in Bangladesh and their link with deforestation in Nepal. The international community considered Nepal to be facing an ecological, social and institutional crisis of enormous proportions which would have far-reaching consequences for other countries in the region, in particular Bangladesh. Thus, it was into this climate of "eco-doom" that community forestry was introduced and the international donor community began putting their funds in restoration of forests of Nepal emphasizing community participation in the management, conservation and utilization of forest resources (Hobley 1996).
- As reflected from the existing indigenous forest management systems, it was indicated that local farming communities have definite interests and experience in forest management. As a result, there was a growing recognition that communities can be as good if not better managers of forest as government or private companies.
- An increased knowledge base on the common property resources management systems both nationally and internationally also exerted some influence to promote community forestry in Nepal.

- While community forestry was moving in its own pace, change in national political system towards more democratic governance creating the environment for the broader participation in the development process in 1990 created the environment to take up community forestry in the country.

6.2.2 Endogenous Factors Supporting Community Forestry

The implementation of Community Forestry (CF) in Nepal has produced promising results in decentralized natural resources management. A considerable progress has been made in developing strong forestry policies. The governance system of community forestry has been advancing with the evolution of a very strong local institutional mechanism and clearer definition of property rights. Organization of CFUGs through networking and federation building is noteworthy, especially for safeguarding the community rights and policy lobbying. Finally, the progress is made in terms of the growing number of hectares of forests under community management and a better understanding and practices of people's participation in forest management. In addition to the exogenous factors the following three contextual factors also contributed to create the conditions for the development of community forestry systems:

- The recognition of legitimate livelihood needs of rural communities and the role of forests, trees and their products (on communal and private land) for sustainable livelihoods and farming systems in Nepal (Hobley 1996).
- Inaccessibility of these forests for commercial exploitation, so the risk of losing power and revenue from the government was minimal.
- Inability of the DOF to manage forests effectively, especially in the hills and mountains where about 3.5 million hectares of potential community forest land is located within an estimated 30,000 forest patches.

The conditions thus established and adaptive practices with the government and donor programs have contributed in establishing the community forestry system, which has further built up the forces for its continuation and advancement. A brief description and analysis on the progress of the four important components of community forestry system is presented below.

6.2.2.1 Development of forestry policy

Decentralization in forestry in Nepal formally commenced in 1978, with the enactment of *Panchayat* Forest Rules and *Panchayat* Protected Forest Rules (1978). This progressive legislation provided authority to the Department of Forests (DOF) to hand over the management responsibility of parts of national forests to local *Panchayats*. These rules were amended in 1980. Since then, the collaborative and adaptive process in advancing community forestry resulted into an exemplary forestry policy. The historical context of Nepal in this regard is summarized in Table 6.3.

The notable policies and legislations supporting community forestry include 1982 Decentralization Act, and its several amendments, 1988 National Conservation Strategy for Nepal, 1989 Master Plan for the Forestry Sector, 1993 Forest Act, and its amendments together with the Forest Regulations of 1995 and the Community Forest Directives of 1995. The Local Self-Governance Act, 1998 further emphasizes the decentralized governance of resources.

Table 6.3
The emergence of community forestry in Nepal (adapted from Hobley 1996)

Period	Form of government	What happened to the forests
1800-1850s	Shah Monarchy	Gift of forests land in lieu of payment for services to state mainly in the hills
1850-1920s	Rana feudal regime	• Gift of tax-free forest lands in lieu of payment for services to state, practice expanded to terai areas • Extraction of terai timber to supply to British India

---

5 Traditionally popular term to refer a council of five for justice, Panchayat used to be the smallest politico-administrative unit of the government until the restoration of democracy in 1990 in Nepal.

Period	Form of government	What happened to the forests
1920s-1960	Rana feudal regime to democratic government to Shah monarchy	• Timber exports to India • Clearance of forests for resettlement • Nationalization
1960-70	Shah monarchy	• Industrialization • Provision of Panchyat Forests (transferring forest management responsibility to local communities) • Protection-oriented laws enacted • Continued resettlement in terai forest areas • Continued timber exports
1970-late 80s	Shah monarchy	• Realization of widespread forest degradation and eco-doom became a talking point • Introduction of community forestry, plantations of Eucalyptus and other fuelwood species • Continued timber exports to India
1990s -2000s	Constitutional monarchy	• New Forest Act emphasizes importance of participatory forestry, still some fundamental contradictions • Emphasis on user groups rather than administrative definitions for local organizations • Decentralization Act emphasis on developed management of natural resources • Federation building and Emergence of NGOs voices-social and environmental activists • Government sanctioned handing over of all biotic resources to identified user groups • Land tenure remains with government • Government retains right to reclaim forests if misused by local people • Timber exports banned

"District Forest Officer (DFO)", according to the 1993 Forest Act, "may hand over part of a national forest to a user group in the form of a community forest, entitling the group to develop, conserve, use and manage the forest, and sell and distribute the forest products by independently fixing their prices, according to an operational plan." (HMG, 1993)

Forest ownership is, however, not transferred to the community Forest User Groups (CFUGs) but remains with the government under central government control. The legislation recognizes CFUGs as self-governing and autonomous entities and entrusts them with the management, control, utilization, and sale of community forest resources in a planned way. The CFUG has the rights to exclude others from using the forest.

Once the forest is handed over to the CFUG, there is no time limit for retaining use rights. The use rights remain with the CFUG for an indefinite period. The DFO can cancel a CFUG's registration if the CFUG fails to implement its operational plan; does not observe the overall provisions of the act; or undertakes any actions that negatively affect the environment significantly. In practice, the cancellation of a CFUG happened less than once in a thousand CFUG certification cases.

6.2.2.2 CFUG system and governance

The evolution of community forestry in Nepal entails different models of community participation. Community forestry in late seventies or eighties included a transfer of forest management rights to local political bodies, called *Panchayats* (now Village Development Committees, VDCs). But this was not effective in bringing the desired people's participation in forest management, as the management rights was practically confined to politically elected members, who were least concerned with forest management and more interested to control the resources rather than to involve local people in use and management of forests. Subsequent studies and experiences indicated a need to identify a well-defined set of users of forest, regardless of their status, i.e. gender, caste, age, socio-economic status or the likes. As a result, the concept of Forest User Group (CFUG) was proposed and tried out.

A CFUG consists of the people who use particular forest(s). The group could include everyone in the village, or just some people, or even some people from another village. The institution is inclusive rather than exclusive of households in the village, and in practice all households of one or more villages become member of a CFUG. As King *et al* (1990:6) describe, "The term users group is really descriptive of a category of people rather than a group."

The Forest Act, 1993 has further strengthened the CFUGs by providing them legal status and more autonomy to mobilize their funds and resources. A CFUG is now a legally recognized, autonomous, corporate entity with perpetual succession and can exercise powers as a legal person. The CFUG governance is defined by their Constitution and community forest management Operational Plan (OP). The constitution is registered in the District Forest Office (DFO). While there are certain standards, guidelines and norms for the group constitutions, each CFUG prepares its own constitution defining the social arrangement and the responsibilities and rights of the group (which may vary from group to group to adapt the local tradition, culture and practices) as well as an OP specifying how the forest is managed and utilized. OP also serves as an agreement between the DOF and the CFUG.

To take care of the daily activities and coordinate with the users, the group elects some members in its committee assigning certain responsibilities in accordance to their Constitution, the time period of the elected members ranges from 1-3 years. On need basis, the group can form many sub-committees to deal with specific issues.

Although the Himalayan communities from a broader perspective are more homogenous, a user group may consist of different interest groups, and there is always a chance of having some persons in a user group with dominating power. Our observations of CFUGs in the study areas show that the majorities were governed by committee, and some others were by chairperson alone or with some other members of the committee, and the rest with a fair degree of group participation. It was also learned that when the appropriate process was not followed to form a CFUG, conflicts arose among users, between CFUGs and between CFUGs and DOF. In many cases, these conflicts turned out to be difficult to manage later on.

To address the situation ideas and mechanisms for assuring wider participation had been developing for quite some time. The process for identifying interest groups within a CFUG and understanding and addressing their needs and concerns while preparing OP have evolved in many cases, and assured that all users including the marginalized groups become fully aware of their rights and opportunities along with their responsibilities to manage the forest. Secondary or tertiary users were also recognized in many instances to account for particular legitimate interests of people beyond the primary users. In some cases, there was growing access of women and other disadvantaged groups to decision making, especially through the stronger representation in CFUG committees, with positive influence in gender sensitive decisions.

Even if a CFUG was specifically concerned with the use, management, and conservation of forest resources, it had also been instrumental to develop social capital for community development. Community decision-making has been gradually democratized, as with progress in the understanding of developmental process, particularly of literate members. In several cases, community fund-raising by charging on the forest products harvested for use by their members as well as sale outside had been reinforced and used in rural infrastructure or social development works that address the needs and concerns of the poor and disadvantaged. Although limited to enterprise oriented CFUGs, they have also been helping to raise individual incomes from the collection and sale of NTFPs.

Thus, the governance system of community forestry has been advancing with the evolution of a very strong local institutional mechanism and more clear definition of property rights. Community forestry system became more established with the progressive legislation, a strong local institutional mechanism -- the CFUG, DFO and their collaborative process, and the more explicit property rights arrangement through the provision of community forest management Operational Plan (OP). The innovative mechanism and process allowed advancing the community forestry system, which then became instrumental for further innovation to take place. In brief, CFUG is a major innovation with regard to participatory management and empowerment of the poor people. It has made the societies living in deep mountains vibrant with activities and hope.

6.2.2.3 Federation and policy advocacy

Networking and federation building by the CFUG are burgeoning activities. CFUGs themselves felt the need of having their own forum to share the experience and knowledge among themselves, and raise their voice to the government to change the national policies and regulation in their favor. CFUGs' initiative in this line was appreciated and supported by the DOF, donor communities, and NGOs. As a result, CFUGs have been able to establish their national level federation called Federation of Community Forest Users, Nepal (FECOFUN). FECOFUN has now spread its network at district and in some districts even at range-post level. In 69 districts, district chapters of the Federation of Community Forestry Users Nepal (FECOFUN) have been formed, and in others they are evolving with support from various agencies.

At the community level, self-initiated inter-CFUG networks are just beginning to be established. To support the continuity and replication of the exemplary works of CFUG, a few policy advocacy forums have been organized. With the initiation of commercial forestry, local networking of the CFUGs producing similar products began at different places. They initiated networking at various levels for sharing information and working collaboratively on NTFP marketing issues. These networks of CFUGs are hoping to be more efficient in dealing with their common challenges.

Through the federation, CFUGs have made significant influence on forestry policy by enabling CFUGs to share learning and experiences on forest management, group mobilization, and entrepreneurship. The federation has made significant influence on forestry policy. They have also carried out capacity strengthening and awareness raising program, and initiated income-generating activities.

With the progress of community forestry, the constituency for advancing the community forestry is getting larger and larger. This includes the CFUGs, FECOFUN, development and environmental NGOs, political leaders, community based enterprises and a large portion of general public.

As of July 2004, more than 1,094,107 ha of national forests have been handed over to 1,509,023 households organized into 13,397 Community Forest User Groups (CPFD, 2004) (Table 6.4).

Table 6.4
Community forestry progress in terms of number of groups, households and community forest area in Nepal

Fiscal year	Number of CFUGs formed	Number of households involved	CF area in ha
Up to 1985-86	126	15,006	7,599
1986-87	127	15,059	7,615
1987-88	128	15,094	7,642
1988-89	138	16,209	8,210
1989-90	180	20,701	10,182
1990-91	267	33,440	15,186
1991-92	617	69,460	35,833
1992-93	1,355	150,467	88,175
1993-94	2,585	293,763	177,065
1994-95	4,234	469,433	294,380
1995-96	6,001	664,879	444,475
1996-97	7,587	841,279	577,785
1997-98	9,024	1,007,867	713,139
1998-99	10,172	1,141,456	812,687
1999-00	11,231	1,261,454	902,842
2000-01	12,065	1,354,732	986,254
2001-02	12,648	1,427,039	1,036,331
2002-03	13,184	1,487,470	1,075,593
2003-04*	13,397	1,509,023	1,094,107

Source: CFDP records, July 2004
Note: CF=Community Forest, CFUGs=Community Forest User Groups

At present, 25 percent of the total forest area is under community forests and more than 35% of the total population of the nation is under CFUGs. These percentages are growing each year (Figure 6.1). The period until 1990 remained mainly the experimental and learning phase during which a better understanding of people's participation in forest management and development of policy took place. The handing over of forest management responsibilities and use rights started to take place in 1990s and accelerated with the support from donors and NGOs subsequently.

Figure 6.1
Number of CFUGs and households and area of forests under community forest in Nepal in relation to time

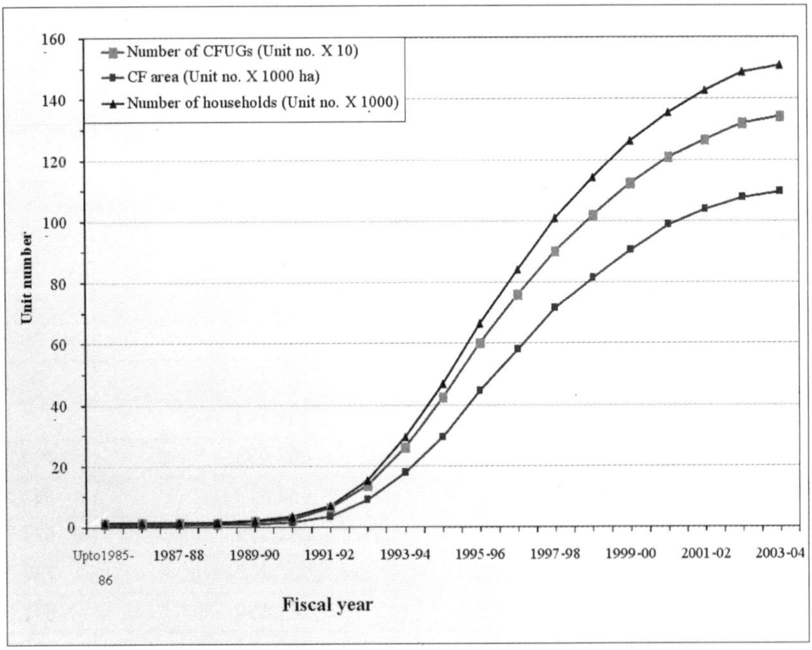

6.2.3 Restraining Factors and Challenges for Local Communities

Community forestry has generally made a good progress in terms of developing good policies, defining appropriate social units, institutionalizing the community system, management planning process and to some extent implementation. However, even with the most progressive policy and legislations on community forestry in Nepal, most of the CFUGs were found not moving beyond the subsistence mode of community forestry. Although there is no size restriction in defining the area of forest to handover to CFUGs, this orientation led in practice to manage small size of forest as community forest. In many cases the forests are not large enough to meet communities' subsistence need. As a result, while the community members protected their community forests, they continued unmanaged/uncontrolled collection of forest products for their use and sale from the adjacent government controlled forests. Restrictions on use and trade of forest products (both timber and non-timber) even from the community forest limited the rights of the users. The existing policy provisions and practices make it difficult to visualize the forest management and use beyond the subsistence, consequently investment in community forestry was out of question. Factors which restrict communities to take initiatives for improving production and production capacity of their forest are outlined as in Table 6.5.

Table 6.5

Factors restricting the communities to take up effective CF management

Area of challenges	Key features
Policy and Legislation Provisions	• Gaps, inconsistencies and contradictions in relation to commercial production, enterprises and marketing • Complex and restrictive regulations (ban, permits, royalties) • Overly bureaucratic process • Low level of stakeholders participation and influence in policy formation process
Distortion in Policy Implementation	• Interest and value clashes between community and government officials • Rent seeking • Discretion on interpretation of regulations • Red tape • Elite dominance: chairperson, committee rather than group
Community Characteristics and Setting	• Lack of awareness and motivation • Inadequate technical capacity • Unjust social structure • Remoteness and physical layout
Inadequate Understanding, Research and Study	• Legitimate community needs and capacity in managing enterprise-oriented forestry • Economic potential of forest resources for poverty reduction and community development • Knowledge on species specific information for sustainable production management
Inadequate Technical Assistance to Communities	• Government services – number, motivation, capability • Limited NGOs and project • Coordination

As given in the Table 6.5 the area of challenges to communities for effective CF management are grouped into 5 different categories with their key features. However, it does not mean that they are "distinct category" to each other. In many cases as found in the study, they operate simultaneously and synergistically resulting disincentives to communities for improving production and production capacity of their forest. They are briefly described as follows.

Policy and Legislation Provisions

First and foremost factor is that in Nepal policies are barely made in consultation with relevant stakeholders and through the reflection of grassroots issues and field realities. This has in many cases had serious implications in terms of CF management. For example, government keeps on changing its policy decision *to and fro* on benefit sharing mechanism in terms of community forests management. What triggered the government to decide 40% levy from the sale of timber from community managed forest? Time to time demonstrated such an ill intention of the government discouraged communities for improving production and production capacity of their community forests.

Moreover, the contents of Operational Plans are wide and emphasize the management of forest for timber, fuelwood and fodder. Although there is provision for the management of medicinal plants, no specific guidelines are given in the section to the development of NTFPs. The scope and opportunities for NTFP management within community forests are not clearly spelled out in the existing forest rules.

Species like okhar (*Juglans regia*) and panchaule (*Dactylorhiza hatagirea*) - have been completely banned for collection and trade by the government. The idea behind this was to help conserve such bio-resources/species from extreme pressure and the threat of extinction. But the ban has not been able to enhance conservation; rather the illegal trade and smuggling has taken place. This has created unfavorable conditions and disincentive for the communities for the conservation of such valuable species in their community forests.

Moreover, nine species are currently banned for exports in crude form including yarshagumba (*Cordyceps sinensis,*) jatamansi (*Nardostachys grandiflora*), sugandhawal (*Valeriana jatamansi*), jhyau (*Parmelia sp*), and sugandhkokila (*Cinamomum glaucescens*) even if they are managed and harvested from community forests. Jatamansi and sugandhawal, in particular, are traded to India each year in significant quantities, and yarshagumba to Tibet. In the case of yarshagumba, the ban is imposed even when any value-added processing is not known. The trade in reality is continuing with increased distortions in legal provisions, providing benefits at the community level resulting to disincentives to the communities.

The royalty rate is to be decided so as to ensure conservation, sustainable utilization and trade of the NTFP resources. The current system of determining royalty rates is arbitrary; for example royalty rate for a kilogram of yarshagumba is NRs 20,000, which is considered high by all key stakeholders and the government is not able to collect any royalty from its collection and trade. The rates remain fixed until the rules are changed. When the royalty rates are changed, there are anomalies in decisions, as it was decided without consultation of the relevant stakeholders. For example, the royalty rate of lauthsalla (*Taxus baccata*) was changed from NRs 0.50 to NRs 25 per kilogram without any consultation with the stakeholders.

The registration and establishment of forest based enterprises including NTFPs requires a complicated procedure. They are not allowed to establish within 3 km in hills and 5 km in terai from the forests, although the provision is set in terms of establishment of saw mills and brick kilns in the environmental conservation regulation (2054). In case, however, CFUGs want to establish and operate such enterprises, this distance limit becomes a major constraint as well as the three party (DFO, Land Survey and Cottage and Small Industry Authority) consensus requirement for enterprise registration. This is one of the important bottlenecks for the promotion of enterprise oriented resource management. Moreover, current regulatory provision states that CFUG can establish industry based on the raw materials from its own CF or a group of CFs. Clarity lacks regarding whether a CFUG can legally get raw materials from other sources like private or government forest lands for operating its own enterprise.

Distortion in Policy Implementation

Master Plan for the Forestry Sector (MPFS) has emphasized the fulfillment local need of fuelwood, fodder and timber from the management of CF, while giving limited attention to enhance income and employment from high value NTFPs. The criteria of 'accessibility' and the size for 'manageability' in case of NTFP focused management of CF differ from traditional forestry that focused on timber and fuelwood. In other words, a group of users maybe in a position to manage larger areas of forest, especially in high altitude regions of Nepal. The 'distance between community and forest' as criterion for forest hand over may not be valid in case of NTFP-focused and enterprise-oriented community forest management. Although there is no legal limit in area of forest to be handed over, the concerned authority hesitates for so doing.

There is a paradox that in most of the cases interest and value clashes between government officials and communities. The rent-seeking behavior and red-tape in the bureaucracy, and the ways the government officials interpret the regulations have discouraged the communities to move towards sustainable and enterprise mode of community forests management. For example, even to renew the operational plan of CFUGs, the DFO staffs may seek bribes from the communities. It is not unusual that if there is no money involved there is little, if not no, interest of the government staff.

Although the overall policy of the government is to promote national and international trade so as to contribute to poverty reductions, in reality the trade of NTFPs has been discouraged by a number of multiple taxes at local level governance units (DDC, VDC). In some cases, such taxes are as high as 200% of the product price. The obvious effect is that the share of collectors has sharply decreased. Even existing Forest Act in many cases contradicts with Local Self-Governance Act resulting in de-motivation to the communities for improving the productivity and conservation of their CF.

Community Characteristics and Setting

In many cases the CFUGs leadership usually has poor representation from the dalits, women, poor, and other disadvantaged group. Even where CF management has been judged "successful", there may be instances where CF activities have unwittingly twisted difficult conditions for some groups especially poor, dalit and women. Lack of awareness among CFUG members and the poor socioeconomic conditions because of the orthodox society have played a catalytic role in many ways so as to continuously marginalize those who are poor and disadvantaged by inheritance. Therefore, services created through CFUG investments are not always equally accessible to all income groups within the community. Moreover, the CFUGs are sometimes found dominated by the chairperson, or executive committee. In such cases the poor community members are de-motivated to taking active part in the management of community forests and in making relevant decisions. Such situation is exacerbated in the distant CFUGs which receive almost no technical assistance from the government staff, NGOs and projects.

Inadequate Understanding, Research and Study

The enterprise-oriented CF management is a relatively new concept. There is a big gap between understanding and realization regarding the potential of this approach to conservation and poverty reduction. As various aspects of CF management have not been adequately investigated grey areas are wide with regard to understanding legitimate community needs and economic activities that can be generated from the forest resources. It requires not only the knowledge of a commercial species, but also the ecosystem dynamics on which the production of valuable products depends. Moreover, the traditional belief that enterprise undermines sustainable use of forest resources is still prevalent among some professionals, advisors, and government and policy makers. This notion has led to a kind of CF programs and policy implementation practices which remain subsistence oriented and several regulatory and market related barriers continue to adversely affect community based enterprises.

Additionally, when subsistence-oriented community forestry moves to enterprise oriented mode, it elevates the concerns of equity, gender, and good governance, and adds on new challenges of enterprise management and marketing, commercial production of forest products, and ensuring biodiversity status. Therefore, it demands studies on the enterprise-oriented community forestry and efforts to increase practical insights into steps along the value chain so as to achieve the success both in conservation and poverty reduction goals.

Inadequate Technical Assistance to Communities

Basically community forestry is a legitimate recognition of traditional and indigenous forest management systems in Nepal in which forest is seen as resource to sustain a subsistence life style. Historically, the system was too primitive to address the issues of enterprise-oriented activities. With appropriate technical facilitation and social mobilization, the initiative could be moved towards enterprising, self-sustaining mode so as to realize proper link between biodiversity conservation and poverty reductions.

The technical assistance available for this field in mountains in general and more remote areas in particular are very limited, and if any technical assistance is available, that is often not useful or appropriate to communities. Very little can be expected from those who are trying to provide technical assistance to these communities with very little understanding of enterprises and their linkages with the conservation. The government agencies often impose unnecessary restrictions, without providing services to communities and acknowledging their status of stewards of the community forest resources. The government staffs are basically de-motivated in working with the communities, and apparently their presence in respect of coverage of community forests is negligible. In this way communities are deprived of getting technical assistance from the government agencies. There are many NGOs in Nepal; but there is handful of them working with the communities in this sector dotted at a small scale. The coordination is poor amongst the government, NGOs and other stakeholders, who could otherwise have brought synergic impacts on the communities in terms of providing technical assistance to the communities and giving a self-sustaining mode of community forests management.

Chapter 7

Impacts of Enterprise-Oriented Community Forestry on Local Livelihood and Conservation

7.1 An Outline of Study Approach

In this chapter an attempt has been made to examine the impact of enterprise-oriented community forest management (EOCFM) with regards to the issues of livelihood and conservation of forest and meadows used. In this participatory action research, interventions of enterprise-oriented community forestry were designed, implemented, reviewed, and several cycles of this interactive process completed and monitored. A broad outline of methods used in this particular study are given in the methodology chapter (Chapter 2), we here refer to certain aspects of the procedures for clarity and immediate reference.

The assessment of the performance of the enterprise-oriented community forest management interventions and synergies among its performance objectives, such as improvement of livelihoods and conservation was based on 37 Community Forest User Groups (CFUGs) from high mountain areas, characterized by the presence of alpine meadows and forests, which are rich in biodiversity and the sources of valuable NTFPs. The districts include Humla, Bajhang, Darchula, Jumla, Dolakha, and Dolpa, most of which are inaccessible from road and suffer from acute poverty. The EOCFM intervention was introduced in 1996 in a participatory action research mode. Of the 37 CFUGs studied, 16 were less than 3 years old, 11 between 3 - 6 years old, and 10 more than 6 years old in 2004.

The data collected pertained to economic performance, biodiversity conservation and resource management, social equity and group governance. The list of CFUGs participating in the PAR is given in Annex 1, and the questionnaire and checklists used for data collection are given in Annex 4. Observations were generally based on 4-8 years of enterprise-oriented community forestry.

Details of methods used to calculate ratings and composite indexes of CFUGs with respect to economic, social, and conservation performances are described in Table 7.1 Based on the data collected for various variables related to a particular aspect, indexes were generated to evaluate the CFUGs on that aspect, details of which are given in Table 7.1. The index for performance on institutional system, as an example was generated by considering practices adopted by the CFUGs in accounting, fund mobilization, and decision making. Index for measuring impact on generating subsistence benefits to households was derived from the ratings on legal access to forest, availability of fuel wood, availability of fodder, availability of timber. Similarly, to measure the performance of the CFUGs on equity aspect, index for access of poor and dalit to subsistence forest products.

Table 7.1

An outline of criteria and methods used to calculate composite indexes of economic, social and conservation performances for CFUGs

Composite indexes	Criteria used	Calculation
Economic	Increase in cash income to Households; subsistence benefits such as availability of fodder, firewood; amount of group funds generated.	For each of the criteria used, ratings were given, such as 4, 3, 2, 1; 4 indicating the highest on performance scale and 1 the lowest. Numbers used for ratings were summed up to determine overall indexes. This was done separately for each of three components-economic, social, and conservation. Since these were very different components, it was difficult to develop synthetic index by combining the three indexes. However, correlations between these were calculated.
Social	Involvement of dalits, women, and other socially deprived people; participation of households in economic activities; access of dalits, women, and poor to forest resources; group fund mobilization and capacity building of CFUGs.	
Conservation	Increase in areas of forest and meadow managed by CFUGs; quality of management plan (assessment of forest resources, harvesting rules, monitoring provisions); improvement in harvesting and regeneration practices; assessment and mitigation of threats.	

Composite indexes were calculated to indicate the overall performance of the CFUGs in the areas of economic benefits, biodiversity conservation and social equity and group governance. The composite index of economic performance was developed from the increase in income as well as subsistence benefits (e.g. such as legal access to forest and availability of fuel wood, fodder, and timber) to HHs. While calculating the composite index of economic performance, 60% weight was given to cash income and 40% to subsistence benefits. Composite index of conservation performance was derived from the ratings on resources assessment practices, awareness of threats to biodiversity, threat identification and mitigation measures, monitoring provisions and practices, grazing regulation, fire control mechanism, tending and other silvicultural practices, regeneration management, harvesting rules in practice, control on immature harvesting, adaptive measures in management, and resource use efficiency. A composite index of social performance was derived from percentage of participants in enterprise activities, women participation in CFUG committees, dalits participation in CFUG committees, access of the *dalits* and other poor to subsistence forest products, and systems and practices adopted by the CFUGs in account keeping, fund mobilization, decision making, and monitoring. The lists of variables and indexes used in PAR analysis are given in Annex 6.

All the 37 CFUGs provided data on the variables related to conservation, institutional system, and economic performance. However in case of variables related to other social performance the number of CFUGs that responded varied from 17 to 37, as not all variables were applicable to a CFUG. In some cases, information was missing on some variables for the period before the intervention, particularly of those CFUGs who initiated EOCFM before this research was designed. Because of the lack of sufficient quantitative data before the intervention, comparison before- and after-intervention situations was not possible for some variables.

Mainly descriptive analysis (frequency, mean, cross tabulation, etc) and correlation have been used for quantitative analysis. Comparisons between the participating CFUGs and the other CFUGs as well as before and after intervention analysis have enriched the analysis of the findings.

While the study compares the performances among the involved CFUGs, examples from other regions and figures of national average are cited to provide a broad perspective and insights as to where these CFUGs stand. In addition, the specific measures applied by the involved CFUGs and factors influencing the CFUGs and their performances are also analyzed to draw conclusions and lessons.

Observations on the performances of the 37 study enterprise-oriented CFUGs are given in the following sections.

7.2 Economic Performance

As described earlier, the economic performance was measured in terms of generation of economic incentives - goods, benefits and services (productivity, employment and cash earning opportunities, group fund and subsidies and provision of social goods). Enterprise-oriented community forestry was found to create benefits in various ways. The individual members got the opportunity to increase their incomes from enterprise activities, especially collection of NTFPs, value adding processing and sale of NTFPs. Some of the community members also got direct employment in community-run forest-based enterprises (CBFEs). The enterprise-oriented CFUGs also generated group funds by charging conservation fee on the harvests from their community forests. Supply of forest products for subsistence purpose also increased, as forests were better managed.

The chief factors affecting the economic opportunity for household income were population density, forest and meadow areas available to communities as CF, and type and abundance of forest products. Because of these differences the CFUGs characters varied across the three altitudinal belts, viz, low (with more than 80% of the forest between 2000-3000m), mid- (with more than 80% of the forest between 2500-3500m) and high (with more than 80% of the forest between 3000-4000m) mountain belts.

7.2.1 Income and Employment to Member Households

7.2.1.1 Economic Participants

As the Table 7.2 shows, while 1,733 households, representing 41% of the total number in the study area were involved in collection and sale of NTFPs before the intervention, the number increased to 3,254

Photo 10. Handmade paper-making at Malika enterprise in Bajhang

households, representing 76% the total households after the intervention. The activities included collection and trade of NTFPs, engagement in value added enterprises, or other CFUGs activities from which the participating households derived cash income. The increment, 88% of the baseline, in the number of households as economic participants in forest enterprise activities within 4-8 years after the EOCFM intervention is remarkable.

Table 7. 2

Changes in the number of economic participants and income to individual households from forest enterprise activities after the intervention

	CFUG Category by Altitudinal Zone			
Elevation zone	**Lower (around 2500m)**	**Mid (around 3000m)**	**Higher (around 3500m)**	**Total**
Number of CFUGs	10	17	10	37
Average number of household per CFUG	218	109	108	138
Total number of households	2180	1847	1080	5107
Number (and percentage) of households engaged in forest enterprise activities				
Before	261 (17%)	676 (35%)	796 (77%)	1733 (41%)
After	823 (53%)	1486 (81%)	945 (93%)	3254 (76%)
Change	562 (215%)	810 (120%)	149 (19%)	1521 (88%)

Elevation zone	CFUG Category by Altitudinal Zone			Total
	Lower (around 2500m)	Mid (around 3000m)	Higher (around 3500m)	
Total annual income to households from forest enterprise activities (in Rs)				
Before	407,300	1,782,940	10,290,250	12,480,490
After	2,385,559	7,453,964	17,657,510	27,497,033
Change	486%	318%	72%	120%
Average annual income per household (in Rs)				
Before	495	1,200	10,889	3,835
After	2,899	5,016	18,685	8,450
Change	1,952 (394%)	3,253 (271%)	7,488 (69%)	4,046 (105%)

Figure 7.1 compares the change in the percentage of households participating in forest enterprise activities before and after the interventions by altitudinal zones. Only 17% of the total households participated in forest enterprise activities from the low altitudinal belt before the intervention, whereas these figures were 35% and 77% for middle zone and upper zone, respectively. The increment in the percentage of households participating in forest enterprise activities after the intervention was significant in all the three zones, but the increment was higher in lower and middle than the upper zone, where the percentage of economic participants was lower before the intervention. The increment was more than three folds in the lower zone, two times in the mid zone and nearly one-fifth in the upper zone. As the availability of commercial products was lower and size of the community forest smaller before the intervention in lower elevation than in higher elevation zone, only small percentage of households used to participate in the collection and sale of NTFPs. With the increased opportunities for the harvesting of NTFPs from the managed community forests after the intervention, the number of economic participants increased significantly.

Figure 7.1
Percentage of households engaged in forest enterprise activities before and after the intervention in relation to altitudinal belts studied

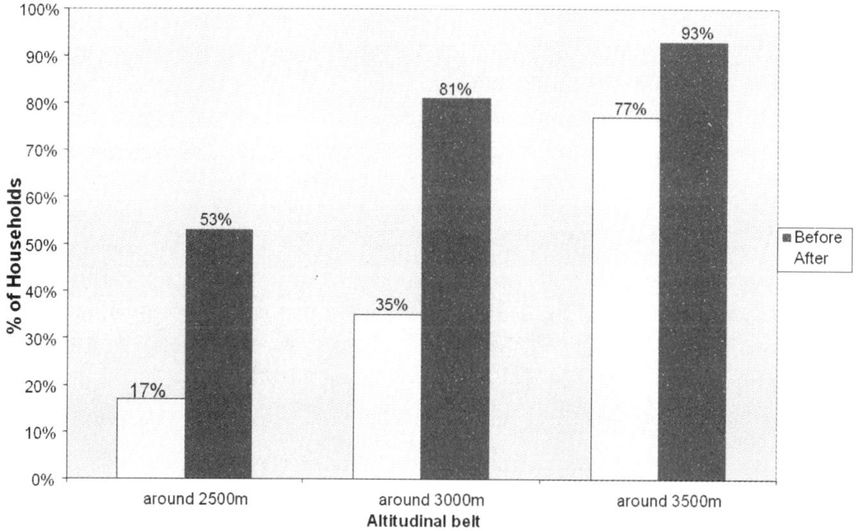

The additional households were attracted to the collection and sale of NTFPs after it became more feasible to do so for them with the support of CFUGs and more remunerative with the organized enterprise activities. For example, in Bajhang Malika handmade paper making enterprise provided direct employment opportunity to 12 local people including 4 women. It has benefited 500 men and women of 240 households of Kailash Pimidada CFUG and 5 adjoining CFUGs, most of whom are also the owners of the enterprise and represent poorest people living in the most remote areas of Nepal. These people earn cash income by supplying raw materials to the enterprise during the supply seasons of the year (Oct-Nov and Mar-Apr). In Humla, Humla Oil Pvt. Ltd. (HOPL) employs a dozen of people in the management and operation of the enterprise. HOPL created employment opportunities for many of the existing 1996 households in its seasonal activities, especially for those who harvest NTFPs and fire wood from the managed community forests. HOPL raised the prices of jatamansi and this substantially increased the incomes of the collectors in the region attracting more number of people to join the collection activities. This has resulted to increase the incomes of the households involved in collecting and processing NTFPs.

The equity section below elaborates the implications of the increased in participation of households in forest enterprise activities and access to benefits in case of to poor, *dalits*, and women, as well as benefit distribution system of the CFUGs.

7.2.1.2 Household Income

The enterprise-oriented community forestry not only created economic opportunities for many more households, but also increased their average annual incomes. All the participating CFUGs created economic opportunities to earn cash income for most of their member households (Figure 7.2). The 37 CFUGs generated Rs. 27,497,033 in 2003 for their member households, and are likely to generate at least the same amount every year in the future. On average, the total income increased by 120% after the EOCFM interventions, and the increase was remarkably high for CFUGs of lower elevation.

Figure 7.2
Change in average household income from forest enterprise activities of the participating CFUGs

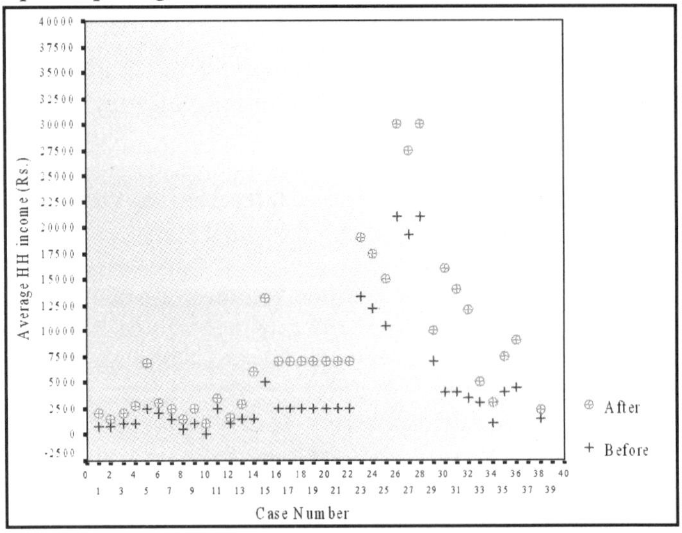

A comparison between before- and after-intervention stages shows that on average the annual household income from forest enterprise activities of the 37 participating CFUGs increased from Rs. 3,835 to Rs. 8,450, the additional income of Rs. 4,046 being 105% of the income

Figure 7.3

Distribution of annual household income for all CFUGs before and after the intervention

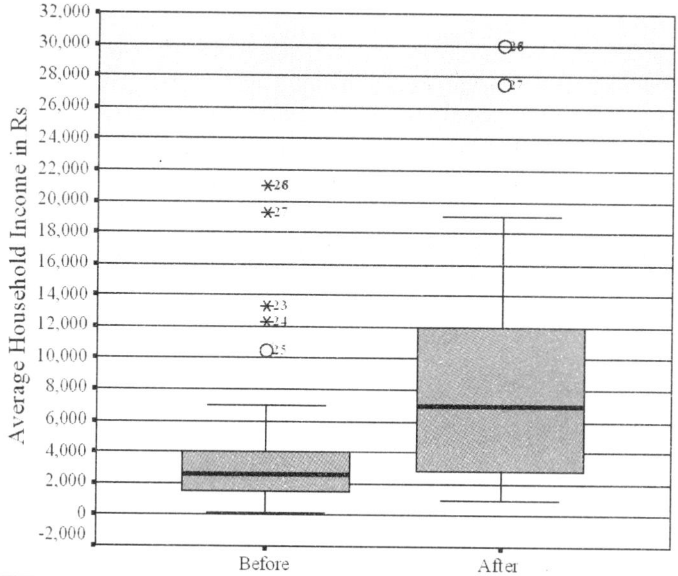

before the intervention stage (Table 7.2). This additional cash income, Rs. 4,046 per household is significant for the area where other opportunities for cash income are severely restricted. The total cash income for 3,254 households of 37 CFUGs, comes to above Rs. 15 million. The total change in annual household income from forest enterprise activities was nearly 500% in lower elevation zone as compared to 318% and 72% in mid and higher elevation respectively.

Box plots in Figures 7.3 and 7.4 present the distribution of annual household income earned from forest enterprise activities before and after the intervention. The box plots show the median incomes and their ranges. Although the overall distribution patterns are similar before and after the intervention, a number of CFUGs with extremely high average household incomes are no longer extreme outliers after the intervention as many households approached the higher side of the income ranges of the pre-intervention stage.

Across the altitudinal categories, the distribution is positively skewed for CFUGs in low elevation belt, but negatively at mid elevation belt.

For high elevation, it is slightly positive before the intervention, and more skewed after the intervention, indicating the range of average household income of the CFUGs above the median was wide.

While all the 37 CFUGs generated some additional income to their member households, some CFUGs generated distinctly more household income than others (Table 7.2; Figure 7.3 and 7.4). In pre-intervention stage the household incomes were much lower in low- and mid-elevation belts than in high elevation belt. The change in income in the post-intervention stage was interestingly in reverse order, very high in low elevation belt, followed by mid- and high-elevation belt respectively. Among the participating CFUGs, the average annual household income from the forest enterprise activities ranged from Rs. 1,000 to 30,000 after the intervention, about 35% of the CFUGs generating an average annual household income of more than Rs. 7,500.

The positive correlation between the household cash income and percentage of households participating in forest enterprise activities

Figure 7.4
Distribution of annual household income by altitudinal categories of CFUGs before and after the intervention

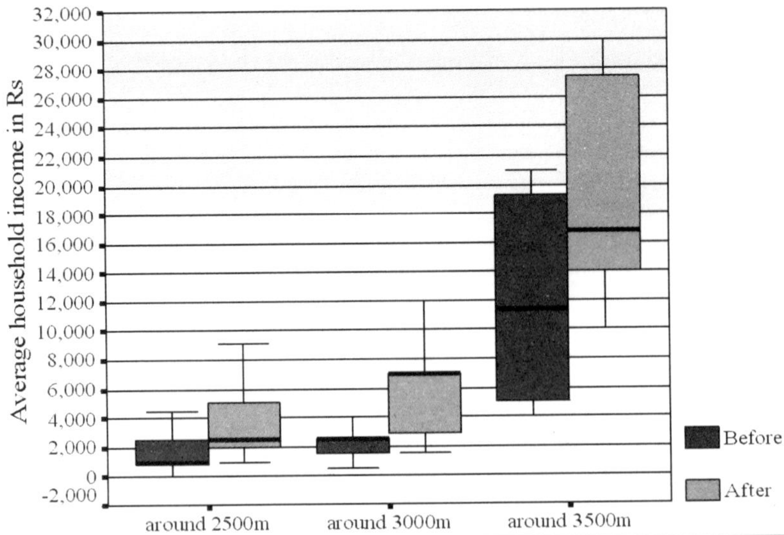

(r = 0.394; significant at 0.05 level) shows that the CFUGs with higher per household income had also provided economic opportunities to higher percentages of the households. One reason for this could bethat the CFUGs creating higher income had larger forest areas and hence more production of commercial forest products, with an improved forest management plans. In addition, these CFUGs had better options for initiating community enterprise activities and improved market linkages and offered more programs for awareness and capacity building.

The major reasons for the increase in individual household income were generally:

a) increased availability of NTFPs with the improvement of forest management;

b) increased selling prices of NTFPs with the availability of marketing information and organized marketing; and

c) processing techniques and enterprises that add values to NTFPs.

As communities began to manage forests and pastures for the production of a variety of commercial products, the member households got opportunity to harvest greater volumes of these products. The increased availability of the products not only resulted in increased harvest per person, but also in increased number of harvesters from households. On average, number of harvesters per household increased from 1.5 to 2.

There was a significant increase in the selling price of NTFPs after the intervention. Some notable examples include yarshagumba in Darchula, morels in Dolpa, Humla and Jumla, and timur in Darchula (Table 7.3). An example of price trends before and after the intervention for one product (yarshagumba) in Darchula is given in Figure 7.5. In Darchula, the Participatory Action Research (PAR) intervention was started in 2000-01, which resulted in the increase of average selling price at collectors' level by 100% in the following year mainly because of the availability of new marketing information and organized trading.

Table 7.3
Average prices of select NTFPs at study district trade centers before and after the intervention

Name of NTFPs and districts	Year (Price per Kg in NRs)				
	1996	1998	2000	2002	2004
Jatamansi (Humla)	13	27	32	40	45
Morels (Humla)		2,000	2,500	3,000	4,000
Silajit (Humla)			40	100	145
Sugandhwal (Humla)		20	30	30	35
Timur (Darchula)			30	40	60
Yarshagumba (Darchula)		30,000	40,000	90,000	130,000
Lokta (Bajhang)	10				24

Source: ANSAB records of field study and marketing information system; HOPL 1994, 1995; MHPL 2000; DFO, Humla 2000; DFO Jumla 1999; Binayak Pimidada CFUG 1999.

A number of community based forest enterprises were established with the EOCFM intervention. Table 7.4 provides the details of CBFEs established and operating as a result of PAR intervention. In an imperfect market, the establishment of CBFEs was instrumental in

Figure 7.5 Trend of average selling price of Yarshagumba at collectors' level in Darchula district before and after the intervention

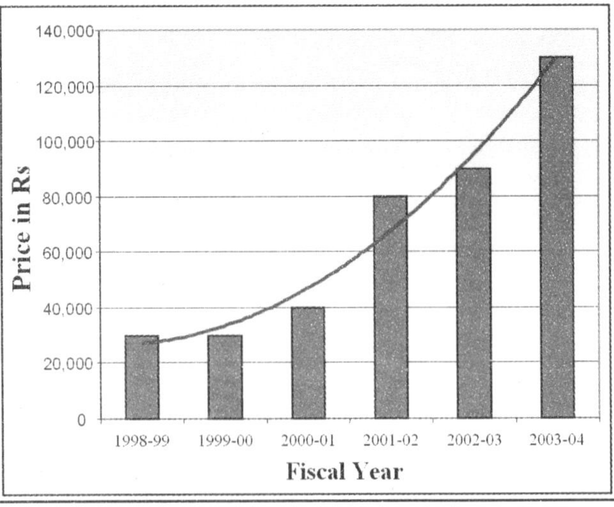

raising the selling prices of NTFPs to local harvesters. For example, as a result of Humla Oils Pvt. Ltd. (HOPL) in Humla, the selling price of dried jatamansi, at collectors' level increased from Rs 15 to Rs 27 per kg in the first year. In two years the price rose to Rs. 50 per kg while the price in the end market in Delhi remained almost the same. Table 7.4 gives the examples of value-added processing enterprises after the intervention. In addition, there were a number of practices adopted by individual households or a group of households that added market value to their products. Some examples are summarized in Table 7.5.

Table 7.4.

Examples of value added processing enterprises initiated with the Participatory Action Research interventions

Name of enterprise	Address	Description	NTFPs	Value added products	Yield (% of raw material)	Value addition (% of raw material value)
Malika Handmade Paper Pvt. Ltd.	Pimi, Kailash, Bajhang	Established in 1999 with a total investment of Rs 1,000,000; owned by 240 HH members of Shree Binayak CFUG; the enterprise's annual target is to produce 3,600 kg of export quality hand-made paper from Lokta barks; raw material collected from 6 community-managed forests of 2596 ha; this CFUG managed company employs 3 persons permanently (for management and production) and 9 on seasonal basis, and benefits 240 households	Lokta bark	Lokta hand-made paper	33.0%	317%
Humla Oil Pvt. Ltd.	Kurrila and Rahadev, Humla	Establishment in 1994 with a total investment of Rs 5,000,000; registered as a community owed private company with 1966 beneficiary housholds; the enterprise's annual production capacity is 500 kg of Jatamansi oil; has two steam distillation units to produce essential oils; employes 7 persons permanelty; target markets of the essential oils are Nepal, India, Europe, and North America	Jatamansi Sugandh-wal, Sunpati	Essential oils	1.3%, 0.5%, 0.4%	200%
Bhitteri Natural Product Enterprise	Boach, Dolakha	Established in 2000 with a total investment of Rs 143,800; owned by 243 shareholders; the enterprise's annual target is to produce 1,000 kg of export quality whiteskin from Argeli stems; raw materials collected from 2 community-managed forests of 670 ha; employees 1 person permanently (for management and production) and 7 on seasonal basis, and benefits 243 households	Argeli bark	Argeli whiteskin	6.0%	500%
Dumling NTFP Trading Cooperative	Rapla, Dumling, Darchula	Established as an information cooperative in 2003; managed by Dumling CFUG with a total investment of Rs 10,000. In 2003 the enterprise marketed 112 kg of Timur from its own community forest; undertakes primary processing such as cleaning, drying, and packaging; the enterprise; employs 2 persons and benefits 86 households; the packaged product is marketed locally	Timur	Packed Timur	5.0%	333%

Name of enterprise	Address	Description	NTFPs	Value added products	Yield (% of raw material)	Value addition (% of raw material value)
Deudhunga Cooperative Distillation Enterprise	Charikot, Dolakha	Established in 2000 with a total investment of Rs 750,000; owned by a CFUG and 25 individual shareholders; the enterprise's annual target is to produce 3,500 kg of essential oils from wintergreen leaves and twigs; raw materials collected from 2 community-managed forests of 1240 ha; employs 7 persons (for management and production) and benefits a total of 897 households	Winter-green,	Essential oils	0.4%	213%

Table 7.5.
Value added processing adopted by CFUG households

Type of value addition	NTFPs	Remarks
Drying	Most of the NTFPs given in Annex 3 except some, such as wintergreen, sunpati, and lokta	With the enterprise development and market information activities, the traders and collectors realized the importance of drying and improved sun drying techniques
Cleaning	morels, yarshagumba, timur,	Although there is improvement in cleaning for all the Annex 3 species, significant value addition by cleaning noticed for few select species
Grading and packaging	timur, yarshagumba, morels, chiraito	
Improved trading	morels, timur, yarshagumba, chiraito, satuwa, atis	Through market information and marketing linkages support, the traders and collectors improved their trade on NTFPs including collective bargaining

CFUGs and CBFEs provided significant cash income mostly with part time employment in forest enterprise activities to more than three-fourth of their member households. This diversification of income sources is critical in remote areas where agriculture production is low and no other industries exist.

7.2.2 Supply of Forest Products for Subsistence

Apart from increasing cash income to individual households, enterprise activities promoted the supply of the subsistence forest products. The availability of all three forest product categories (timber, fuel wood and fodder) to the households for subsistence purpose increased for more than 80% of CFUGs. Only in case of 8% CFUGs the availability of fodder decreased (Table 7.6).

Table 7.6.
Change in access to and availability of forest products to member households of the 37 participating CFUGs after the intervention

Particular	Number of CFUGs		
	Improved	**Same**	**Decreased**
Availability of fuel wood	36	1	
Availability of fodder	30	4	3
Availability of timber	32	5	

Correlations between cash income and subsistence benefits to households at post-intervention stage was positive in terms of availability of fuelwood ($r = 0.624$, $p<0.01$), fodder ($r = 0.591$, $p<0.01$) and timber ($r = 0.484$, $p<0.01$). As shown in Figure 7.6, subsistence benefits to households increased with the increasing enterprise activities.

Availability of these products increased because of the improved harvesting practices. After the introduction of the EOCFM and exposure to the opportunities of the enterprise activities, all 37 CFUGs took up a number of initiatives to increase the forest productivity, value added processing, and improved trading.

With the handing over of forests and establishment of enterprise-oriented CF management forest products became easily accessible to local communities. Unlike other CFUGs, the enterprise-oriented CFUGs showed interest in managing larger areas of forests. With the support from ANSAB they received larger forest areas under their management responsibility. They were able to devise management system for the production of both commercial and subsistence forest products. For example, in Shree Binayak Pimi Danda Community Forest of Bajhang, there was no systematic harvesting of timber and other products before the intervention, but in the post-intervention stage they designed the harvesting system and practices that specified the technical and social rules for a number of commercially valuable NTFPs as well as timber, fuelwood and fodder. As a result, the availability of fuel wood, fodder, timber and other subsistence forest products improved and became easily accessible even to poor.

Figure 7.6 Number of CFUGs by cash income to household and subsistence benefits.

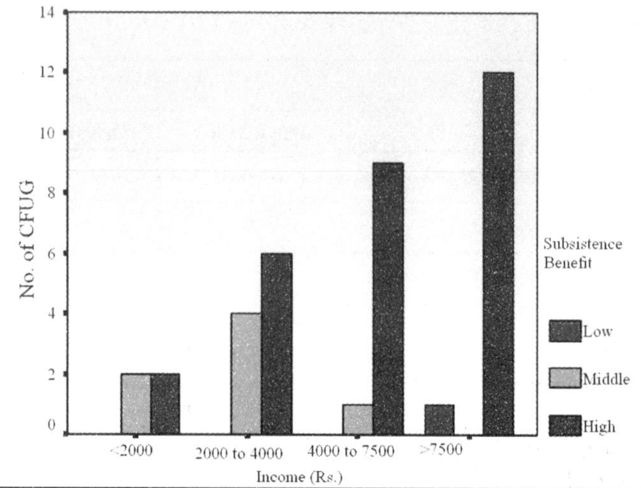

Earlier, the communities had difficult time to receive legal approval for harvesting forest products as the district forest offices and range posts were located far from their settlements, they could hardly find responsible forest officers at the duty station, and even if they find they could hardly convince them about their needs of forest products. Though there was a legal restriction to harvest any forest products from government managed forests, for all practical purposes, the most of the communities, even before the handover of the community forests, were harvesting the needed forest products without any approval of the forest office. Unaware of the legal provisions, the communities had to live in terror and had to suffer, when they had to harvest forest products for their household purposes, especially the timber.

7.2.3 Generation of Group Funds

Enterprise-oriented CFUGs not only provided cash to individual households, but also helped generating group funds. Table 7.7 and Figure 7.7 give information on group fund generated by the participating CFUGs. The size of group fund as of 2003 ranged widely across the participating CFUGs, from Rs. 6,200 to Rs. 470,700, with mean balance of Rs. 115,572 and standard error of mean of Rs. 18, 554.

Table 7.7
Group funds by CFUGs categories in 2003 (in Rs)

Number of CFUGs	Minimum	Maximum	Sum of 37 CFUGs	Mean	S. E. Mean
37	6,200	470,700	4,276,174	115,572	18,554

The CBFEs and other forest enterprise activities enabled CFUGs to create and increase group funds. The majority of CFUGs generated a significant portion of the group funds by levying fee to their members and concerned traders on commercial forest products, specifically NTFPs harvested from the community forests. Some CFUGs also sold forest products to their members and outside and charged forest management fee to members on use of forest products, especially timber for construction. Additional sources of funds for many of the participating CFUGs included membership fee, donation and charity, prize, profits from enterprises and marketing, and penalties imposed on the violation of their social and conservation rules and regulations.

With the establishment of enterprise-oriented community forestry, the money generated through conservation fee increased substantially

Figure 7.7
Group fund of participating CFUG by altitudinal categories in 2003

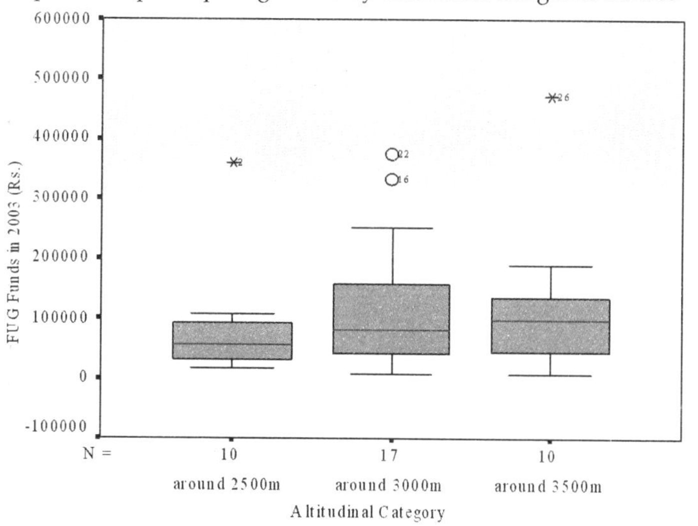

as the community-based enterprises paid the conservation fee to the CFUGs for the entire quantity of NTFPs they bought. CFUGs-based enterprises operated legally, and were willing to contribute to conservation activities so that supply of raw materials continued. Earlier, the practice was to pay the royalty to the government by contractors, who had nothing at stake with regards to conservation, and therefore took all measures to avoid paying royalties in legal way to government.

Some community-based enterprises, such as Humla Oils Pvt. Ltd. (HOPL) in Humla, Malika handmade paper in Bajhang, Rocha NTFP trading cooperative in Humla, and Dumling NTFP trading enterprise in Darchula have been contributing substantially to the funds of CFUGs associated with the enterprises. As a result of HOPL purchasing jatamansi from the 19 associated CFUGs, the income of the CFUGs showed a distinct increase. HOPL, a community based enterprise that involves over 1966 households (3096 collectors) from 19 CFUGs, has two distillation units to produce essential oils. In 1998 it purchased 18,300 kg of jatamansi from collectors and paid a conservation fee to the CFUGs at the rate of 15 Rs/kg, which implies that from jatamansi alone the 19 CFUGs earned Rs 274,500 for the community funds. The records of 19 participating CFUGs in Humla shows that they have collected Rs. 2,340,000 from 1996 to 1998.

As Table 7.8 shows, there are significant, positive correlations among various income related variables. In a CFUG, it is likely to have a higher percentage of households participating in forest enterprise activities when they earn higher incomes from these activities. The household income was also positively correlated with the supply of subsistence products and CFUG funds. The higher the level of household income in a CFUG, the higher is the availability of subsistence forest products (timber, fuel wood, and fodder) to its all member households. However, there was no significant relationship between the CFUG fund and supply of subsistence products. It is interesting to note that there was negative correlation between the total number of household in a CFUG and percentage of household participating in forest enterprise activities. The bigger the group the lower is the percentage of household participating in forest enterprise activities.

Table 7.8
Pearson correlation coefficients between certain economic and social parameters measured at CFUG level after the interventions

	Availability of fuel wood	Availability of fodder	Availability of timber	% of economic participants
Average HH income	.624(**)	.591(**)	.484(**)	.394(*)
% of economic participants	.572(**)	0.289	.365(*)	

Notes: * significant at the 0.05 level (2-tailed); ** significant at the 0.01 level (2-tailed).

7.3 Social Equity and Community Development

One of the primary concerns of enterprise-oriented community forestry is whether or not they have a favorable impact on social equity. Social performance was measured in terms of equity, more specifically benefit distribution among wealth-classes, gender and caste; participation and access to women, dalits and poor; and inter-community equity. Within the CFUG, impacts on gender, dalits and income class were of primary concerns. Since enterprising CFUGs operate through linkages with a number of stakeholder groups at various levels of value chain in or beyond the community, how community-based forest enterprises (CBFEs) contribute to the participants downstream is also an equally important equity concern.

7.3.1 Distribution of Benefits: Access to and Participation of Women, Dalits and Poor

As Table 7.9 and Figure 7.8 show there is clear improvement on participation of women and dalits in CFUG executive committee, which is a decision-making body during the implementation of CFUGs policies and plans finalized by the assembly.

Table 7.9

Percentage of dalits and women in executive committee by income category among the 37 participating CFUGs

CFUG category by average HH income (Rs.)	Dalits' representation in CFUGC in proportion to their population (%)								Women's representation in CFUGC (%)						
	Before				After				Before			After			
	<30%	30 - 60%	>60%	Total	<30%	30- 60%	>60%	Total	<30%	30 - 60%	Total	<30%	30 - 60%	>60%	Total
<2000	6			6			11	11		9	9	3	5	3	11
2000 to 4000	24	6		29	4		25	29	9	18	27	3	11	14	27
4000 to 7500	12			12	7	11	11	29	9	9	18	5	14	8	27
>7500	35	6	12	53	7		25	32	36	9	45	11	14	11	35
Total	76	12	12	100	18	11	71	100	55	45	100	22	43	35	100

CFUG activities are outside households, and most of the activities involve no direct compensation. Besides, most of the CFUG activities have been volunteered by males, which women can hardly afford in view of their heavy burden of household work. This is the reason why the representation of women in the CFUG committees remains low.

Seemingly similar enterprises can have different degrees of women participation, depending upon the type and extent of work a given enterprise offers to them. Women can contribute to in some enterprise activities more than others. For example, women's involvement was found high in collection and sale of wintergreen leaves and allo fiber as the plant sources are available nearby their settlements and are easy to collect. Many women were attracted to allo cloth making following the identification of enterprise opportunities. Enterprises that involve cleaning, grading and packaging, have a more favorable gender impact. Similarly, if the traditional skills of women are used in the enterprise process, that is likely to have a better impact on women.

Enterprising CFUGs have created employment opportunities for both men and women. In lokta papermaking, both men and women are engaged in collecting barks from forests as well as in papermaking. Among the diverse forms of enterprise works, men and women worked synergistically through combining their unique traits, expertise and social roles. But the concern is that these enterprises may raise

Figure 7.8 Representation of dalits and women in executive committee (EC) of CFUGs (Representation shown as: proportion in EC divided by proportion in CFUG population)

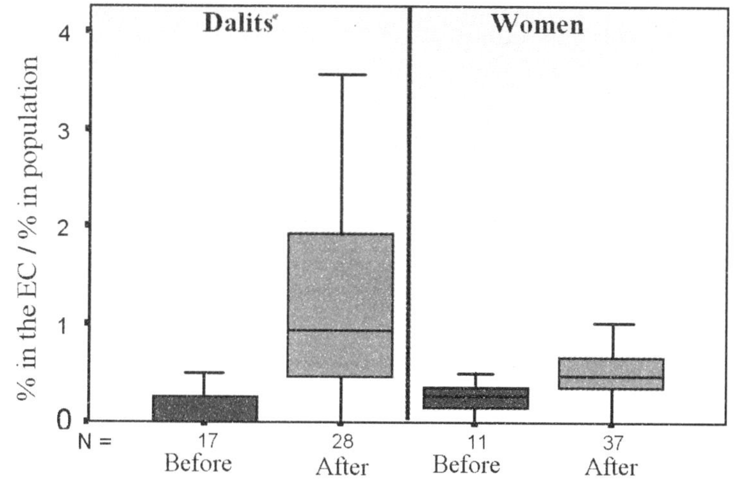

women's workload. On the other hand, when an enterprise is based on centralized processing and is located away from settlements, such as a distillation plant, women's participation declines.

In many cases, both men and women have been involved in collection and marketing, although men dominate the management. HOPL benefited both men and women in terms of increased incomes from the sale of raw materials to the enterprise, but men were found to dominate in the management and decision making. Similarly, in Malika, the enterprise created benefits to both men and women but decisions was mostly made by the men who occupy the managerial positions of the enterprise and CFUG. This issue of social domination men through superior job opportunity can be addressed only by improving women education.

This study shows that enterprises can trigger varied forms of social advancements in women life. Women of the study region traditionally remained confined to household chores. Now they have begun to participate in activities outside the traditional chores with the development of enterprise activities and the income generated from them. For example, in Bajhang, they were found to actively participate in a processing enterprise, producing hand-made paper, and in Humla, they traveled to urban markets and began to control pricing and cash flow. Very poor women in these villages were also able to weave and sell their products with the enterprise opportunities. Women's access to cash is likely to benefit the children in the long run.

7.3.2 Equity across different stakeholders, from harvesters to big traders

The current pattern of profit distribution is highly uneven with generally a high return to external stakeholders, and a low return to stakeholders close to resource base, i.e. collectors of NTFPs and village traders. Based on 13 products traded from Nepal Edward (1996) reported that harvesters of NTFPs in Nepal received only 32% of the final price in India. In Karnali zone, it was found that regional traders generated the largest profit, followed by airport traders; harvesters were the least profit makers. For some products the price received by local harvesters was less than their labor wages (Subedi 1999; Subedi and Ojha 2001). Similar pattern of benefit distribution was also seen in other parts of the country.

Obviously, this is an unfavorable condition from both social and conservation points of view. The reasons for this unfair distribution of benefits include the characteristics of stakeholders themselves, policy and regulatory environment, market conditions, and available technology and services. An analysis of variation in equity indicats that policy (local, national or international provisions as well as their implementation) along with appropriate technical assistance to communities in improving forest management and enterprise development can play a significant role in addressing inequity (Table 7.10).

When ban on the trade of a given NTFP imposed, it leads to illegal trade in which much of the profit goes to big traders at the cost of small traders and collectors. An analysis of the of ban of NTFPs on distribution of income is presented in Figure 7.9, using the case of kutki roots (permitted products) and the jatamasi rhizomes and roots (banned to export without processing). For example, with the ban on export of jatamansi and sugandhawal in unprocessed form, margins and profits of exporters in Nepalgunj rose cnspicuously (Figure 7.9). It was very difficult for small traders to enter this illegal business.

Table 7.10

Some prevailing policy and regulatory environment and their equity implications in Nepal

Policy Issues	Equity Implications
Arbitrary royalty rates for NTFPs and absence of well-developed system of determining royalty	Increased business costs for internal stakeholders
Lengthy and costly export formalities	Internal stakeholders excluded from export functions
Ban on collection and trade of commercially valuable NTFPs that can be harvested on a non-destructive basis	Destructive harvesting, illegal trade and reduction in share of internal stakeholders on profits
Contradictions between forest acts and local governance acts regarding control over NTFP use and management	Excessive taxes by local as well as central government and increased business costs of internal stakeholders
CFUG rights for NTFPs withheld in forests where DOF has separate agreements with other companies	Reduction in incomes of local communities
Absence of NTFP management directives and guidelines for community forests	NTFPs controlled centrally and permits given to big contractors, reducing local income
Inadequate fiscal incentives to community based NTFP enterprises	Business opportunity goes untapped at local level
Impractical enterprise registration and establishment formalities	Business opportunity goes untapped at local level
Bureaucratic harassment on commercial use of community forest resources	Lost or reduced income of local communities
Distorted implementation of regulatory provisions – e.g. royalty for NTFPs from private forests and cultivation, mis-identification of species etc.	Individual cultivators discouraged to grow, trade barriers to small-businesses and earn money

At the international level, Iqbal (1995) found a striking pattern that developing countries are the major producers and exporters of raw or semi-processed products and developed, industrialized countries are the major importers and enjoy high profits.

Figure 7.9 Comparison of profit margins for different operators of legally and illegally exported NTFPs

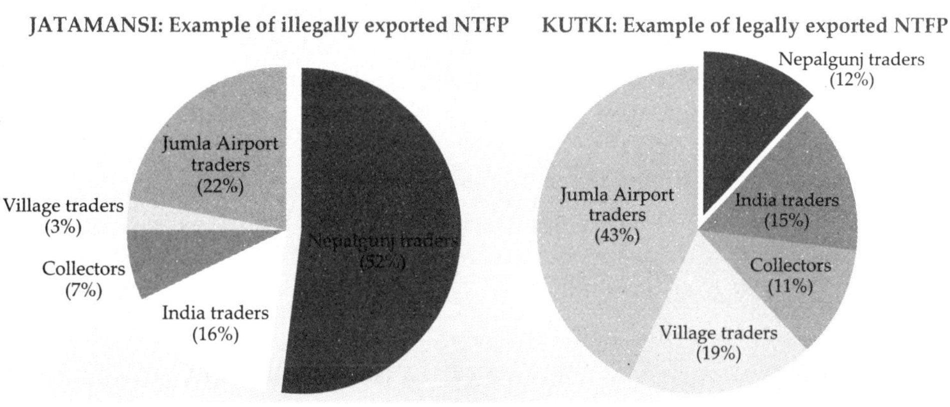

7.3.3 Mobilization of Group Funds and Group Efforts in Addressing Poverty and Social Welfare at Local Level

From the equity and governance point of views, we have made an attempt to assess how the group fund was mobilized. Once the fund is generated, a challenge ahead is how to mobilize the fund that is fair and just. In very few cases a mechanism of involving all interest groups in making fund mobilization decision has been evolved; fund mobilization proposals have to be presented at CFUG level, and CFUG assembly must approve all programs related to fund management. The income and expenditure accounts are presented at the general assembly. In several cases these records are accessible to members. With the prevailing corrupt system, auditing of accounts by certified auditor alone does not guarantee the misappropriation of fund. As the democratic governance of CFUG is fostering, the concept of public auditing is being considered. But this is far from reality for most cases.

The funds generated by CFUGs are being used for forest development as well as community services such as schools, literacy classes and others. Other additional benefits accruing from the enterprise oriented CFUGs activities to their members include sharing of knowledge and skills on entrepreneurship, technology transfer and market information and linkages. The common practices of making investment of group funds (in some cases they combined cash investment with members' voluntary labor and forest products) by the participating CFUGs were as following:

- All CFUGs invested some of their group funds along with their labor in forest management and conservation activities (raising NTFP nurseries, fire control, planting of tree saplings near villages to control soil erosion and prevent landslides, and employing forest watchers).
- Most CFUGs also used their funds in building community infrastructure (e.g. construction of trails, construction and maintaining community buildings, developing drinking water system, irrigation, and solar electricity generation, health post, etc.).

- Some invested in social development and social welfare activities (water mills to reduce women drudgery, hiring school teachers, running public health programs, helping the people affected by natural disaster); in these cases, the decision to where to invest more was guided by social justice as well.
- A few also invested in community-based value-added enterprises (such as distillation units to produce essential oils, hand-made paper production, small-scale presses for edible oils, etc.), generating income and employment opportunities to community members.

Investment in poverty reduction and equity

Here a few examples are cited to show that CFUGs have begun to address the equity issues. Initiatives were taken to address the issues of poverty and social injustice through the benefit sharing acceptable to all members of the group.

- Special benefits to *dalits* and women. Bhitteri CFUG in Dolakha supported its around 20 poor member households to organize into a group and get involved in its Argeli whiteskin production enterprise. In some cases, poor people within a CFUG were allowed to grow NTFPs in community forest area. The poor people sold the products and earned their livelihoods, while a portion of the income was paid to the CFUG fund.
- Giving high priority to poor and needy members of the community while employing persons in forest management, plantation nursery, harvesting, and distribution activities.
- Distribution of forest products based on the real needs of the households (timber, firewood, grazing, fodder, charcoal, etc.). In other cases, contribution of a household in forest management and/or in sustainable harvesting was also considered.
- Free or discounted distribution of forest products for culturally important events. Most CFUGs have practice of providing several types of forest products and other services as a subsidy to local community members and institutions. Timber, poles and other forest products are provided to forest users at prices lower than in market.

In addition to their role of creating direct provision of social goods, the CFUG enterprises also played a role of stimulators in entrepreneurship development. MHPL in Bajhang freely shared and demonstrated their experiences and skills with other community members. These demonstrations influenced their neighbors, who initiated small dairy cooperative to sell milk at the district headquarters.

A success story from Darchula

To illustrate in more detail how enterprise-oriented CFUGs have addressed the issue of poverty at local level – providing finance and access of CF resources to the poor for enterprise activities, we describe a case study from Darchula.

After the PAR intervention, the six CFUGs in Darchula expanded their community forest area enormously from 706 ha to 13,908 ha for conservation and management. The EOCFM allowed them to exclude outsiders from the community forests and manage it through their group members.

In Dumling CFUG, poor people of the communities were more dependent on NTFPs to sustain their livelihoods. However, they did not benefit from NTFPs to improve their livelihoods because of the shortage money required to cover the cost of food during the period of NTFPs collection and trading. These poor people usually go to India for labor works and maintain their daily needs from what they "earn" from the very day. So ANSAB facilitated the poor and other community members to create a community fund to enable the poor to participate in collection and trade of NTFPs. For creating a group fund (revolving type), the individual members collected Rs.10/month/household. The poor people were particularly encouraged to actively involve and contribute to decision making regarding fund mobilization.

With a capitalization fund from ANSAB at the beginning, and their monthly collections, Dumling CFUG began to revolve the fund to the selected 15 poor people for NTFP enterprises at a time. Within a span of about 1 year, there was a visible livelihood outcome along with a number of positive impacts with regard to conservation (Table 7.11). This initiative was replicated by other community members as well, resulting in a substantial growth in NTFP activities in the area.

The revolving fund scheme decreased the financial dependency of the NTFPs collectors on the traders, who used to exploit them, and increased their bargaining power and share of benefits. It was observed that Rs. 22,600 investment generated income and wealth worth over Rs. 95,000 within a year.

Table 7.11
Fund raised and invested by CFUGs for improving livelihoods of the poor through enterprise activities in Darchula (fund raised out of monthly contribution of CFUG members)

Name	Loan from CFUG fund in 2002 (Rs.)	Amount paid back in 2003 (Rs.)	NTFPs based enterprise activities	Livelihood improvement (In terms of wealth and income)
Mr. Netra Singh Buthathoki	2000	1000	250 bundles of grass and 40 kg of timur collection and selling;	Made house of 3 rooms of worth Rs. 22,000.
Mr. Utttam Singh Buthathoki	2000	1500	Grass and allo collection and selling	Goats worth Rs. 5000.
Mr. Jaya Singh Buthathoki	2000	1000	Allo, grass, chiraito collection and selling	Poultry worth Rs. 4000; Increased domestic purchases.
Mr. Indra Singh Budhthoki	2000	2000	Grass, okhar, allo collection and selling	A cow and calves worth Rs. 4000.
Mr. Jituwa Singh Budhathoki	3000	---	Grass, timur collection and selling	An ox and incomes from it worth Rs. 5000.
Mr. Jaspal Bhandari	2000	----	Grass collection and selling	Goats worth Rs. 21,000.
Mrs. Banga Bhandari	800	----	Allo, timur collection and selling	Poultry and cows worth Rs. 4000.
Mr. Rajendra Bhandari	1000	----	Allo, timur collection and selling	A cow and calves Rs. 4000.
Mr. Raghu Singh Budhathoki	1000	----	Grass collection	Goats worth Rs.5000; Increased domestic purchases.
Mr. Baru Singh Budhathoki	2000	----	Chiraito collection	Land worth Rs. 4000.
Mr. Niranjan Singh Budhathoki	1000		Timur collection	Goat worth Rs. 11,000.
Mr. Matusingh Budhathoki	300	----	Allo ropes	Increased domestic purchases.
Mr. Krishna Singh Budhathoki	2000	----	Guchi chyau	Poultry worth Rs. 4000.
Mrs. Huntaya Budhathoki	1000	----	5000 okhar fruit collection and selling	Goat worth Rs. 2000.
Mrs. Dalpati Budhathoki	500	500	Guchi chyau collection	Increased domestic purchases.
Total (Rs.)	**22,600**	**6000**		**95,000**

Benefits to Downstream Stakeholders

Natural products from enterprising CFUGs are mostly sold outside the community area, including international markets. From the communities to market place, there is a long chain of traders, manufacturers and exporters that further add place, time and product utilities, thus providing a forward link to the products. Creation and operation of CBFEs have some socio-economic impacts on participants that live downstream. For example, the handmade paper ultimately goes to Europe and America in the form of hundreds of finished goods that are prepared by Kathmandu based companies. Essential oils produced by HOPL also go to India, Europe, Gulf countries, and America. Allo cloth has also market outside the country. NTFPs, mainly MAPs sold by many CFUGs enter India and beyond. In carrying these products several parties in downstream areas are involved and seek return on the investment that they make.

The several related enterprises downstream get benefits because of the enterprise development in high mountain districts. As the enterprise-oriented CFUGs enhance their production and sale, the downstream stakeholder groups benefit through increased opportunity to undertake trading functions in the value chain.

7.4 Conservation Measures: Stewardship, Management Plan, Practices and Monitoring

Conservation impacts were measured in terms of changes in stewardship of resource base (area under community management); management objectives in relation to the type and range of products; quality of forest management operational plan; resource use and management practices (system, pattern, behavior); conservation awareness (realization, identification and assessment of threats to biodiversity); plan for addressing threats and biodiversity enhancing activities; monitoring system and practices.

7.4.1 Stewardship and Area under Active Management

With the introduction of enterprise-oriented community forestry, communities became interested to be the steward of forest. The existing CFUGs became interested to expand their CF areas and include provisions for the use and management of additional forest products in their management plan. The enterprise development and livelihood opportunities it generated worked as a driving force for rapid CFUG formation in the study region (Table 7.12).

As compared to the national average of 81.7 ha of community forest per CFUG, the average for the 37 CFUGs studied in detail is 1,614 ha. More importantly, the studied CFUGs earlier used to manage only 90 ha/CFUG which was similar to the national average. Thus, they have already achieved nearly 17 times of expansion in CFs. The national average of CF area per household is 0.73 ha whereas in the study CFUGs it is 11.7 ha/HH, with the range of 1 - 89.5 ha/HH. As of 2003 December, these 37 CFUGs were managing 59,716 ha of forest and meadow ecosystems. It may be pointed out that the region is part of a global hotspot of biodiversity (according to Norman Myers' conservation priority setting). Before the interventions, these communities were managing just 1,898 ha as community forest.

Table 7.12

Comparison of areas under CFUGs before and after the intervention

	CFUG Category by Altitude			Total
Elevation zone	**Low (around 2500)**	**Mid (around 3000m)**	**High (around 3500m)**	
Number of CFUGs				
Before	8	6	7	21
After	10	17	10	37
Total number of households				
Before	1272	702	710	2684
After	2180	1847	1080	5107
Total CF Area (ha)				
Before	931	363	604	1898
After	6835	27877	25004	59716
Times it increased	6	72	40	29
Average CF area/HH (ha)				
Before	0.73	0.52	0.85	0.71
After	3.1	15.1	23.2	11.7
Times it increased	2	27	25	15

Note: CFUG = community forest user group; CF = community forest; HH = household; OP = CFUG's Operational Plan for forest management.

Before the interventions, the average area of community forest per household was similar across the altitudinal zones, but after the interventions it increased markedly with the increasing altitudes, the value in high altitude zone being more than 7 times greater than in low altitude zone (Table 7.12). There are two reasons for it: first, there are larger areas of forest and meadow available for community forestry in the high altitude zone, and second, a variety of high value NTFPs are scattered over a large area of habitats in this zone. With the enterprise orientation, the CFUGs became interested in taking over the management responsibility of large areas of forest and meadow and making both the short and long-term investments for the conservation. The community stewardship saved significant areas of forestland from becoming open-access property. Earlier, as the government was unable to enforce and control, let alone to manage the forest, many areas became degraded. The impressive success in initial stage in demonstrating CFUGs' capacity and commitment to sustainable and cost effective management of forests greatly influenced government officials, who readily agreed to handover large chunks of the forest land. Hence, the newly organized CFUGs participating in the PAR were found having larger forest areas, expanded property rights, and better forest management practices.

The communities that were not getting meaningful benefits from forest resources were found uninterested to be the stewards of the resources. For example, in Humla before the enterprise intervention local people used to burn their forests and pasture lands, destroying valuable MAPs such as jatamansi (*Nardostachys grandiflora*), to promote growth of grasses for subsisting livestock. With the introduction of an enterprise in their locality, they became interested to get tenure of forest for assured regular income from the NTFPs. After the establishment of the enterprise-oriented community forestry, CFUGs

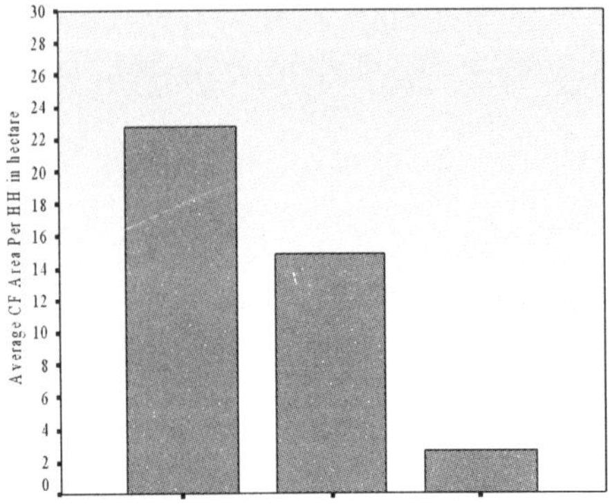

Figure 7.11 CF area by year of formation of CFUGs

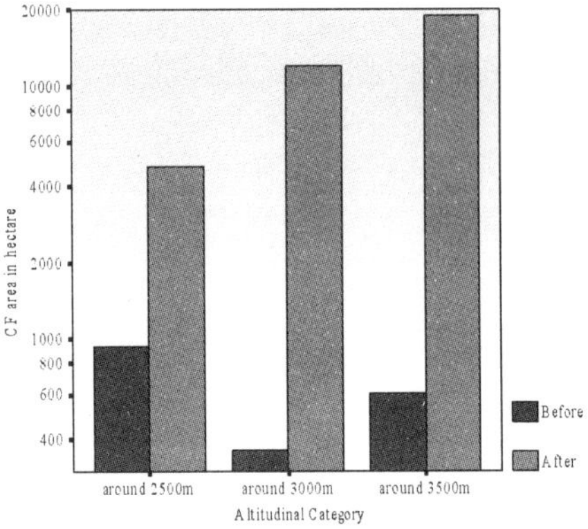

Figure 7.11 Changes in CF areas by altitudes after the intervention

were able to exclude outsiders and manage forest and meadows by making rules and imposing self-regulations at community level. The enterprise development and management of larger forest areas contributed also to ensured supply of timber to member households.

7.4.2 Management Plan

7.4.2.1 Management objectives: range of products particularly of NTFPs under management

The enterprise-oriented CFUGs not only had to manage larger areas of forest and meadow but also to manage them for a variety of goods including Non-Timber Forest Products (NTFPs), as well as those traditionally used for subsistence living. The focus of the participating CFUGs shifted more towards commercial products than the non-commercial products. For example, in an exercise conducted during this study people simply listed the names of species in case of non-commercial products like agricultural implements, whereas they made detail management plans for use and conservation of each specie in case of commercial products. Obviously, money generation and conservation positively liked in this case.

When needed technical support was available, the participating CFUGs were interested to include additional species of plant for the use and management. The CFUGs, in fact, were seen searching for more species of which they could make commercial uses (Table 7.13). This expansion in use of biodiversity is likely to contribute significantly to its conservation, because CFUGs have begun to develop detail plans for use and conservation of many more species than they did in the past. Earlier, people's focus was on a few timber, firewood and fodder species, now a much larger fraction of biodiversity is part of their knowledge and management.

Table 7.13

Number of NTFP species managed by the 37 participating CFUGs after the intervention

Elevation zone	Lower (2000-3000m)	Mid (2500-3500m)	Higher (3000-4000m)	Overall
Average number of species listed in OP	16.0	13.8	11.9	13.4
Average number of species with a detail management plan in OP	2.8	3.4	3.3	3.2

Note: OP = CFUG's Operational Plan for forest management

Thali CFUG of Humla was first in Nepal to incorporate (in 1996) management and use provisions of NTFPs beyond subsistence purpose in its OP. The government agreed to the interpretation that Forest Act and Rules can allow CFUGs to include NTFPs in their management plan and harvest for sale. The communities became interested to get management and use rights of these products so that they could earn revenue for their group funds, which would otherwise go to the government. The individual members could earn cash income from harvesting and sale of NTFPs from their community forests. As a result, there became a large number of communities interested to be organized as CFUGs and convert government forests into community forests. The number of request was much more than the project staff could handle and provide technical assistance.

7.4.2.2 Inventory, resources assessment and planning process

Unlike traditional CFUGs, all the 37 participating CFUGs carried out forest and forest product inventories with the support of professionals in a participatory way, generating the information required for making management decisions. They carried out detailed resource inventory of the target forest species for commercial use and devised an elaborate forest management plans. A list of plant species of which detailed inventory and assessment have been made for timber and non-timber products by the participating CFUGs is given in Table 7.14. Box 7.1 gives an example of assessment of lokta (*Daphne* spp) in Binayak Pimidada Community Forest of Bajhang district in Far-Western Nepal.

Table 7.14

List of plant species included in management provisions with detailed assessment for NTFPs by the participating CFUGs after the intervention

SN	Local Name	Scientific Name	Life form	Managed for
Species primarily for NTFPs for sale and household use				
1	Allo	*Girardinia diversifolia*	Shrub	Fiber for thread and cloth
2	Argeli	*Edgeworthia gardnerii*	Shrub	Bast fiber for paper
3	Atis	*Delphinium himalayai*	Herb	Root for medicine
4	Bajradanti	*Potentilla fulgens*	Herb	Whole plant for medicine
5	Bhutkesh	*Selinum tenuifolium*	Herb	Whole plant for medicine and food
6	Bikh	*Aconitum spicatum*	Herb	Tuber, flower, leaves for medicine
7	Biojadi	*Tanacetum dolicophyllum*	Herb	Roots for medicine

SN	Local Name	Scientific Name	Life form	Managed for
8	Chiraito	*Swertia chirayita*	Herb	Whole plant for medicine
9	Dhatelo	*Prinsepia utilis*	Shrub	Fruit for edible oil
10	Guchchichyau	*Morchella conica*	Fungus	Whole plant for food
11	Guras	*Rhododendron spp.*	Shrub	Leaf, flower for incense and medicine
12	Jatamansi	*Nardostachys grandiflora*	Herb	Rhizome for essential oil, medicine
13	Jhyau	*Parmelia nepalensis*	Lichen	Whole plant
14	Kutki	*Neopicrorhiza scrophulariiflora*	Herb	Root for medicine
15	Lokta	*Daphne bholua*	Shrub	Bark fiber for paper
16	Majitho	*Rubia cordifolia*	Herb	Whole plant for dye
17	Nigalo	*Drepanostachym intermedium*	Shrub	Stem for sticks and handicrafts
18	Padamchal	*Rheum australe*	Herb	Root and stem for medicine and food
19	Satuwa	*Paris polyphylla*	Herb	Tuber and root for medicine
20	Soti grass	*Cymbopogon jwarancusa*	Herb	Leaf for essential oil
21	Sugandhawal	*Valeriana jatamansii*	Herb	Root for essential oil
22	Sunpati	*Rhododendron anthopogan*	Shrub	Seed and leaves for essential oil and incense
23	Timur	*Zanthoxylum armatum*	Shrub	Fruit for spice and flavor
24	Yarsagumba	*Cordyceps sinensis*	Fungus	Whole plant for medicine
25	Lauthsalla	*Taxus baccata subsp. Wallichiana*	Tree	Leaf and bark for medicine
26	Panger	*Aesculus indica*	Tree	Fruit for detergent, leaf for fodder, fuel wood
27	Okhar	*Juglans regia*	Tree	Fruit, bark, root for food and dye
28	Bhojpatra	*Betula utilis*	Tree	Bark for natural paper, roofing
Species primarily for timber, fuelwood and fodder				
1	Bajh	*Quercus spps*	Tree	Fuel wood, fodder, grass
2	Dhupi	*Juniperus indica*	Tree	Wood , fruits for medicine and essential oil
3	Gobresalla	*Pinus wallichiana*	Tree	Timber, fuel wood
4	Kaulo	*Persea odoratissima*	Tree	Timber, fodder, bark for sale, food
5	Kharsu	*Quercus spp*	Tree	Timber, fuel wood, fodder
6	Ranisalla	*Pinus roxburghii*	Tree	Timber, resin and gum
7	Thingresalla	*Tsuga dumosa*	Tree	Timber, fuel wood
8	Tilalo	*Acer spp*	Tree	Timber, fodder, wooden bowl
9	Utis	*Alnus nepalensis*	Tree	Timber and fuel wood
10	Jhule-salla	*Abies pindrow*	Tree	Fuel wood and timber
11	Jhule-salla	*Abies spectabilis*	Tree	Fuel wood and timber

The operational plans of the CFUGs included information about the current stock of the product by species and area, with a projected stock table for five to ten years and the annual harvestable quantity under a defined harvesting regime (e.g. minimum size of cutting, rotational interval, etc.).

Box 7.1 Inventory of Lokta in Binayak Community Forest, Bajhang

Preliminary mapping: The community prepared a participatory resource map showing forests and its legitimate users. Community members also demarcated the forest boundary on a topographical sheet.

Boundary survey and blocking: Using topographical map sheet, forest boundary was tentatively delineated. The boundary was verified with a compass and tape survey. The community forest area was calculated from the map (912 hectares), and was divided into seven blocks, based on the existing natural boundaries and forest types.

Sampling and measurement: Using a stratified random sampling method, the group completed a participatory inventory of the forest tree species and NTFPs in the forest. Several strata were made based on forest types by dominant species and other conditions. The sampling intensity was around 1% and 136 plots were observed. Twenty major tree species and twenty NTFP species were recorded, and seven tree species and lokta were inventoried in a greater detail. Stock of lokta was recorded by diameter class (below 3 cm; 3 to 6 cm; 6 to 9 cm at around 30 cm above the ground) to identify sustainable harvesting levels. Only individuals of certain diameter class were harvested.

Estimation of sustainable harvest levels: Using the data from the inventory and available secondary sources (on growth rate, stem diameter and bark yield relations etc.), sustainable yield was prescribed for five years. Each year the CFUG could obtain approximately 11,000 kg of lokta bark that produces 3,600 kg of hand made paper, that is 33% of weight of bark. Sampling error could occur but experiences afterwards showed that the estimates provided a fairly accurate basis to judge the potential of lokta supply, upon which enterprise decisions were made.

Incorporation of NTFP provisions in management plan: The above information was used to prescribe harvesting system for timber as well as NTFPs used in subsistence and/or income generating activities. The plan included a separate section on the harvesting of NTFP, particularly lokta. The 5-year operational plan described the forest management and harvesting activities.

7.4.2.3 Identification of threats to biodiversity and mitigation plan

After the enterprise-oriented forest management interventions, as Table 7.15 shows, all the CFUGs bcame aware of the threats to biodiversity; 92% had identified the major threats; 86% had designed threats mitigation measures; and 49% had been regularly reviewing the threats and effectiveness of mitigation measures.

Table 7.15
Status of threats assessment and mitigation among the participating CFUGs as of December 2003

Threat related activities completed	Number of CFUGs	Percentage of the total CFUGs
Threats awareness	37	100
Threats identification and assessment	36	97.3
Threats mitigation measures	31	83.8
Threats review	18	48.6

Encouraged by the economic benefits they received from the enterprises using the products from their CF, the CFUGs began to link their harvesting and other management practices with biodiversity conservation. They started analyzing the threats to biodiversity, both internal and external. As it was almost impossible to ascertain all factors of sustainability beforehand, most of them decided to keep the track of what they had been doing and their impacts on conservation. In most of the cases, the CFUGs site-specific threats analyses were done as part of the CFUG's forest management operational plan development. The CFUG operational plans noted specific threats and designed action plan to abate the threats. Communities used the threat analysis framework to monitor their performance with regard to threat abatement and periodically reviewed the changes in the status of the threats. A generalized example of the major threats to biodiversity identified by the participating CFUGs and how the CFUGs and other partners have been addressing them is summarized in Table 7.16.

Table 7.16
Major threats to biodiversity identified by the participating CFUGs and abatement steps being considered

Threats	How the Threat is being Addressed
Destructive collection of NTFPs (due to outsider intrusion, absence of local ownership, unscientific collection)	CFUGs (Forest User Groups) which enable the community to protect the forest by giving them rights to prohibit outside collectors, creating a sense of ownership over the resources, and generation and sharing of scientific information for sustainable harvesting.

Threats	How the Threat is being Addressed
Encroachment and slash and burn (by locals as well as transhumance for cultivating food crops for self consumption)	CFUG agreements give communities the power to restrict slash and burn activities in their lands. CFUG management plans typically prohibit slash and burn, and provide alternate income generating opportunities through sustainable NTFP collection that gives people an economic incentive to stop destructive land use practices.
Overgrazing (by outsiders and locals)	CFUGs prohibit outside grazers. Overgrazing by community members is addressed in CFUG operational plans. Also, as more and more CFUGs across Nepal are formed, migratory herds are decreasing as herders can no longer move animals to lower altitudes in winter. This threat is being addressed indirectly in providing alternative income from NTFPs.
Fire from natural and intentional causes (intentional fire for clearing grasses and bushes, and accidental fire from heating, cooking and smoking)	Conservation education and emphasis on NTFPs for income generation has encouraged communities to stop pasture burning. No efforts yet on controlling natural fires. CFUGs initiating to plan and implement fire prevention education for accidental causes.
Removal of fuelwood and timber (for local use)	CFUG operational plans determine the sustainable rate of harvest in agreement with DFO (District Forestry Official). The CFUG would monitor the harvesting impact and take corrective action to adjust harvest practices (rates, methods, etc.) if necessary.
Lopping and removal of leaf litter (excessive and unsystematic collection for fodder and bedding materials)	Operational plan would regulate the lopping and leaf litter collection for maintaining sustainability. The existing practices would be improved through adaptive management based on the new knowledge and experience.
Illegal hunting (of wild animals)	Included in CFUG management plans, this threat would be discussed in the overall biodiversity education.
Insects, diseases and pests	No direct interventions are planned.

Threats	How the Threat is being Addressed
Soil erosion and landslides	No direct interventions are planned. DFOs and CFUGs are engaged in some replanting activities.
Natural calamities	No direct interventions are planned. However, it is important to note: In 1999 there was severe drought in Humla. Socioeconomic monitoring indicated the people who had NTFP income options faired better and were less likely to expand biodiveristy-threatening activities, such as slash and burn and overgrazing.

7.4.3 Management Practices

7.4.3.1 Harvesting regulation (time, block, quantity, method)

Following the initiation of enterprise activities by the CFUGs, majority of their members became more concerned about the sustainable use of NTFPs. As a result, all the participating CFUGs included new provisions in the operational plan, particularly relating to the harvesting system. Block-wise rotation and specific systems of collection were mentioned in the plan. In some cases, block-specific stocking was taken as part of the forest management planning. Prescriptions were made for each block on yearly basis. As a result, quality of management was getting improved (Table 7.17).

Table 7.17
Grading of CFUGs with regard to quality of management practices as applied to grazing, fire control, and harvesting (percentages are of 37 participating CFUGs)

Quality of Management Practice	Grazing management	Fire management	Application of Harvesting Rules	Regulation on Harvesting of Immature Plants
Very Low	2.7	0	0	0
Low	32.4	2.7	10.8	13.5
Good	64.9	97.3	64.9	83.8
Very Good	0	0	24.3	2.7
Total	100	100	100	100

The CFUGs also began to think of the efficiency of harvesting operation and timing. In many cases, regular firewood needs were fulfilled through pruning or thinning operations, which earlier were hardly considered, as people were used only to felling whole trees, particularly young ones. In most of the enterprise-oriented CFUGs, now the fallen trees and their parts satisfied much of the requirements. CFUGs in general have yet to employ practices such as harvesting at an optimal stage of plant growth and time when the chemical compounds in question peak in concentration. This requires scientific study, which is not available in most of the cases. Generation of knowledge in this subject can bring about a conspicuous improvement in sustainable harvest practices.

The CFUGs established nurseries and carried out enrichment plantations. When nurseries were not successful, because of severe drought and other factors, people who curious to know more about the reasons why it failed. They could not get any technical advice from the forestry staff. In other cases, CFUG established nurseries but they could not manage well as they were discouraged by poor survival in plantations. More scientific inputs are required in nursery raising.

CFUGs in Darchula have banned cutting of tree branches while collecting jhyau (lichens) from trees. Likewise, practices such as leaving a substantial part of population for regeneration and recovery of biomass at the time of harvest are being promoted. In Dolakha, after the intervention, CFUGs members stopped felling Taxus trees for harvesting leaves.

Following the establishment and operation of HOPL, the CFUGs in Humla realized that the forest and pasture could not be depended on to supply raw materials sustainably if the proper resource management system was not applied. In order to reinforce the resource conservation efforts made by local communities, the company increased purchasing prices of jatamansi from collectors and paid to the concerned CFUGs the conservation fee of Rs 15 for each kg of herb purchased. These communities have instituted the harvesting practices, such as rotational harvesting and group harvesting following the prescribed methods, rates, seasons, etc. Before 1996, the grasses including jatamansi in alpine pastures of Humla used to be burned to hasten the growth of summer grasses for livestock. As a result of the enterprise, these herbs later turned out to be important cash generating products for local people, and the above burning practice has been drastically reduced.

In addition to giving more time for conservation activities, the CFUG invested the group fund in assisting natural regeneration, employing forest watchers, enrichment plantations, etc. (Table 7.18). CFUGs have also assisted in cultivation and artificial regeneration of forest resources. Some enterprise oriented CFUGs have already adopted, and many others are planning to adopt the following practices to protect the regeneration:

- Most CFUGs instituted rotational grazing practices to allow natural regeneration;
- About one-third CFUGs initiated stall feeding and reducing the number of livestock substituting them with improved breed, many feel it is necessary but difficult to practice due to socio-economic condition;
- About 90% CFUGs have practiced rotational harvesting systems (including leaf litter, grass, and fodder) to allow seeding, coppicing, etc.,
- Most CFUGs have a system of inspecting forest area on rotational basis;
- About one-fifth CFUGs protected mother seed trees of some critical species, e.g. oak and sugandhkokila; and
- Three CFUGs have demarcated and fenced regeneration areas.

These initiatives have become exemplary activities in community forest to revive the lost habitats and improve the forest stockings while saving the costs of other alternative programs such as plantations and providing the communities with constant supply of necessary forest products. Department of Forests does not have a history of undertaking any natural regeneration management activities. They were primarily constrained by their staff capacity and motivation. There were virtually no any silvicultural practices applied in the forests of Nepal.

Table 7.18
Grading of 37 participating CFUGs according to involvement in regeneration management and efficient resource use practices

Quality Grading	Regeneration Assistance %	Efficient Resources Use Practices %
Very Low		
Low	15	23
Good	85	77
Very Good		
Total	100	100

7.4.3.2 Resource use practices

When the communities received the enterprise oriented forest use rights and management responsibilities, they began to see the potential impact of their use pattern on their forest resources. They became interested to conserve the resource base and improve the productivity of their forests. At the same time, they started trying out the innovative ways of minimizing wastage and alternative practices to increase the efficiencies of forest product use. Examples of efficient resource use practices they adopted include improvement in house building, tree felling and sawing, firewood collection and using, and in grazing practices.

7.4.4 Conservation Monitoring and Condition of Forests

CFUGs started to raise the concern on the sustainable harvest rate as well as practices such as finding out appropriate seasons, methods, and tools for each of the products in question. A few participating CFUGs have worked out a harvesting plan based on the preliminary estimates, and devised a monitoring system to test the assumptions and make adjustment (if necessary). A case in Humla illustrates that sustainable harvesting is more than knowing the amount to be harvested. Judgment should be made on how and when the product is harvested and all other impacts on the ecosystem (Box 7.2 from Subedi and Koonz 1999).

The CFUGs of Humla wanted to monitor harvesting practices so that they can adapt better practices that will improve production of commercial products while conserving the biodiversity (Table 7.19).

Box 7.2: Reconciling social factors with ecological factors: when is best to harvest jatamansi?

Jatamansi is dormant from late Autumn until early Summer. During the Winter, plants are covered in snow, making harvest impractical. The plants sprout in early Summer, after the Winter snow melts, and grow until Autumn. The social and ecological effects of Autumn (mid-October to mid-December) versus Summer (mid-May to mid-July) harvesting were examined to determine when it is best to harvest jatamansi. Both seasons are similar in terms of spare time available to the collectors.

From the collectors' point of view, Summer is comfortable weather for harvesting work. Whole roots can be pulled up easily from the moist and less compact soil during Summer. During Autumn, the soil is very hard due to freezing and it is difficult to pull out the roots. The collection of jatamansi is a hardship on collectors during cold weather. There is also a high risk that collectors may have to return empty handed if snow falls early.

As it is easy to pull or dig up the plants during Summer, collectors have a tendency to harvest a higher percentage of plants at this time. Loosening of soil surface and the trampling damage by the grazing animals after Summer harvests also accelerate soil erosion during the rainy season. Harvesting in Summer is also detrimental to the remaining plants and propagules as most of them decay after the harvest during the rainy season. Finally when jatamansi is harvested during the beginning of its growing season (Summer), its annual yield is reduced.

The quality of jatamansi harvested in Autumn was found to be better than that harvested in Summer. The jatamansi harvested in Autumn has low moisture content, is less likely to be damaged by fungi and other factors, and produces heavier high quality essential oils. The jatamansi harvested in Summer contains high moisture, is likely to be damaged by fungi, and produces poor quality essential oils. Therefore, Autumn is recommended as a more appropriate season of harvesting from the biological point of view.

Appreciating the tradeoffs that must be made between the social and ecological factors, the method of harvesting and other management considerations (e.g. grazing practices, burning, etc.) is important when devising management plans.

Source: Subedi and Koonz 1999

The interventions by ANSAB involved defining the criteria, indicators and verifiers of monitoring, and developing formats for recording and analyzing the information. In some cases, a detailed process was developed to enforce the planned activities, monitor the deviation, and take corrective action. However, monitoring is still in very preliminary stage and will take a long time before it is fully integrated with CFUG management plans and practices (Table 7.20).

Table 7.19
Summary of certain monitoring initiatives taken by CFUGs of Humla after the intervention

Activity	Results	Adjust for the Specific Area
With an experienced mapmaker, the community demarcated their resource area by ecosystem type (forest, pasture, farmland, rock face etc.)	The group's total resource area is 2,000 hectares composed of 500 ha forest, 700 ha pasture, 300 ha farmland, and 500 ha rock face.	Adjust the ecosystem types to reflect the resource area. For example, primary and old growth forest, tree plantation areas, or open brush land.
A group discussion was held to determine where everybody has collected natural products in the last three years.	Each group indicated the pasture and forest areas where they collected. This land was marked on the map. Groups were harvesting 10% of the pasture area and 20% of the forest area. This provided information on where to focus biological monitoring activities.	If outsiders have been collecting products, then mark these areas as well. Try to quantify the information and mark on the actual maps. If the product has not been collected before, skip to activity four.
Information was gathered on the amount of product harvested in the past three years. This was done through collector interviews, collecting data from the Department of Forests about forest royalty collections, and obtaining information on kilos of natural product cargo handled at the local airport.	Data collected for jatamansi indicated that 150 tons were harvested in 1995; 50 tons in 1996; and 180 tons in 1997. The early snows of 1996 forced collectors to stop jatamansi harvesting.	While each source of information is biased on its own, the combination of three sources of information gives an indication of the magnitude of natural products harvested. Do not worry about obtaining an exact number. Instead focus on understanding the trend in harvesting and magnitude of harvest level.

Activity	Results	Adjust for the Specific Area
At this point the group knows **where** the natural products are being harvested and the **amount** of harvesting over the past three years. Next they need to know the **general condition of the harvesting areas** and threats to the ecosystem. Group discussions obtained this information.	The group indicated that harvesting areas were in decline and the major threats to the ecosystems were: uncontrolled natural product harvesting burning of pastures overgrazing by migratory livestock	Finding more than three threats is fine. Threats can be from inside or outside the community. The judgement on the condition of the resource base is perception-based and will provide guidance for field-based biophysical data collection.
Preliminary information assessed.	The group's perception was that the resource base is declining, but overharvesting of natural products is only one threat. Harvesting levels appear to be increasing annually, but the group is only harvesting from a small percentage of the resource base. To ensure optimal regeneration, the group will explore rotational harvesting from a larger base and investigate harvesting methods. Interventions will be implemented to address other threats.	Note all threats, match them against the group's activities and compare to current field conditions. Use this information to determine supply conditions for the target product, and to develop sustainable resource use plans. Notice how gathering information on one product area provided preliminary information to preserve the health of the overall resource area.

Table 7.20
Grading of 37 participating CFUGs with regard to certain aspects of monitoring

Quality Rating	Threats Review	Monitoring Policy	Monitoring Practices	Adaptive Management Practices
	%	%	%	%
Very Low	51			3
Low	49	23	44	72
Good		56	56	26
Very Good		21		
Total	100	100	100	100

7.4.1.1 Condition of forests and meadows

Most of the participating CFUGs and local stakeholders perceived that with the introduction of the harvest regulation and distribution system, the condition of the community forests improved. The management plan specified the appropriate harvesting time, quantity, methods, and forest blocks for harvesting of different forest products. With the introduction of exercise on management and training activities, awareness of the individual households increased and improved harvesting practices.

Improved forest management activities in many CFUGs have improved the overall condition of community forest as indicated by apparent increase in tree basal area and crown cover. An evaluation carried out in 2003 in three of the five districts of the project area s

Photo 11. Biodiversity monitoring and mountain landscape in Humla

howing that the community forests were in better condition than even many areas of adjoining parks and protected areas (Burch *et al.* 2003). Several of the CFUGs were close to completing forest stewardship (FSC) certification for their forest areas in 2004. The communities were already harvesting products prior to the start of the PAR interventions, but with declining returns and detrimental impact on the overall biodiversity. In many areas this trend has been arrested or reversed. The rotational harvesting systems, effective protection of the forest, plantation, thinning, pruning, nursery management and similar silvicultural operations have helped to revive the forest condition.

7.4.1.2 Relationship between enterprise development, economic growth, social equity and conservation

As the correlations given in Table 7.21 show the CFUGs with higher economic performance were also able to perform better in conservation.

Table 7.21
Correlation matrix among composite indexes of economic, social and conservation performance across the 37 participating CFUGs

	Economic Index	Social Index	Conservation Index
Economic Index	1	.287	.487(**)
Social Index	.287	1	.497(**)
Conservation Index	.487(**)	.497(**)	1

** Correlation is significant at the 0.01 level (2-tailed).

As Table 7.22 shows, both the subsistence benefits index (availability of timber, fuel wood, and fodder) and average HH income are positively correlated with the conservation index. This indicates that the increment in household income and subsistence benefits served as incentives to CFUGs members to manage and conserve the forest resources.

With the increased economic benefits and awareness of the contribution of forests to community members, livelihoods and ways of managing forest resources improved. Communities opted for bringing larger forest areas under management and improved their management plans and practices. The community owned enterprises as well as the forest dependent communities committed to conservation of the resources once they learned that they could sustain the benefits only when they have appropriate management system and sustainable harvesting practices in place. For example, the establishment and operation of HOPL increased the benefits to collectors and also helped in cultivating more conservation friendly behavior (while collecting products) and a sense of ownership over the resources. With the increase in sense of ownership over resources and an awareness of the scope of benefits from the enterprise, the CFUGs demonstrated an ability and commitment to mitigating threats to natural resources.

Table 7.22
Correlation matrix of variables related to economic, social, and conservation performances of the 37 participating CFUGs in 2003

	Subsistence benefit index	Average HH income (Rs.)	Conservation index	Social index	CF area per HH (ha.)	% of economic participants	Index for access of poor and dalits to subsistence products
Subsistence benefit index	1	.605(**)	.632(**)	.526(**)	.387(*)	.427(**)	.552(**)
Average HH income (Rs.)		1	.601(**)	.323	.266	.394(*)	.632(**)
Conservation index			1	.497(**)	.496(**)	.295	.378(*)
Social index				1	.435(**)	.835(**)	.318
CF area per HH (ha.)					1	.409(*)	-.081
% of economic participants						1	.283
Index for access of poor and dalits to subsistence products							1

* Correlation is significant at the 0.05 level (2-tailed); ** Correlation is significant at the 0.01 level (2-tailed).

In brief, the study shows that the improvement in economic performance of the CFUGs contributes to increasing the forest areas that communities manage, management practices, monitoring, and threat mitigation. Observations on other case studies where all key factors were not considered show that the high income alone may not lead to conservation.

Though the correlation between economic index and social index is not significant (Table 7.21), the individual parameters of the economic index (subsistence benefits, annual household income) are significantly, positively correlated with the key social performance indicators, such as percentage of economic participants and index for access of poor and dalits to subsistence benefits (Table 7.22). This may imply that the enterprise-oriented CFUGs made some progress in linking social equity and economic conditions.

There was a significant positive correlation ($r = 0.49$, $p<0.01$) between social index and conservation index, indicating that the CFUGs with higher social performance also performed better in conservation. With the higher level of participation which was augmented with the improved decision making and institutional practices, the CFUGs were able to prepare more practical and effective forest management plans and became successful to implement and monitor the forest management activities and enforced the harvesting rules and regulations.

Chapter 8

Discussion and Conclusions

This work primarily embodies a participatory action research on enterprise-oriented community forest management (EOCFM) in Nepal with focus on field experiments carried out with 37 community forest user groups (CFUGs) of high mountain areas (generally between 2000-3000m altitudes). These mountain areas are remote, mostly inaccessible, rich in biodiversity (part of one of the global hotspots), and have sparse populations suffering from acute poverty, isolation and lack of economic opportunities. The main questions which were addressed in this study were 1) whether EOCFM works? 2) if it works, then under what conditions?

To address the first question, we examined whether EOCFM can improve people's economic conditions as well as conservation of biodiversity, which provides raw materials to enterprises. To address the second question, we looked at the performance of enterprise-oriented CFUGs in relation to concerned external factors, viz., policy, market, financial incentives and technical assistance. However, it was not possible to examine the effect of any one external factor in isolation from other factors, as the CFUGs work under the influence of several factors working simultaneously.

As shown in Figure 8.1, enterprise-oriented community forestry management system is under the influence of several external factors as described above. Within this system there is a continuous interplay among the three sub-systems, referred to as local communities, biodiversity and enterprises. It is assumed that interplays among community, biodiversity and enterprise can be managed in such a way that they contribute to biodiversity conservation, uninterrupted supply of ecosystem services, and social harmony, if the EOCFM approach works well. The assumption is also that improvement both in economic conditions and ecosystem health would have positive social impact not only on local people living in upstream areas, but also those of downstream areas receiving ecosystem services. Any social discontent in upstream areas because of poverty and discrimination is likely to affect all the connected populations. In a way, this approach is an exercise in exploring positive linkages between generation of money and conservation. This approach was first experimented in a big way by Biodiversity Conservation Network (BCN, a Washington based international program) in a number of countries (Salafsky *et al.* 1999), of which not many tested this approach over sufficiently long period. The present study was carried out to test the above hypothesis over a relatively extended period involving sufficiently large samples. Though the present work encompasses analysis of number of studies carried out by various agencies in different parts of the country, it focuses on detailed investigation on 37 CFUGs of 6 remote high mountain districts.

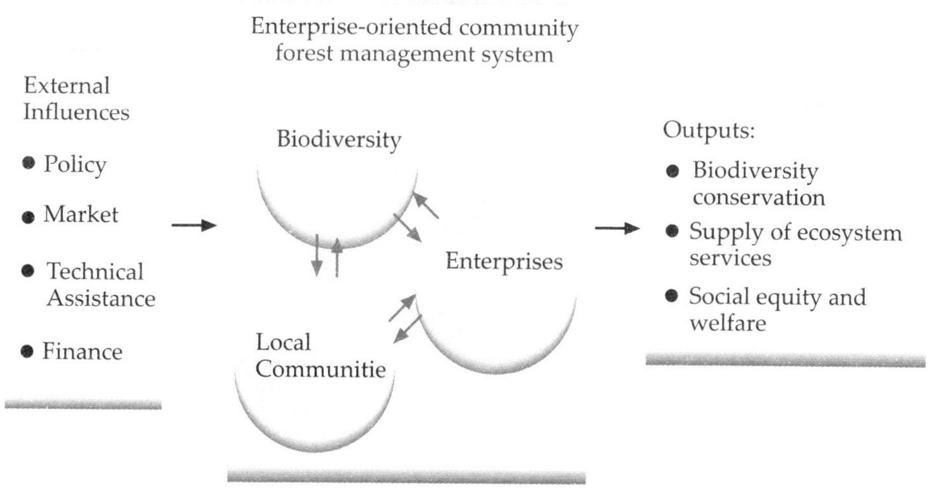

Figure 8.1 A schematic representation of the external factors that have influences on enterprise-oriented community forest management system and likely outputs of a well managed interactions between the sub-systems (shown by circles)

The approach of this study is different from the traditional approach of conservation, which is primarily based on creation of protected area model, regulatory measures with restrictions and bans, limited property rights to communities, and focus on subsistence use of biodiversity. Our hypothesis is that by developing synergy among local communities, biodiversity and enterprises, it is possible to generate enough economic incentives to local communities for biodiversity conservation.

8.1 What is at stake?

Having one of the biodiversity hotspots, Nepal is one of the important biodiversity centers of the world. Nepal's 6 phyto-geographical provinces, 11 bioclimatic zones and 198 forest and vegetation types house not only remarkably diverse biota (plants and animals), but also some unique and economically valuable plants and animals. Nepal represents only 0.1% of the earth's land area, but 2.6% of all the flowering plants (7000 species), of which 5% are only found in Nepal. It also hosts 9.3% of all birds and 4.5% of all mammals. A large number of diverse forest and grassland communities cover more than 50% of the total area of Nepal (147, 141 km^2), many of them are good sources of NTFPs with high demands. NTFPs harvested from more than 160 plant species are traded in and from Nepal, and about 1000 species have known economic uses.

Although the precise economic valuation of Nepal's usable biodiversity is difficult to make, there is a strong indication that considerable economic benefits can be generated from it. Even the anecdotal, partial accounts of estimations on economic value indicate how important biological resources are in Nepal's rural economy. Ministry of Forest and Soil Conservation estimates a lost opportunity of forestry sector at NRs. 42 billion per year. Our rough estimation of export value of major NTFPs alone is more than NRs 2.5 billion annually.

Our findings show that most of rural farming people depend on forest products (both timber and non-timber) for their livelihoods whether it is for their own use (at home and farm) or for earning cash income. For many of the communities of high mountains, NTFPs are the only source of cash income, and in some cases these are more important source of income than timber. However, ecological zones rich in biodiversity have also some of the world's poorest people.

These poor people depend on natural resources around them for both production and extractive purposes, and the issues of environmental sustainability are of immediate relevance to poor people as they directly depend on the viability of the resource base for their day-to-day living.

The upstream forest ecosystems provide significant services not only to local communities, but also people living in downstream areas. Hydrological functions of these ecosystems to lower hill areas and the terai are of direct relevance to the country. It is because of the downstream flows of ecosystem services from the forests of Nepal and Uttranchal (India) that the adjacent Gangetic plain is able to support over five hundred million people, and has been sustaining one of the greatest agriculture systems of the world for last several thousand years (Singh 2000).

8.2 Threats to Biodiversity

Using PRA methods we analyzed people's perception about threats to biodiversity in three areas, viz., around meadows, forestlands around villages, and forestlands away from villages. The analysis showed that communities considered man-made fire, unmanaged harvest of NTFPs and other forest products (timber, fodder and firewood), and overgrazing as major threats to the biodiversity in all the three study areas. Apart from these common threats, conversion of forestland into crop land was a major threat in areas near village settlements and slash-and-burn-farming in far off areas. Communities felt that though poaching was a threat to wild animals, it was manageable. More often than not a site at a given time is affected by more than one factor. For example, a jatamansi stand is often degraded by over-harvesting, as well as burning and overgrazing. The regeneration of *Quercus semecarpifolia* is disturbed by cumulative effect of overgrazing and biomass extraction. Once a site is degraded, many exotic invasive species come to occupy that. For example, *Eupatorium's* expansion has already become a common threat to biodiversity. Lack of basic technology may also degrade forests because of the inefficient harvest practices. In remote areas, like Dolpa and Humla, as an example, young trees are cut and used as logs because there is no availability of sawing.

However, the root cause of forest degradation is acute poverty, which in combination with several other factors, such as uncertainty about tenure, external market demand for forest resources, lack of knowledge, skills and capacity to address livelihood issue, and lack of awareness and education constrain the efforts that are required for the conservation of biodiversity. To summarize, the issue of livelihood is required to be addressed to make people to value biodiversity conservation. One of the ways to address this issue is to use biodiversity efficiently and sustainbly for improving livelihood. In this anthropogenically dominated world, people's issues get priority, particularly when societies elsewhere are hugely consumptive.

8.3 Community-Based Approach and its Evolution

Our analysis of historical changes in the biodiversity conservation of Nepal and the key stakeholders' dependency on forest suggest that community-based conservation approach is a viable option to slow the rate of biodiversity loss. Even if the Protected Area System (PAS) is effective and efficient for the conservation, it is not practical to bring all the important areas of biodiversity hotspots under PAS. A vast area of globally significant biodiversity is outside the PAS and conservation problems are prominent even inside the national parks because of the high dependence of local communities and ineffective enforcement capacity of the concerned agencies.

We analyzed community forestry from a broader perspective to find out how to sustain community's interest in management and conservation, economic incentives required for enterprise-oriented management, and need of rights and technical support for improving institutional capabilities. There are many challenges and weaknesses in community forest management, some arise with its formation and some are inherent to social structure. Experience of two decades of formal community forestry indicates that there is a need to expand local community's rights over forest resources. Mountain communities in Nepal are heavily dependent on forests for livelihoods, therefore they face problems arising from forest degradation.

According to an FAO assessment, over 80% of the closed forest area in the Third World is under public control (Lanly 1982). In Nepal, government owns almost all forest land and community forestry that was formally initiated in 1978 represents a kind of common property resource governance system. A community forest is not a common property with open access; it allows the community forest user group to exclude all others from the forest handed over to it by the government. The factors that have led to the CFUG formation are as following:

A. Exogenous factors

- Since late 1970s increasing attention has been given to the multiple relations between forestry and rural development. International organizations like FAO and World Bank played major role in drawing attention to previously neglected aspects of community participation in forest management. Subsequently, the eighth world forest congress held in Jakarta in 1978 contributed significantly to this idea of "forest for people" as its main theme.
- Also, during 1970s international attention was drawn to the floods in Bangladesh and their so called link with deforestation in Nepal.
- It was in this climate of "eco-doom", that the community forestry was introduced and international donors began funding the concerned program.
- The realization that the local farming communities had definite interest and experiences in forest management began to get world-wide support. There was a growing recognition that communities can be as good if not better manager of forest as government or private companies.
- An increased knowledge base on the common property resource management positively influenced the community forestry in Nepal.
- Changes in national political system toward more democratic governance created a conducive environment for a greater participation of communities in development processes.

B. Endogenous factors

- Livelihood needs of rural communities and role of forest in sustainable livelihood were increasingly recognized (Hobley 1996).

- Since many of these forests are inaccessible for commercial exploitation, the risk of losing power and revenue for government was minimal.
- Department of Forests was unable to manage forests in mountains, where presently 3.5 million ha of potential community forests occur (about 30,000 patches).

Subsequently, steps were taken to create community forest user groups with clearly defined concept and functioning. A CFUG represents a group of people, who use a particular forest land. In this there is a freedom to include all villagers or part of them or also some individuals from other villages. According to King et al. (1990) "the term user group is actually descriptive of a category of people, rather than a group". The Forest Act, 1993 strengthened CFUGs by giving legal backing and autonomy to theme to mobilize funds and resources. Thus, a CFUG became legally recognized, autonomous corporate entity with on-going succession. Its governance is defined by its constitution, which is registered in DFO and community forest management operational plan. CFUGs have also freedom to develop their constitution consistent with their needs and constraints. It represents a major innovation in participatory management of natural resources and empowerment of the poor people. This institution has made the poor communities living in remote mountains vibrant with hope and activities. The number of CFUGs and households involved and area under their management have increased dramatically during last 12 to 13 years (Figure 8.2).

Since 1978 about 1.1 million hectares or 25% of the total of forest area of Nepal has been handed over to about 13,000 CFUGs that represent nearly one-third of the total population of Nepal. Such an approach was being promoted in the entire developing world, where also nearly one-fourth of total forest area was brought under community forestry (Scher *et al.* 2003), and likely to double by 2015 (Bull and White 2002). Many positive forces have been created with the progress on power devolution in forestry through community forestry (CF) policy, procedures and practices.

Figure 8.2 Increase in number of CFUGs and households and forest area under community management during past 13 years (1991-2003) in Nepal

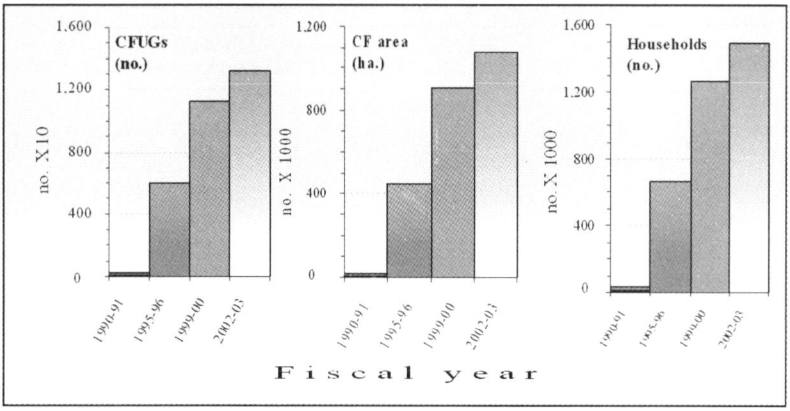

The organization of CFUGs proved handy for incorporating enterprise oriented initiatives. Gradually, more and more CFUGs began to opt for NTFPs-based enterprises in Nepal, in which NGOs like ANSAB and government played a facilitative role. Currently, more than 100 CFUGs are involved in EOCFM activities. However, it does not mean that the hurdles in the path of EOCFM have been removed and CFUGs progress is smooth. CFUGs are still confronted with several problems relating to uncertainties in policies and legislations and distortions in their implementation. The overly bureaucratic functioning of the government and negative interpretation of regulations continue to hamper the progress of EOCFM. Then, the technical assistance required to enable EOCFM to make progress is still rudimentary.

8.4 Potentials of NTFPs in Nepal: harvest, uses and marketing

Nepal has nearly 1000 plants species of known uses (i.e. 14% of total vascular plants): 700 medicinal species, 440 wild food yielding species, 30 spice yielding species), 71 fiber yielding species, and over 100 fodder species. Of these more than 160 are collected for NTFPs of commerce. Many of these, however, are also used locally.

The high mountain areas supporting forests as well as meadows particularly in western part of Nepal are most important for NTFPs from the standpoints of commercial values and local livelihood. Some of the valuable species of these areas are: *Swertia chirayita* (chraito), *lichens, Taxus* (lauthsalla), *Neopicrortiza scrophulariflorra* (kutki), *Nardostachys grandiflora* (jatamansi), *Aconitum heterophyllum* (Atis), *Valeriana jatamansi* (Sugandhawal), *Daphne bholua* (Lokta), Edgeworthia *gardnerii* (Argeli), *Arundinaria falcata* (Nigalo), *Morchela spp.* (morels), and *Cordyceps sinensis* (yarshagumba). Interestingly, these areas have some of the poorest people. There is a need to understand the relationship between rich biodiversity and the poverty of people and to take necessary steps to develop positive linkages between biodiversity and economic welfare.

The taxonomy of NTFPs uses is quite rich in Nepal: medicinal and aromatic products, spices and flavor, wild-mushrooms, fruits, dyes and tans, fibers used in handicrafts, tea, brooms, leaf plates, rosin, turpentine, gums, edible fats and oils, shampoos and creams, bamboo and rattan products.

Natural populations of NTFP species vary widely in size and capacity to tolerate disturbance. Some of the species used as NTFPs have inherently small populations in nature, (e.g. *Podophyllum hexandrum*), there are some which used to have large populations in the past, but have depleted because of selective harvest and habitat deterioration (*Neopicrorhiza scrophulariiflora*), and there are still others that have been able to withstand disturbance (harvest) more successfully (*Nardostachys jatamansi*). Unfortunately, population ecology and life history characters of these species are poorly known. ANSAB (1999) has developed improved sets of practices for jatamansi, kutki and others based on field experiences, but this calls for undertaking valid and replicable experiments to develop reliable harvest methods. However, such improved harvest methods as developed by ANSAB are useful as they emphasize on uncomplicated and feasible harvest practices which people can use (Table 8.1).

Although information on species uses is helpful, this is only the first step in understanding the role of forests and meadows in the life of poor people of the world, the significance of harvest in economic (and ecological) terms has largely remained hidden (Campbell and Luckert 2002). Finding these values is important for policy reasons. Since they are not valued economically policy makers think they have no value. However, many studies have shown that NTFPs and other environmental goods play a significant role in household welfare of forest dependent societies (Jodha 1986 e.g., Bojo 1993, Wollenberg and Nawin 1998).

Table 8.1
Certain features of harvest practices (derived from ANSAB 1999) for jatamansi, kutki (both are rhizomatous species and in both rhizomes are harvested), sunpati (leaves harvested) and juniper (leaves and berries harvested)

Recommended proportion of harvest

- Leave about 20% of the plant population while harvesting in case of jatamansi and kutki
- Leave 30% of foliage and handpick while harvesting in case of sunpati
- Handpick berries and leaves from small branches in case of juniper

Use of tools

- Restricted and careful use of cutting tools recommended

Rotational cycle

- 5 years in case of jatamansi rhizome
- 3-5 years for kutki rhizome
- Annually for sunpati

Season of collection

- Fall, i.e. when growth cycle is completed for jatamansi and kutki rhizomes

There is a need for interdisciplinary research to understand various issues related to sustainable use of NTFPs, their economic values and marketing. There are several problems, both conceptual and methodological to undertake a truly integrated interdisciplinary research. It calls for understanding the biology of species, their harvest practices, social attributes of communities that depend on them, economic valuation and technological improvements. Developing knowledge in all these areas to make a sound plan for EOCFM is very challenging and difficult to achieve even at a small scale. There are also serious problems related to the specialized language of different disciplines. For example, words such as system, regime and niche are used across disciplines with different meaning (Sithole, *et al.* 2002). Our approach was to apply relatively simple methods that can work well with local communities with limited education and technological understanding.

Use of technology in processing the raw material is still low, that is why value addition attained, in most cases in Nepal still remains only a small fraction of the potential one. The common practices include: sun and fire drying (e.g., medicinal and aromatic plants), steam distillation (e.g. essential oil from jatamansi), solvent extraction (e.g. oil from castor, cinnamon, jatropha), extraction of active compounds (e.g. Taxus), sapogenin extraction (e.g. soap bearing plants), oil expelling (e.g. jatropha, dhatelo), detoxification (e.g. chiuri), packaging bulk (all raw NTFPs), plate-making (e.g. sal leaves).

Though NTFPs from Nepal are sold to 30 countries of Asia, Europe and north America, the bulk of NTFPs end up in Indian markets. There is a long trade chain starting from local collectors, village traders to retailers in India (Figure 8.3).

Though traders play a crucial role in the distribution of products which is an important component of marketing, their shares of profit are disproportionately higher than that of poor collectors, who often get payment only for their labor. Some reforms have begun to occur with the organization of CFUGs and their networks, but scope for improvement is still huge. Of the total value of NTFPs exported from Nepal, the raw form accounts for 85% and among the processed form hand made paper (about 11%) and essential oils (about 2%) are important ones.

There is a great scope for increasing export of NTFPs in a processed form, as growth of natural products market is increasing in a range of 3-20 % (Grundwald 1994), which is 3 to 4 fold higher than average national economic growth of countries. There are several constraints which need to be addressed in order to improve marketing: i) imperfect wholesale market with wide fluctuations, ii) exploitation at different levels along the market chain, iii) poorly developed marketing information system particularly with regard to prices, iv) low marketing knowledge and skills of collectors, v) poor infrastructure of storage, transportation, testing laboratories, etc, vi) lack of certification in regard to organically produced products, and vii) mismatch between demand and supply.

As per entrepreneurs' perceptions, regulatory hassles in transport, sale and export, impractical government bans and restrictions, illogical royalty rates and multiple taxation, and lack of certainty of policies and regulations on NTFPs are principal hurdles. The number of entrepreneurs affected by lack of certainty of policies and regulations on NTFPs has increased rapidly from 1995 to 2002. Interestingly, lack of sustainable supply of products which was a minor issue in 1995 became a major issue in 2002.

Figure 8.3 A simplified schematic representation of market chains of NTFPs from Nepal

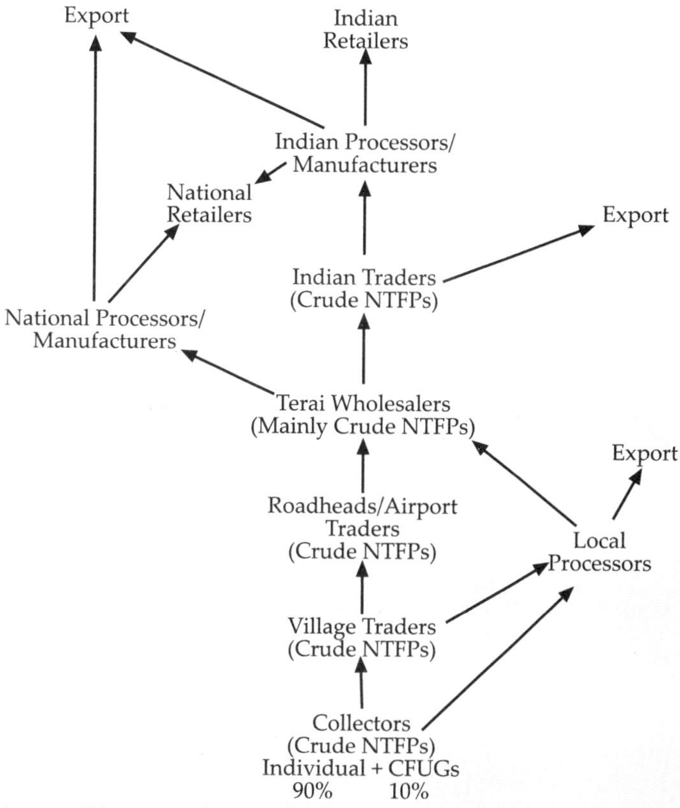

In inaccessible remote districts like Dolpa and Humla, there are no roads. Therefore, NTFPs are transported by airplanes.

8.1 Does Enterprise-Oriented Community Forest Management Contribute to Local Livelihood as well as Social Equity and Conservation?

The results of this study based on 37 CFUGs of high altitudinal areas of Nepal indicate that EOCFM can contribute to all the three components, economic, social and conservation (Table 8.2). Normally, one would expect that since an NTFPs-based enterprise causes additional pressure on forests and meadows, which are already subject to biomass extraction for meeting daily needs of firewood and fodder, it should degrade them. Obviously, there are several factors which come to play positive roles as indicated in Table 8.2 and Figure 8.1. It seems that when people suffering from acute poverty come to get cash from forests and meadows, they take steps to conserve them. This relationship between biomass extraction and ecosystem degradation is not straight forward, it can be greatly modified by appropriate silvicultural practices and other conservation measures taken. Forests can be degraded even if the harvest rates are well within the carrying capacity of their productivities, if steps for species regeneration are not taken. In the study areas, forest degradation in the past was not only because of over-harvesting, but also because of poor silvicultural practices and disregard for regeneration. With some improvement in livelihood conditions through forest enterprise activities, people seem to begin to understand the importance of conservation measures, such as control of fire, leaving enough plant population for regeneration while harvesting, avoiding whole tree cutting and collecting branches from pruning for firewood, and protecting mother seed trees to assist natural regeneration. This may particularly apply to communities suffering from acute poverty and lack of economic options (Table 8.3). However, people need support from an NGO, government and other agencies so that necessary atmosphere of certainty and assurance with regard to resource use is created (Table 8.3).

Table 8.2
Summary of impact of enterprise-oriented community forest management in 6 remote districts of Nepal (based on 37 CFUGs)

A.	**Conservation**
●	Increased use of thinned and pruned branches as firewood so that whole tree cutting is reduced – at an initial stage

- Initiation of nurseries and enrichment plantations – in a few CFUGs
- Reduced cutting of tree branches while collecting lichens (jhyau) – in CFUGs of Darchula
- Reduction in indiscriminate burning in meadows so that jatamansi populations are not damaged – in most of CFUGs of Humla and Jumla
- Increased practice of leaving a part of plant population for secured regeneration – introduced
- Increased practice of harvesting in appropriate season – getting common
- Increase in practice of rotational/block-wise harvesting – getting common
- Institutionalization of CFUG funds raised from the contributions of their members out of income from forest enterprise activities - common
- Increased protection of community forest by employing watchers - common
- More stall feeding – about 30% CFUGs already practicing
- Increased rotational grazing – most CFUGs are following to a certain extent
- Protection of mother seed-trees for ensuring regeneration – in a few CFUGs
- Concept of monitoring introduced – still in early stage
- A dramatic increase in areas of forest and meadows under community management – from 90 ha/CFUG to 1,614 ha/CFUG, which amounts to 0.73/HH to 11.7 ha/HH (because of cash income CFUGs were willing to take responsibility of managing larger forest areas)
- Increased number of species under use and management, hence improved perception of biodiversity value – on average across all altitudinal belts the species number increased from 3.2 to 13.4
- Reduction in indiscriminate harvesting to ensure uninterrupted supply of resources for enterprises – beginning made

- Increased awareness of threats to biodiversity – change is visible

B. Economic

- Increased selling price of NTFPs at collectors' level – e.g. in the case of jatamansi it increased three times without corresponding increases at other levels along the trade-chain
- Increased by an average of Rs. 4000 in household income from forest enterprise activities largely because of improved organization of collectors' and marketing and technological inputs from the NGO
- Increased supply of forest products for subsistence – perceptible change
- Generation and use of group funds for economic activities – some funds in all CFUGs
- Direct employment in the enterprises – a few jobs in all CFUGs

C. Social equity

- Mobilization of group funds and group efforts in addressing poverty and social welfare al local level – in some CFUGs
- Increased participation of women, dalits and other disadvantaged people – getting common
- Increased access of women, dalits and poor to forest resources - common
- Allowing dalits and other poors to grow NTFPs in community forest areas – in a few CFUGs of Dolakha
- Distribution of forest products based on real needs of households - common
- More employment to poor and needy in forest activities – in a few CFUGs
- Providing finance and access of CF resources to the poor for enterprise activities – e.g. in 6 CFUGs in Darchula
- Reduced dependence on outside traders for loan – to some extent
- Increased bargaining power of collectors with traders - common

EOCFM represents a kind of cooperative with an element of an entrepreneurship. Individuals are so poor that they cannot run their own enterprises; therefore they need support of their communities as well as external support of NGOs and government. Advantages of collective efforts may include low transaction costs, generation of a sufficient volume of goods, and a greater bargaining power. When such poor people come to have access to some cash earning opportunity from forest and assurance of access to forest resources, they conserve forests and meadow ecosystem so that their enterprises have uninterrupted supply of raw materials. However, when enterprise is not integrated with the conservation of ecosystem which provide raw material and stake of communities and individuals is low, the system is likely to fail. For example, the paper makers of Naglibang have now no resource and they are fully dependent on other villages for supply of raw materials. A few years ago when handmade paper was in high demand, the resource base was drastically depleted, as the paper was produced by individual with no legal ownership of the resource, they had little concern for resource management. Now the collectors and paper makers are facing two main problems. First, they had to travel several days to get to the forest sites where lokta grows; and second, communities around those sites restricted the access of these outsiders. This indicates that enterprises having no linkage with conservation and have no ownership tend to over-exploit resource (Subedi *et al.* 2000).

In most of the CFUGs and enterprises, sharing of the profits with dalits and other poor people is already in place. It seems that the activities, such as collection of NTFPs are so labor intensive that only limited amounts can be collected by individuals, therefore joining the economic activities by more individuals does not reduce one's profit. In other words, the opportunity cost is low. Moreover, in many situations a larger group of participants is required to run an enterprise, therefore sharing with poor, dalits and other deprived people becomes necessary for improving individual's income. It is quite possible that because of the current socio-political conflicts and tensions, people have become more sensitive to equity issues and need to address the problem of acute poverty. This was evident from the gestures like allowing poor to cultivate NTFP species on community forest lands and financing them for micro-enterprises.

The biggest change that is associated with EOCFM is dramatic increase in the areas of forest and meadows handed over by government to communities. Availability of sufficiently large size and certainty of property rights are pre-requisite for conservation by communities. Earlier, when community forest areas were small, people used to exploit surrounding government forests indiscriminately. However, with the access to sufficiently large forest areas and assured rights, people were able to plan and implement conservation practices on a long-term basis. Availability of adequate resources might have also contributed to sharing with the poor members of CFUGs.

8.6 Relationship Between Livelihood, Equity and Conservation

In this section, we discuss how social factors and conservation interact within and across CFUGs. As described in Chapter 2 and 7, a composite index based on several parameters was developed for each of the components and relationship among them was examined. Furthermore, we also examined relationship between various parameters used to develop composite indexes. Each of the correlations among the three composite indexes (economic, social and conservation) was positive and significant except between economic and social indexes. These correlations show that economic incentives or some amelioration in economic hardship is necessary to make community interested in conservation. Hypothesis of this kind has been made in several studies, but not many studies have been able to show it on the basis of sufficiently large samples and over a long time period as done in this study. However, we are aware of limitations of our observation, particularly because economic incentives to the people from enterprises were generally small and within a limited range. This may also explain the lack of significant correlation between economic incentives and social well being. In time, when some CFUGs are able to attain clearly more success than others and the range of income widens sufficiently, it can be expected to establish conclusive relationships between these parameters. Furthermore, most of the parameters used to measure CFUGs performances with regard to conservation were based on introduction or initiation of conservation measures. The social transformation in this regard is still remote. As given below conclusive results can be achieved only after taking observations over sufficiently long periods.

- The observations of this study were based on limited periods (4-8 years) during which it was not possible to achieve enough economic growth, local communities' day-to-day struggle for survival still limited their capacity to put more efforts for conservation. Bringing changes in provisions and practices of policy and market that favor local communities and small producers is difficult to make in a short period of time.
- Conservation requires making people educated and aware of various aspects which is difficult to achieve in 4-8 years time with the limited man power and funding.
- For several factors which are critical for conservation of the species being used for NTFPs, ecological knowledge is still scarce and needs to be developed. For example, detail knowledge about the ecology and life-history characters and their response to harvest in the ecosystem is hardly known.

These are some of the areas which need to be addressed to achieve the goal of the conservation. Nevertheless, this research has shown clearly that the increase in value of NTFPs through enterprises makes people more conservation-oriented. The species yielding NTFPs at a commercial scale were more conserved by people than other species. It is also clear that one component without the synergy with the others cannot produce positive incentives for the conservation and improved livelihoods.

Table 8.3

Main features of the background of 37 CFUGs studied and measures included to make EOCFM work

A. Background features

- Acute poverty
- Low human development index
- Inaccessibility and isolation
- Lack of economic options
- Sufficiently large resource base

- Limited farm land and low agricultural productivity
- High dependence on forest and meadow resources
- Orthodox social structure

B. Accessory measures included to enable CFUGs to establish enterprises

- Sensitization and awareness – legal, economic, social and conservation
- Organizing communities to form CFUGs and providing technical assistance for planning and management of community forest
- Allowing CFUGs to have significantly larger areas of forests and meadows
- Certainty with regard to land tenure and resource use
- Providing technical assistance for enterprise development and management
- Capacity building in processing and marketing of NTFPs
- Promoting participation of women, dalits and other disadvantaged groups in EOCFM
- Capacity building in improved conservation practices and resource monitoring
- Providing access to markets, information, finance and technology
- Promoting ownership of communities in enterprise and forest management activities from the beginning
- Networking and policy support
- Continued support of responsible NGO – not only in improving provisions, but also proper implementation

Correlation matrix of various parameters used indicated significant positive relationships in many pairs. One of the encouraging observations was that access of poor and dalits to subsistence products increased with increase in subsistence benefits and average household incomes. Evidently, EOCFM is not going to adversely affect the weaker section of the society. Conservation index was found positively correlated with subsistence benefits, household income, community forest area, as well as access of poor to subsistence products. The significant positive correlation between the percentage of economic participants and conservation suggests that it is important to create economic opportunity for as many as possible to improve the management of forest and meadows (Table 7.22).

8.7 Conclusions

This study on community based NTFP enterprises and conservation provides an analysis at two levels. The first deals with the potential of NTFP enterprises and community forestry in Nepal. In the second, an in-depth analysis of enterprise-oriented community forest management was made by sampling 37 CFUGs of high mountain areas where other economic options were negligible. The country-level analysis shows that Nepal has extraordinarily wide range of NTFPs uses and the dependence of local communities on them would continue for long time. The in-depth analysis of 37 CFUGs indicated that through enterprise oriented community forest management, it is possible to develop synergy between improvement of livelihood and conservation. EOCF gave economic power to local people to choose an action that they think will be more rewarding in the long-run. People conserve more the species from which they generate cash income than the species which they use for their subsistence. The hope of earning cash is the major driving force in a society suffering from lack of it. Though this kind of behavior of community is encouraging from enterprise point of view, it may lead to reduction in biodiversity pool. It is situations like these where better understanding and education may help in addressing the problem. For example, communities need to be educated about the linkages between the species and ecosystem conservation. Though the limitations of this study are many, the fact that it was carried out in collaboration with 37 communities involving more than 5,000 households give convincing evidence in support of the above conclusion.

It may be pointed out that the relationship between enterprise development and conservation of resources which the enterprises use is not straight forward, it requires several prerequisites and efforts and constant monitoring over sufficiently long period. For example, lack of knowledge about the ecology of the NTFP species and responses of their populations to harvesting, realistic assessment of market and social dynamics, and 'total' values of the environmental goods is still a major constraint in this area and may continue to hamper the progress of enterprise oriented community forest management. The importance of this gap needs to be recognized and necessary steps to address it should be taken before it is too late. This also emphasizes that the enterprise oriented community forest management, though promising, requires a much higher level of efforts than the presently being taken. It is important to provide useful and appropriate external assistance that fosters the link between enterprise development and conservation. While undertaking such programs, necessary steps should be taken to allow people to play active role, and feel ownership. The government agencies are required to play primarily a role of service delivery to communities, instead of only imposing restrictions.

References

Adhikari, M. 1999. Global Affinity of Nepalese Mycoflora. Scientific World 1(1):105-112

Adhikari, MK. 2000. *Mushrooms of Nepal.* Adhikari Publication.

Akiyama, S, Yonekura, K and Ohba, H. 1998. New Records and Treatment of Nepalese Flowering Plants. *Newsletter of Himalayan Botany* 23:18-25.

ANSAB. 1999. *Socio-economic and Institutional Impacts of Community-Based Ecosystem Management Project in Humla, Nepal.* A socio-economic monitoring report to BCN. ANSAB/Enterprise Works Worldwide/SEEPORT, Kathmandu, Nepal.

Aryal, M. 1993. Diverted wealth, the trade in Himalayan herbs. *Himal Magazine,* Jan - Feb. 1993.

Bajracharya, DM, Joshi, RM, Rajbhandari, KR, Shakya, PR and Shrestha JB. 1988. Endemism in Nepalese Flora. In: *Proceedings of National Conference on Science and Technology.* Royal Nepal Academy of Science and Technology, Kathmandu, Nepal.

Baral, SR. 1995. *Enumeration of the Algae of Nepal. Biodiversity Profile Project,* Publication No. 11, Department of National Parks and Wildlife Conservation, Kathmandu, Nepal.

Bawdin, R. 2002. The Hawkesbury Experience: Tales from a road less traveled. A paper presented for the "Workshop on New Directions in Agroecology Research and Education"

Binayak Pimidanda CFUG. 1999. Operational plan of Binayak Pimidanda. forest user group, Kailash, Bajhang, Nepal.

Biodiversity Conservation Network (BCN). 1997. *Annual Report 1996.* World Wildlife Fund, Washington, DC (also available at .

Bojo, J. 1993. Economic valuation of indigeneous woodlands. In Bradley, PN and McNamara, K (eds) *Living with trees: Policies for forestry management in Zimbabwe,* World Bank Technical Paper No 210, World Bank, Washington, DC, PP227-41.

Box, EO. 1995. Factors determining distributions of tree species and plant functional types. *Vegetatio* 121: 101-116.

BPP. 1995. Biodiversity profile of the midhills physiographic zone. Biodiversity Profiles Project, Department of National Parks and Wildlife Conservation, Kathmandu, Nepal.

Branny, P. and Yadhav KP. 1998. Changes in community forest condition and management 1994-1998: Analysis of information from the forest resources assessment study and socioeconomic study in the Koshi Hills. Nepal UK Community Forestry Project. Project Report G/NUKCFP/32, Kathmandu Nepal.

Bull, G. and White, A. 2002. Global forest in transition: challenges and opportunities. In *Proceedings of Global Perspectives on Indigenous Forestry: Linking Communities, Commerce and Conservation*, 4-6 June 2002. Vancouver, Canada.

Campbell, BM and Luckert MK (eds). 2002. *Uncovering the hidden harvest: valuation methods for woodland and forest resources.* People and Plants Conservation Series, Earthscan Publications Ltd, London.

Castellanet, C. 2003. *Participatory Action Research in Natural Resource Management.* Taylor & Francis Group, ISBN: 1-56032-979-3.

Chhetri, RB and Pokhrel, BK. 2000. Income Generating Activities and Non-Timber Forest Product Management. Issue Paper 3. Paper prepared for the Joint Technical Review Committee on Community Forestry, Ministry of Forests and Soil Conservation.

Costa MH and Foley JA. 2000. Combined effects of deforestation and doubled atmospheric CO2 concentration on the climate of Amazonia. *Journal of Climate* 13:18-34.

CPFD. 2004. DOF Database. Community and Private Forestry Division, Department of Forests, Kathmandu, Nepal.

DFO, Humla. 2000. Forest Resources and Community Forestry Development in Humla.

DFO, Jumla. 1999. Introduction to Community Forestry Development. District Forest Office, Jumla.

Dobremez, JF. 1976. Le Nepal Ecologie et Biogeography – Editions du Centre National de la Recherche Scientifique, Paris France.

Edwards, DM. 1994. *Non-Timber Forest Products and Community Forestry.* Project Report G/NUKCFP/12. 36pp.

Edwards, DM. 1996. Non-Timber Forest Products and Community Forestry: Are they Compatible? *Banko Janakari* 6(1): 3-8.

Edwards, DM. 1996. *Non-timber Forest Products from Nepal: Aspect of the Trade in Medicinal and Aromatic Plants.* FORESC Monograph 1/96, Forest Research and Survey Center, Ministry of Forests and Soil Conservation, Kathmandu.

Foley JA, Costa, MH, Delire, C, Ramankutti, N and Snyder, P. 2003. Green surprise? How terrestrial ecosystems could affect earth's climate. *Frontiers in Ecology and the Environment* 1:38-44.

FRISP. 1999. Forest Resources of Nepal.(1987-1998). Department of Forest Research and Survey, Ministry of Forest and Soil Conservation, Nepal and Forest Resource Information System Project, the Government of Finland. Pp 33+.

FRISP. 1999. Forest Resources of the Hilly Area of Nepal (1994-1998). Department of Forest Research and Survey, Ministry of Forest and Soil Conservation, Nepal and Forest Resource Information System Project, the Government of Finland. Pp 33+.

Furuki, T and Higuchi, M. 1995. Hepatics from Nepal Collected by the Botanical Expedition of the National Science Museum, Tokyo in 1988; (2) Metzgeriales and Marchantiales. In Watanabe, M. and Hagiwara, H. (eds) *Cryptograms of the Himalayas*, vol. 3, Nepal and Pakistan, pp 143-149. Department of Botany, National Science Museum, Tsukuba, Japan.

Gautam, AP, Webb, EL, Shivakoti, GP, Zoebisch, MA.2003. Land use dynamics and landscape change pattern in a mountain watershed in Nepal. *Agriculture Ecosystem and Environment* 99: 83-96

Gilmour, DA & Fisher, RJ. 1991. *Villagers, forests and foresters: the philosophy, process and practice of community forestry in Nepal.* Kathmandu, Sahayogi Press.

Grimmet, R, Inskipp, C and Inskipp, T. 2000. Birds of Nepal. Helm Field Guide, Prakash Books, New Delhi.

Grunwald, J. 1994. The European Phytomedicines Market: Figures, Trends, Analyses. *HerbalGram*, 34: 60-65pp.

Hertog, WD. 1995. *Trees and people in balance: Forest utilization in Salyan District.* SNV-Nepal.

Hertog, WD. 1996. Non-Timber Forest Products in Dolpa. Karnali Local Development Project.

HMGN and IUCN. 1988. Building on Success: The National Conservation Strategy for Nepal. Kathmandu: The National Planning Commission and the World Conservation Union (IUCN) Nepal.

HMGN. 1982. Medicinal Plants of Nepal. 3rd edition. *Department of Medicinal Plants Bulletin* No. 3, Ministry of Forests, Kathmandu.

HMGN. 1982. Wild Edible Plants of Nepal. *Department of Medicinal Plants Bulletin* No. 9, Ministry of Forests, Kathmandu. 286 pp.

HMGN. 1984. Medicinal Plants of Nepal – Supplementary Volume. *Department of Medicinal Plants Bulletin* No. 10, Ministry of Forests, Kathmandu. 98 pp.

HMGN. 1988. *Master Plan for the Forestry Sector, Nepal: Main Report.* Kathmandu: MOFSC

HMGN. 1993. Forest Act. 1993. Nepal Law Book House, Babarmahal, Kathmandu, Nepal.

HMGN. 1995. Forest Regulations, 1995. Nepal Law Book House, Babarmahal, Kathmandu, Nepal.

HMGN. 2002. Statistical Pocket Book. Central Bureau of Statistics, Kathmandu, Nepal.

HMGN. 2002. Tenth Plan, 2002-2007. National Planning Commission.

HMGN. 2003. Poverty Reduction Strategy Paper, 2002-2007. National Planning Commission.

Hobley, M. 1996. Participatory Forestry: The Process of Change in India and Nepal. Rural Development Forestry Study Guide 3, Rural Development Forestry Network, London.

HOPL. 1994. Business Development Plan of Humla Oil Private Limited, Simikot, Humla, Nepal.

HOPL. 1995. Records of Humla Oil Private Limited, Simikot, Humla, Nepal.

HPPCL (Herbs Production and Processing Co. Ltd.). 1999. An unpublished Report.

Imanishi, K. 1953. Nature in Nepal Himalaya. *Kagaku* 23: 405-416.

Iqbal, M. 1995. *A study of trade restrictions affecting international trade in non-wood forest products*. FAO, Rome.

IUCN. 2000. National Register of Medicinal Plants. IUCN Nepal.

Ives, J and Bruno M. 1989. *The Himalayan Dilemma.* London: Rourledge.

Iwatsuki, K. 1988. An Enumeration of the Pteridophytes of Nepal. In Ohba, H and Malla, SB (eds) The Himalayan Plants, vol.1, pp 231-239. University Museum, University of Tokyo Bulletin 31, University of Tokyo, Japan.

Jackson, JK. 1994. Manual of Afforestation in Nepal. Forest Research and Survey Center, 2nd edition.

Jackson, WJ, Tamrakar, RM, Hunt, S and Shepherd, KR. 1998. Land use changes in two middle hills districts of Nepal. *Mountain Research and Development.* 18 (3): 193-212.

Jodha, NS. 1986. Common property resources and rural poor in dry regions of India. *Economic and Political Weekly* 21: 1169-81.

Joshi, AR and Joshi, DP. 1991. Endemic Plants of Nepal Himalaya: Conservation, Status, and Future Direction. *Mountain Environment and Development* 1(2):1-35.

Kanel, KR. 1999. *Analysis of policy and regulatory constraints in the development of non-timber forest products in Nepal* (with special reference to EFEA project area). A special study report submitted to World Wildlife Fund USA.

Kanel, KR. 1999. Strategic Review of Medicinal and Aromatic Plants and their Utilization in Nepal, Mimeograph, International Development Research Centre (IDRC), New Delhi

Kanel, KR. 2004. Twenty five years of community forestry: contribution to millennium development goals. A paper presented at the 4th national workshop on community forestry in Nepal held August 4-6, 2004 in Kathmandu, Nepal.

Karki, S. 1996. Investigating non-timber forest products (NTFPs) opportunities in Nepal. Nepal Australia Community Forestry Project. 16p.

Kattel, LP and Adhikari, MK. 1992. Mosses of Nepal. Natural History Society of Nepal, Kathmandu.

Kihara, H. (ed.) 1955-1957. Scientific results of the Japanese expeditions to Nepal Himalaya, 1952-1953. 3 vols. Kyoto.

Kihara, H. (ed.) 1957. Peoples of Nepal. Kyoto.

Koba, H, Akiyama, S, Endo, Y and Ohba, H. 1994. Name List of Flowering Plants and Gymnosperms of Nepal, 1. The University Museum, University of Tokyo, Japan.

Kolb, DA. 1976. *The Learning Style Inventory: Technical Manual.* McBer and Company. Boston.

LFP. 2003. Hill livelihoods baseline study. Part 1: Main Report of Quantitative Findings with Supplementary Qualitative Information. A Report prepared by Livelihoods and Forestry Programme (LFP) in collaboration with TANGO International, Inc. USA and Development Vision, Nepal.

LFP. 2003. Hill livelihoods baseline study. Part II: Report of Qualitative Findings. A Report prepared by Livelihoods and Forestry Programme (LFP) in collaboration with TANGO International, Inc. USA and Development Vision, Nepal. Majesty's Government of Nepal and the Government of the Netherlands.

Malla, SB and Shakya, PR. 1984. Medicinal Plants, In: Majupuria, TC (Ed), *Nepal-Nature's Paradise.* White Lotus Co. Ltd., Bangkok, Thailand. 261pp.

Malla, SB, Shakya, PR, Rajbhandari, KR, Bhattarai, NK and Subedi, MN. 1995. *Minor forest products (NTFPs) of Nepal: General status and trade.* FRISP Project Paper No. 4. HMGN/FINNIDA. 27p+.

McNeely, J. 1988. *Economics and Biodiversity: Developing and Using Economic Incentives to Conserve Biological Resources.* Gland, Switzerland: International Union for Conservation of Nature and Natural Resources.

MFSC. 2002. Nepal Biodiversity Strategy. Ministry of Forests and Soil Conservation, Singhadurbar, Kathmandu, Nepal.

MHPL. 2000. Business Development Plan of Malika Handmade Paper Processing Pvt. Ltd Kailash, Bajhang, Nepal.

Mittermeier, RA, Myers, N, Thomsen, JB, da Fonseca, GAB, and Olivieri, S. 1998. Biodiversity hotspots and major tropical wilderness areas: Approaches to setting conservation priorities. *Conservation Biology* 12 (3): 516-520.

Mizutani, M, Amakawa, T, Kitagawa, N, Furuki, T, Yamada, K and Higuchi, M. 1995. Hepatics From Nepal Collected by the Botanical Expedition of the National Science Museum, Tokyo, in 1988 1. Jungermanniales. In Watanabe, M and Hagiwara, H. (eds) Cryptograms of the Himalayas, vol.3, Nepal and Pakistan, pp 127-141. Department of Botany, National Science Museum, Tsukuba, Japan.

MOPE. 1998. State of the Environment, Nepal. Ministry of Population and Environment, Kathamandu.

Murphree, MW. 1991. *Communities as Institutions for Resource Management.* Harare: University of Zimbabwe.

Myers, N. 1988. Threatened biotas: "hot spots" in tropical forests. *Environmentalist* 8(3): 187-208.

Myers, N. 1990. The biodiversity challenge: expanded hot-spots analysis. *Environmentalist* 10(4): 243-256.

Ohashi, H. 1975. Notes on Himalayan Hedysarum, Leguminosae. In: J. Jap. Bot. 49: 161-167.

Olsen, CS and Helles, F. 1997. Making the poorest poorer: policies, laws and trade of medicinal plants in Nepal. *Journal of World Resource Management,* Vol. 8:137-158.

Olsen, CS. 1997. Commercial Non-Timber Forestry in Central Nepal: Emerging Themes and Priorities. Ph. D. Dissertation. Department of Economics and Natural Resources. Royal Veterinary and Agricultural University, Denmark.

Sakai, A and Malla SB. 1981. Winter hardness of tree species at high altitudes in the east Himalaya, Nepal. *Ecology* 62:1288-1298.

Salafsky, N, Cordes, B, Parks, J and Hochman, C. 1999. Evaluating Linkages between Business, the Environment, and Local Communities: Final Analytical Results from the Biodiversity Conservation Network. Biodiversity Support Program, Washington, D.C. USA.

Sapkota, IB. 2000. Social Equity and Community Forestry: A Case Study in Kaski District of Nepal. MSc Thesis, Wageningen University and Research Centre, The Netherlands.

Scherr, SJ, White, A, and Kaimowitz D. 2003. A new agenda for forest conservation and poverty reduction: Making markets work for low-income producers. Forest Trends, Washington D.C.

Selener, D. 1997. Participatory Action Research and Social Change, 2nd ed., Ithaca, NY: The Cornell Participatory Action Research Network, Cornell University. ISBN: 9978-95-130-X.

Shah, K. 1995. Enumeration of the Amphibians and Reptiles of Nepal. Biodiversity Profile Project Publication No. 2, Department of National Parks and Wildlife Conservation, HMGN, Kathmandu, Nepal.

Sharma, LR. 1995. Enumeration of the Lichens of Nepal. Biodiversity Profile Project Publication No. 3, Department of National Parks and Wildlife Conservation, HMGN, Kathmandu, Nepal.

Sharma, P. 1996. *Non-wood forest products and integrated mountain development: Observations from Nepal.* Business Seminar on Medicinal Herbs, Essential Oils and other Non Timber Forest Products, held in Kathmandu, December 1996. DEG/NGCCI. 11pp.

Shrestha, J. 1995. Enumeration of the Fishes of Nepal. Biodiversity Profile Project Publication No. 10, Department of National Parks and Wildlife Conservation, HMGN, Kathmandu, Nepal.

Shrestha, J. 2001. Taxonomic Revision of Fishes of Nepal. In Jha, PK., Karmacharya, SB., Baral, SR, and Lacoul, P. (eds) Environment and Agriculture: At the Crossroad of the New Millennium, pp 171-180. Ecological Society (ECOS), Kathmandu, Nepal.

Shrestha, TB. and Joshi, RM. 1996. Rare, Endemic and Endangered Plants of Nepal. WWF Nepal Program, Kathmandu, Nepal.

Silverstein, M. 1993. *The Environmental Economic Revolution: How business will thrive and the earth survive in the years to come.* I ed. New York: St. Martin's Press.

Singh, JS and Singh, SP. 1992. *Forests of Himalaya.* Gyanodaya Prakashan, Naini Tal India. Pp 294.

Singh, SP, Adhikari, BS and Zobel, DB. 1994. Biomass, productivity, leaf longevity and forest structure in the central Himalaya. *Ecological Monograph* 64:401-421.

Sithole, B, Frost, P, Veeman, TS. 2002. Searching for synthesis: integrating economic perspectives with those from other disciplines. Pages 199-227 in uncovering the hidden harvest (B, Campbell and MK, Luckert, eds.)

Smith, C. 1994. *Butterflies of Nepal.* Craftsman Press, Bangkok.

Smith, C. 1997. Butterflies of Royal Chitwan National Park, Nepal. Tecpress Books, Bangkok.

Song, Y. 1995. On the global position of the evergreen-broadleaved forests of China, pages 69-84 in Box, EO, ed. *Vegetation science in forestry: global perspective based on forest ecosystems of East and Southeast Asia.* Handbook of Vegetation Science Vol. 12/1. Dordrecht (the Netherlands), Kluwer Academic Pub.

Stainton, JDA.1972. *Forests of Nepal.* John Murray & Co. London.

Subedi, BP and Binayee, SB. 2000. *Linking Conservation to Business and Local Communities: An Approach to Sustainable Management of in situ Biodiversity in Nepal.* A paper presented in the 3rd SEANN Workshop on Community-Based Non-timber Forest Products Management, April 7-8, 2000, Kathmandu, Nepal.

Subedi, BP and Khanal BB. 1996. *Analysis of Productivity, Equity and Sustainability of User Group Managed Community Forestry.* A research report prepared for the Community Forestry Management Project, Institute of Forestry, Pokhara, Nepal.

Subedi, BP and Koonz, A. 1999. Sustainable harvesting means more than amount harvested. *Himalayan Bioresources*: 3(1)

Subedi, BP and Ojha, HR. 2001. *Commercial Use of Biodiversity and Equity: Are they Compatible?* In Bhattarai, N and Karki, M (eds) Sharing Local and National

Experience in Conservation of Medicinal and Aromatic Plants in South Asia. Proceedings of the Regional Workshop held in Pokhara, Nepal, 21-23 January 2001. pp 145-162.

Subedi, BP, Ojha, HR, Nicholson, K and Binayee, SB. 2002. An Assessment of Community Based Forest Enterprises in Nepal: Case Studies, Lessons and Implications. ANSAB and SNV Nepal, Kathmandu. Pp 109+.

Subedi, BP. 1996. Indigenous knowledge of tree and forest resources in the eastern Nepal terai. In: *Proceedings of the Second International Congress of Ethnobiology*. The International Society of Ethnobiology. Pp. 79-90.

Subedi, BP. 1996. *Participatory Forest Management: Principles and Practices of Community Forestry in Nepal*. A report submitted to Nepal Australia Community Forestry Project, Kathmandu.

Subedi, BP. 1997. Utilization of Non-Timber Forest Products: Issues and strategies for environmental conservation and economic development. Workshop theme paper presented in the Workshop on "The Utilization of NTFPs for Environmental Conservation and Economic Development in Nepal" organized by ANSAB held March 29, 1997 in Kathmandu.

Subedi, BP. 1998. Participatory utilization and conservation of medicinal and aromatic plants: A case from western Nepal Himalaya. Paper presented in the International Conference on Medicinal Plants, February 16-19, 1998, Bangalore, India.

Subedi, BP. 1999. *Monitoring the effects of community based conservation & commercial utilization of natural products on biodiversity in Humla, Nepal*. A Biological Monitoring Report to BCN. ANSAB/EnterpriseWorks Worldwide.

Subedi, BP. 1999. NTFP sub-sector in Karnali, Nepal: opportunities for leveraged intervention for the benefits of local communities. A paper presented at the National Workshop on the Management and Sustainable Utilization of Medicinal and Aromatic Plants in Nepal, July 16, 1999, Kathmandu, Nepal. ANSAB/CBED/CECI.

Suwal, RN. and Verheugt, WJM. 1995. Enumeration of the Mammals of Nepal. Biodiversity Profile Project Publication No. 6, Department of National Parks and Wildlife Conservation, HMGN, Kathmandu, Nepal.

Tempesta, MS and King, S. 1994. Tropical plants as a source of new pharmaceuticals. In Barnacal, PS. (ed) *Pharmaceutical Manufacturing International: The International Review of Pharmaceutical Technology Research and Development*. Sterling Publications Ltd., London.

Thapa, VK. 1995. Enumeration of the Spiders of Nepal. Biodiversity Profile Project Publication No. 5, Department of National Parks and Wildlife Conservation, HMGN, Kathmandu, Nepal.

WCMC. 1992. Protected areas of the world: a review of national systems. World Conservation Monitoring Center, London.

Wells, M, and Katrina B, with Lee H. 1992. *People and Parks: Linking Protected Area Management with Local Communities.* Washington, DC: The World Bank.

WHO. 2002. *WHO Traditional Medicine Strategy 2002-2005*. World Health Organization, Geneva.

Wiersum, KF. 1999. Social Forestry: Changing Perspectives in Forestry Science or Practice? PhD Thesis, Wageningen University and Research Centre, The Netherlands.

World Bank. 1996. From Plan to Market, World Development Report. World Bank, Washington, DC.

Yonzon, P. 1993. Raiders of the Park. *Himal*, 6(1): 22-23.

Zobel, DB and Singh, SP. 1997. Himalayan forests and ecological generalizations. *BioScience* 47:735-745.

Annex 1: A list of enterprise-oriented CFUGs involved in participatory action research

SN	CFUG Name	Address
1	Binayak Pimidanda	Kailash 1-7, Bajhang
2	Hemantawada	Hemantawada 1-9, Bajhang
3	Binayak	Gadaraya 8,9, Bajhang
4	Ranada	Kotdeval 1,2,3, Bajhang
5	Latun	Rilu 4, Bajhang
6	Phurkisalla	Patarasi 1,2, Jumla
7	Lamteli	Patarasi 3-6, Jumla
8	Syalapatal	Chhumchaur 1-3, Jumla
9	Bagjale,	Dillichaur 7-9, Jumla
10	Bhagawati	Patmara 9, Jumla
11	Jadikausi	Darma 7-9, Humla
12	Baghedhunga	Darma 1,2, Humla
13	Syali Kocheni	Mimi 3,4, Humla
14	Rocha	Mimi 1,2, Humla
15	Lepche Dangsile	Melchham 1-9, Humla
16	Thali	Raya 5-9, Humla
17	Mauri	Raya 2-4, Humla
18	Rahadev	Rodikot 1, 2, 3, Humla
19	Paksibada	Rodikot 7-9, Humla
20	Gopka	Lali 1-4, Humla
21	Hilsa	Chhipra 1, 5, 6, 7, Humla
22	Ripa	Sarkideu 1, 2, 3, 9, Humla
23	Devisthan	Shoon 5-6, Dolpa
24	Devi	Shoon 1-4, Dolpa
25	Shoon	Shoon 7-9, Dolpa
26	Pokepani	Majhphal 3-5, Dolpa
27	Rolagad	Majhphal 6-7, Dolpa
28	Meli	Majhphal 8-9, Dolpa
29	Juphal	Juphal 1-5, 9, Dolpa
30	Dumling	Rapla 7-9, Darchula
31	Namjung	Rapla 1-4, Darchula
32	Gorakhnath	Rapla 4-5, Darchula
33	Sampal rani	Sunsera 4-6 , Darchula
34	Bramha lekh	Sunsera 6, 7 and Dhaulakot 1, Darchula
35	Sidheshwor	Sunsera 1, 2, 3, 9, Darchula
36	Bhitteri	Boch 1-3, Dolakha
37	Bhatekhola	Jhyaku-7-9, Dolakha

Annex 2. Lists of community based forest enterprises and NTFP entrepreneurs studied

A. Lists of community based forest enterprises

SN	Enterprise name	District	Product	Plants used	Ownership	No. of HHs benefitted				Annual Average		Started (Year)
						Employees		Collectors	Owner	Income (Rs)	Production	
						Regular	Seasonal					
1	Malika Handmade Paper Pvt. Ltd.	Bajhang	Paper	Lokta	Corp of FUGs	2	7	735	235	4,00,000	325 kori	1999
2	Shree HERBIL Multipurpose Cooperative Ltd.	Bajhang	Trading of NTFPs, Paper,Thread	Different NTFPs	Coperative			1099				2003
3	Masta Bhatekhola Krishi Tatha Ban Multipurpose Cooperative Ltd.	Bajhang	Trading of NTFPs	Different NTFPs	Cooperative			100	25			2003
4	Allo Enterprise	Bajhang	Fibre	Allo	Conrt of FUGs			2328	2358			2004
5	Himalayan Nepali Hate Kagaz Udyog	Bajhang	Paper	Lokta	Sole	1	10	300	3	4,00,000	350 Kori	1999
6	Bajhang Gharelu Kagaz Udyog	Bajhang	Paper	Lokta	Sole	2	9	400	1	3,25,000	300 Kori	1985
7	Surmadevi Nepali Kagaz Udyog	Bajhang	Paper	Lokta	Sole						closed	1991
8	Chaya Kagaz Udyog	Bajhang	Paper	Lokta	Sole						closed	1995
9	Dharmodaya Nepali Kagaz Udyog	Bajhang	Paper	Lokta	Sole						closed	1996
10	Masta Gharelu Kagaz Karkhana	Bajhang	Paper	Lokta	Sole	2	11	300	1	4,00,000	350 Kori	
11	Himali Hate Kagaz Udyog	Bajhang	Paper	Lokta	Sole						closed	1998
12	Humla Oil Pvt. Ltd.	Humla	Essential oils	Different MAPs	Corp	2	3	1966		13,75,000	250 kg	1994
13	Rocha FUG Trading Cooperative Ltd.	Humla	Trading of NTFPs	Gucchichyau, Jatamasi	Cooperative		1	38	38	1,38,000	15 kg Gucchichyau, 18 qtl Jatamasi	2001
14	Jadikausi FUG Trading Cooperative	Humla	Trading of NTFPs	Gucchichyau, Jatamasi	FUG		1	76	81	2,05,000	20 kg Gucchichyau, 30 qtl Jatamasi	2000
15	Deudhunga Multi Purpose Cooperative Ltd.	Dolakha	Essential oil	Wintergreen	Cooperative	1	2	897	25	2,88,000	360 kg	2000
16	Bhitteri Ban Paidabar Prasodan Pvt. Ltd.	Dolakha	Argeli white skin	Argeli	Corp/FUG		17	57	243	2,10,000	300 kg	2000
17	Pandit Kamala Ban Paidabar	Dolakha	Paper	Lokta	Corp/FUG	5	4	1000	555	1,14,000	76 kori	2000

SN	Enterprise name	District	Product	Plants used	Ownership	No. of HHs benefitted				Annual Average		Started (Year)
						Employees		Collectors	Owner	Income (Rs)	Production	
						Regular	Seasonal					
	Prasodan Pvt. Ltd.											
18	Kalinchowk Forest Products Production & Processing Multipurpose Coop	Dolakha	Different NTFPs					2659				
19	Talfi Edible Oil Processing Enterprise	Jumla	Edible oil	Dhatelo	FUG			5661	151			
20	Rinmochha Forest Product Processing Pvt. Ltd.	Jumla	Essential oil	Jatamasi	Corp			195	18			
21	Karnali Jadibuti Processing Ltd.	Jumla	Essential oil	Jatamasi	Sole	4			1			
22	Bhagwati Edible Oil Processing Mill	Jumla	Edible oil	Dhatelo	FUG	2		1500	90	73,906	2319 kg	2002
23	Tripurasundari Herbs Conservation & Processing Pvt. Ltd.	Dolpa	Essential oils	Soti grass, Jatamasi	Corp	2	1	500	48	3,38,666	33 kg Jatamasi oil, 40 L Soti grass oil	
24	Rara Soap Enterprise	Mugu	Soap	Pagar	FUG/CBOs	2	3	400	308	10,000	800 pcs	2003
25	Chankheli Buga FUG NTFP Trading	Mugu	Trading of NTFPs	NTFPs	FUG		1	82	82	1,65,000	50 kg Gucchichayu	
26	Dumling NTFP Collection and Trading	Darchula			CBO			87	87			2003
27	FUG NTFP Trading	Darchula	MAPs	Timur	FUGs		13	10	86	22400	112 kg	2003
28	NTFP Nursery Enterprise	Darchula	MAPs	Timur,Okhar, Chiraito	FUGs			87	87			2003
29	Jan Pragati Cooperative	Baglung	Paper	Lokta	FUG	6		209	209			
30	Surya Pakho FUG	Baglung	MAPs	Lycopodium	FUG							
31	Alternative Herbal Company Pvt. Ltd.	Bhaktapur	Bael Juice, Herbal tea	Bael, Cinnamom, Gurjo, Lemon grass	Corp of NGOs, Individuals	4	30	300	12	33,50,000	25,000 bottles juice, 10,000 kg tea	1999
32	Santoshi FUG	Bardiya	Fuelwood/Timber	Sal/Khayar	FUG	2		66	66	1,10,000		1997
33	Praja NTFP Co-operative Ltd.	Chitwan	Trading of NTFPs	Different NTFPs	Cooperative	3	1	300	240	2,87,746	8774 kg	1998
34	Ajinggare FUG	Chitwan	Timber, Fuelwood	Sal	FUG	4	3		980	6,36,000	2000 cft timber, 68,800 kg fuelwood	1997
35	Kangkali FUG	Chitwan	Timber, Fuelwood	Sal	FUG	5	4		1612	8,38,000	3500 cft timber,	1996

SN	Enterprise name	District	Product	Plants used	Ownership	No. of HHs benefitted				Annual Average		Started (Year)
						Employees		Collectors	Owner	Income (Rs)	Production	
						Regular	Seasonal					
											80,000 kg fuelwood	
36	Herbal Laliguransh Sarbat Enterprise	Dadeldhura	Juice	Laliguransh	Conrt of FUGs		6	500	500	1,20,000	1200 L	2004
37	Tripurasundari FUG	Dadeldhura	Timber/Raw	Salla/NTFPs	FUG			500	500	23,25,000	62,500 kg	1999
38	Jagadamma FUG	Dadeldhura	Timber	Sal	FUG			200		10,00000	2850 cft	2000
39	Durga Bhawani FUG	Dadeldhura	Timber	Sal	FUG			350		12,00000	3430 cft	2000
40	Allo Entrepreneurs Group	Dadeldhura	Fibre	Allo	Sole			14	14	60,957	183 kg	2000
41	Chyuri Ghee & Honey Enterprise	Dadeldhura	Honey, Ghee	Chyuri	CBOs			191	191	7,00,000	5360 kg	2002
42	Nava Durga Enterprise	Dadeldhura	Handicrafts	Bamboo, Nigalo	CBOs		7	35	125	60,000		
43	Baghmara FUG	Dang	Timber	Sawn timber	FUG							
44	Dumresanne FUG	Dhankuta	Resin	Salla	FUG							
45	Cash Crop Producer & Trade	Ilam	Tea, Cardamom, v	Tea, Cardamom, v	Sole	1	2	1	1			
46	Large Cardamom Producer	Ilam	Cardamom	Cardamom	Sole	1	1	1		89375	100 kg	2001
47	Himalayan Bio Trade Pvt. Ltd.	Kathmandu	Marketing of NTFPs	Different NTFPs	Corp	14	3	350		17,87,000		
48	Shiva Shakti Hate Kagaz Udyog	Kathmandu	Different Prodcuts of Lokta Paper	Lokta	Sole	30		100	1	20,00,000	Different products	1993
49	Puskar Handmade & Wallpaper Ent.	Kavre	Paper	Lokta	Sole	6				50,000	100 pcs	2002
50	Chaubas Bhumlu Saw Mill	Kavre	Sawn timber	Salla	Const of FUGs	4	7	305	305	17,50,000	7000 cft	1995
51	Iccha Devi Saw Mill	Kavre	Sawn timber	Salla	FUG	5	10	215	215	15,00000	6000 cft	2001
52	Sundari FUG	Nawalparasi	Sawn timber	Sal	FUG	2			1200	10,50,000	3000 cft	2001
53	Chautari FUG	Nawalparasi	Sawn timber	Sal	FUG	2			1400	8,75,000	2500 cft	
54	Narjamandap Herbal Soap Udyog	Nuwakot	Soap	Chyuri	CBOs		3	11	4	1,35,000	9000 pcs	2002
55	Lokta Handmade Paper Producers	Parbat	Paper	Lokta	Sole							
56	Jimruk Herbal Soap Enterprise	Pyuthan	Soap	Chyuri	CBOs			100	27	37,333	2666 pcs	2003
57	NTFP Collection and Trading Enterprise	Pyuthan	Trading of NTFPs	Ritha, Timur, Cinnamom	CBOs			61		2,00,575		2003
58	Bamti Jadibuti Kheti Udyog Samuha	Ramechhap	Trade of NTFPs	Lathsalla, Chiraito	FUG			25	25	5,25,000	1500 kg	2002

SN	Enterprise name	District	Product	Plants used	Ownership	No. of HHs benefitted				Annual Average		Started (Year)
						Employees		Collectors	Owner	Income (Rs)	Production	
						Regular	Seasonal					
59	Himchuli Tea Producers Cooperative	Ramechhap	Orthodox tea	Tea	Cooperative			20	70	3,00,000	100 kg	1997
60	Bamti Alainchi Producers Samuha	Ramechhap	Trading of Cardamom	Cardamom	CBOs			50	100	10,00,000	5000 kg	1995
61	Shankarnagar FUG	Rupandehi	Timber/Fuelwood	Sal, Sisso	FUG	11	8	1967		15,00000		1996
62	Bhimeshwor Nepali Handmade Paper Pvt. Ltd.	Sindhupalchowk	Paper	Lokta	Sole							
63	Dandapakhar NTFP Network	Sindhupalchowk	Trading of NTFPs	Lokta, Argeli, Chiraito	Const of CFUGs			800	500	5,00000	10 qtl	2000
64	Allo Enterprise	Shankhuwasabha	Fibre/Knitted cloth	Allo	CBOs			50	1200	8,00000		2001
65	Lakuwa Product Association	Shankhuwasabha	Bamboo & Rattan	Handicrafts	Sole/Coop							
66	Chiraito Trading Network	Taplejung	Trading of chiraito	Chiraito	CFUGs			500	700	1,80,000	1200 kg	2000
67	Pathivara CFUG	Taplejung	Raw trade of Lokta	Lokta	CFUG			70	70	1,00,000	4000 kg	2000
68	Sidhingba Siddhi Hate Kagaz Udyog	Taplejung	Paper	Lokta	Sole		5			5,40,000		
69	KaliKhola Hate Kagaz Udyog	Taplejung	Paper	Lokta	Sole		27			6,00000		
70	Lama Pahadi Hate Kagaz Udyog	Taplejung	Paper	Lokta, Argeli	Sole		72			15,00000		
71	Kunfen Ausadhalaya	Kathmandu	Ayurvedic Medicine	Different medicinal plants	Sole							

B. Name and address of the enterpenuers surveyed for the study

1. Abdul Ahat : Ghorahi, Milan chowk, Dang
2. Abdul Samad Jogi: Ghorahi, Dang
3. Ahasan Khan: Krishnagar, Panitanki, Kapilbastu
4. Ambika Prasad & Co: Jawabari, Rupandehi
5. Amrit Aurved Aushadhalaya: Tersapatti, Palpa
6. Ansari Kirana Merchant : DSP road, Banke
7. Anup Nursery: Basamadi, Makwanpur
8. Arogya Bhavan Works: Dillibazar, Kathmandu
9. Arun Traders: Dhulabari, Jhapa
10. Asal Bijuwal: Ghatle lek, Mugu
11. Atmaram Kanu: Birta, Parsa
12. Babu Ansari : Fultekra , Banke
13. Babu Galla Pasal: Tulsipur, Dang
14. Baburam Rai: Hile, Dhankuta
15. Badri Prasad Shah: Dhulabari, Paanchthar
16. Bal Bahadur Limbu: Basantapur Bazar, Tehrathum
17. Bam Bahadur Shrestha: Barbote , Ilam
18. Bansal Laghu Udhyog: Birtamod, Paanchthar
19. Bheri Kirana Store : Ghositole, Banke
20. Bhim Bahadur Karki: Mude Sanischare, Tehrathum
21. Bindal Enterprises: Birtamod, Paanchthar
22. Birsingh Tamang: Belawa, Makwanpur
23. Chandra Bahadur Shrestha (Gore sahu): Barbote, Ilam
24. Chandrabhan Agrawal: Dharan, Prithivimarga, Sunsari
25. Cosmos Herbal Products (P) Ltd.: Baluwatar, Kathmandu
26. Dabur Nepal (P) Ltd.: Tinkune, Kathmandu
27. Deepchand Traders: Ilam, Ilam
28. Dev Narayan Shrestha: Lothar , Makwanpur
29. Dhan Bahadur Bhandari: Fikkal, Ilam
30. Dhorpatan Traders: Kalanki, Kathmandu
31. Dinesh Kirana Store: Lothar, Makwanpur
32. Ekbal Ahamad Ansari : Eklaini, Banke
33. Everest Herbal Processing Pvt. Ltd.: Buddhanagar, Kathmandu
34. Everest Paper Mill: Chanauta, Dhanusha
35. Everest Product: Dharan, Buddha Marg, Sunsari
36. Fleur Himalayan Ltd: Jeetpur, Bara
37. Gajendra Traders: Makhan Galli, Kathmandu
38. Ganapati Oil: Tulsipur, Ganesh chowk, Dang
39. Ganapati Rosin and Terpentine (P) Ltd. : Gadagauda, Kapilbastu
40. Ganesh Poudel: Basantapur, Tehrathum
41. Ganga Rosin and Terpentine P. Ltd. : Ganapur , Banke
42. Gangaram Chaudhari: Mude Sanischare, Tehrathum
43. Gautam Kucho Udhyog: Birtamod, Charali, Paanchthar
44. Gopal and Govinda Store: Birtamod, Paanchthar
45. Gopal Bhujel: Mathillo Hile, Tehrathum
46. Gorkha Ayurved Co.P.Ltd.: Goganbu, Kathmandu
47. Gorkha Exim.P.Ltd.: Balaju, Kathmandu
48. Grihalaxmi Kucho Udhyog: Dhulabari, Paanchthar
49. Haji Kirana Store : Sadarline, Banke
50. Hark Bahadur Bam: Khalanga, Bangabagar, Darchula
51. Hark Bahadur Katuwal: Dharan, Amarhat, Sunsari
52. Herbs Production & Processing Co. Ltd.: Koteswor, Kathmandu
53. Herbs Production and Processing Co. Ltd.: Tarahara, Sunsari
54. Herbs Production and Processing Co. Ltd. : Salyanibag, Banke
55. Himalai Zinger Factory: Tanahun
56. Himalayan BioTrade (P) Ltd: Baneswor, Kathmandu
57. Himalayan Herbs Processor: Ghositole, Banke
58. Himalayan Herbs Traders: Baluwatar, Kathmandu
59. Indra Aurved Aushadhalaya: Tersapatti, Kaski
60. Indra Tamang: Hile, Dhankuta
61. Jadibuti Bhandar: Trisuli, dhunge, Nuwakot
62. Jagannath Shrestha: Inarwa, Sunsari
63. Jagdish Shah: Hile, Dhankuta
64. Jamil Ahamad : Devigunj, Banke
65. Kamalakant Sony: Ghorahi, Dang
66. Khanal Rosin and Terpentine P. Ltd. : Ganapur, Banke
67. Khaptad Aroma: Putalisadak, Kathmandu
68. Kirana Traders : Sadarline, Banke
69. Kishor Agrawal: Birtamod, Jhapa
70. Kriparam Agrawal: Ilam, Ilam
71. Kulani Herbal Pvt. Ltd.: Indreni Chowk, Sunsari
72. Kumar Shrestha: Mude Sanischare, Tehrathum
73. Kushal Suppliers: Mahendranagar, Kanchanpur
74. L. S. and Sons: Birtamod, Paanchthar
75. Laddan Miyan: Fultekra , Banke
76. Laxmi Rosin and Terpentine P. Ltd. : Ganapur , Banke
77. Machhapuchhre Herbal (P) Ltd.: Basamadi, Makwanpur
78. Man Singh Bohora: Khalanga, Bangabagar, Darchula
79. Manoj and Brothers: Dharan, Chhatachowk, Sunsari

80. Md. Hussain Halwai : Ghositole, Banke
81. Mittal International Traders: Birtamod, Paanchthar
82. Mohan Dev Bhatta: Attaria, Kailali
83. Mordhoj Ram Kumar: Dharan, Laxmisadak, Sunsari
84. Namdar Khan : Ganeshpur, Banke
85. Natural Goods Collection: Sannantar, Makwanpur
86. Natural Goods Store: Ghositole, Banke
87. Natural Nepal: Mahaviroad, Tulsian Market, Parsa
88. Natural Product Industry: Chanauta, Kapilbastu
89. Nepal Herbs Traders: Ghositole, Banke
90. Nepal Liver Ltd.: Makwanpur
91. Nepal Rosin and Terpentine Ltd. : Attari, Kailali
92. Nepali Herbs Enterprises: Chaughada, Makwanpur
93. New Faruq Enterprises: Ghorahi, Dang
94. Nirub Subedi Medical: Attaria, Godabri road, Kailali
95. Padam Lal Taude: Kabhrepalanchowk
96. Pawan Traders: Tulsipur, Kha line, Dang
97. Pemba Lama: Basantapur, Tehrathum
98. Popular Trading Concern: Kailali
99. Raj Bahadur Shahi: Rola, Mugu
100. Rajendra Shah: Dhulabari, Paanchthar
101. Rajesh Shah: Dhulabari, Paanchthar
102. Ram Chandra Joshi: Chapagaun, Kathmandu
103. Ram Chandra Shrestha: Chhetrapati, Kathmandu
104. Rarendra Prasad Jaiswal: Dharan, Chhatachowk, Sunsari
105. Renuka Herbal (P) Ltd: Panitanki, Parsa
106. RJN Enterprises: Dharan, Sunsari
107. Royal Drugs Ltd.: Babar Mahal, Kathmandu
108. S.I.O.N. TRADES: Lalitpur, Lalitpur
109. Sahwaj Traders: Ghositole, Banke
110. Sama Enterprises: Ramnagar Road, Banke
111. Satya Herbal Products : Salyanibag, Banke
112. Shambala Herbal and Aromatic Industries (P) Ltd: Kathmandu
113. Shashi Overseas International: Gyaneswor, Kathmandu
114. Sher Bahadur Rai: Hile, Dhankuta
115. Shiv Shanker Prasad Gupta : Janakpur, Shivpath, Dhanusha
116. Shree Agro Processing: New road, Maisthan, Parsa
117. Shree Kapi Herbal Traders: Fultekra, Banke
118. Shree Krishna Aushadhalaya: Bagbazar, Kathmandu
119. Simki Trade Center: Gharbari Tole, Banke
120. Singhdurbar Baidhkhana Sameeti: Anamnagar, Kathmandu
121. Sisuwa Medical Hall: Sisuwa, Kaski
122. Sitaram Rangalal Agrawal: Ilam, Ilam
123. Subash Chandra Krishna Kumar : Bhalwari, Rupandehi
124. Sunita Aurved Aushadhalaya: Tersapatti, Kaski
125. Surendra Kumar Baniya : Amarpath, Rupandehi
126. Surya Rosin and Turpentine Co.: Kathmandu
127. Swadeshi Herbs Links : Janakpur, Shivpath, Dhanusha
128. Taparia Export : Panitanki, Morang
129. Tarachand Agrawal: Birtamod, Paanchthar
130. Taudale Khadya Store: Banepa, Kabhrepalanchowk
131. Tej Prasad Rai: Hile, Dhankuta
132. Thakur Prasad Pathak: Lothar, Chitwan
133. Tulasa Galla Pasal: Ghorahi, Dang
134. Unani Aushadhalaya: Bagbazar, Kathmandu
135. Usha Traders and Suppliers: Khalanga, Talli bazar, Darchula
136. Vaishnu Devi Oil Suppliers : Bhairahawa, Rupandehi
137. Wortaula Suppliers: Manahari, Makwanpur

Annex 3. List of NTFP species traded in and from Nepal

S.N.	Botanical Name	Vernacular Name	Price (NRs/kg) 2003	Life Form	Distribution			Parts Used	Commercial Use
					Regional	Alt . zone	Altitude		
1	*Abies spectabilis*	talispatra, gobresalla	33	T	WC	H	2400-4400m	L,W,Tg	essential oil, woods & crafts, medicine
2	*Abies densa*	gobresalla		T	E	H	3000-4000m	L,W	medicine, woods & crafts
3	*Acacia catechu*	khair	850	T	WC	T	100-1000m	W,B	food, dye
4	*Acacia concinna*	shikakai	15	Cl	W	T	400-800m	P,L	medicine, cosmetic
5	*Acer caesium*	putali phul,phirphire		T	W	M	1200-2400m	W	woods & crafts
6	*Aconitum bisma*	bikhama		H	WC	H	3000-4000m	Rt	medicine, tonic
7	*Aconitum spicatum*	bikh	55	H	WCE	H	3300-4300m	Tu,Fl,L	medicine
8	*Aconitum ferox*	Seto bikh	55	H	CE	MH	2100-3800m	Tu,Fl,L	medicine
9	*Aconitum heterophyllum*	atis	300	H	C	MH	1800-4100m	Rt,Tu	medicine, tonic
10	*Acorus calamus*	bojho	32	H	WCE	TM	500-2300m	Rt	medicine, essential oil
11	*Adhatoda vasica*	asuro	15	S	WCE	TM	500-1600m	W,L	medicine

S.N.	Botanical Name	Vernacular Name	Price (NRs/kg) 2003	Life Form	Distribution			Parts Used	Commercial Use
					Regional	Alt . zone	Altitude		
12	*Aegle marmelos*	bel	50	T	WCE	T	600-1100m	Fr,B,L,Rt	food, medicine , Juice
13	*Aesculus indica*	pangar	50	T	W	MH	1200-3000m	Sd,W	detergent, medicine
14	*Amomum subulatum*	alainchi	320	H	CE	M	1000-2000m	Sd	spices & flavours
15	*Agave americana*	ketuki		S	W	MH	1200-3700m	L	plant fibre, biopesticide
16	*Allium hypsistum*	Jimbu	30	H	WCE	H	2500-4500m	L	spices & flavours, medicine
17	*Allium wallichi*	banlasun	80	H	WCE	H	2400-4650m	Rt,L	spices & flavours, medicine
18	*Antidesma acidum*	archal, odal		S	CE	T	100-900m	Rt	medicine
19	*Argemone mexicana*	thakal		H	W	TM	100-1500m	Wp	medicine
20	*Artemisia vulgaris*	titepati	2	S	CE	TM	300-2400m	St,Rt,L	essential oil, medicine
21	*Artemisia dubia*	titepati	2	S	WCE	MH	1200-3400m	St,Rt,L	essential oil, medicine
22	*Artemisia indica*	titepati	2	S	CE	TM	300-2400m	St,Rt,L	essential oil, medicine
23	*Arundinaria falcata*	nigalo,	25	S	WC	MH	1800-2700m	St,Sh	□oods & crafts

S.N.	Botanical Name	Vernacular Name	Price (NRs/kg) 2003	Life Form	Distribution			Parts Used	Commercial Use
					Regional	Alt . zone	Altitude		
24	*Asparagus racemosus*	kurilo, satawari	150	H	W	TM	600-2100m	Rt,St	food, medicine , vegetable
25	*Astilbe rivularis*	thulo okhati		H	WCE	MH	1800-3600m	Rz	medicine
26	*Azadirachta indica*	neem	60	T	CE	T	100-900m	Sd,L,B	medicine, biopesticide
27	*Bassia butyracea*	chiuri	45	T	CE	TM	200-1500m	Fr,Sd,L,B	edible oil & fat, medicine, food
28	*Bauhinia vahlii*	malupat, bhorla	15	Cl	WCE	TM	200-1300m	Sd,B,L,Rt	food, woods & crafts, medicine, Juice
29	*Bauhinia purpurea*	Rato koiralo		T	WCE	TM	100-1500m	B,L,Tg,Bu	dye, food, pickle
30	*Bauhinia variegata*	Seto koiralo		T	WCE	TM	100-1700m	Bu,L,Tg,B	food, medicine , pickle
31	*Berberis asiatica*	chutro	80	S	C	M	1200-2500m	Fr,Rb,B,L	dye, medicine, food
32	*Berberis aristata*	chutro	80	S	WC	MH	1800-3000m	Fr,Rb,B,L	dye, medicine, food
33	*Berberis wallichiana*	baarhamaase chutro	80	S	C	MH	1900-3300m	Fr,Rb,B,L	dye, medicine, food
34	*Berberis chitria*	chutro	80	S	WC	MH	2000-3700m	Fr,Rb,B,L	dye, medicine, food
35	*Bergenia ciliata*	pakhanbed	12	T	WCE	MH	1200-3300m	B,Rz	medicine

S.N.	Botanical Name	Vernacular Name	Price (NRs/kg) 2003	Life Form	Distribution			Parts Used	Commercial Use
					Regional	Alt . zone	Altitude		
36	*Butea monosperma*	palans		T	WCE	TM	150-1500m	Sd,L,B,Fl	medicine
37	*Betula utilis*	bhojpatra	35	H	WC	MH	1600-3200m	B,Rs	plant fibre, medicine
38	*Bombax ceiba*	simal		T	CE	TM	100-1500m	Sd,Rt,B,La	stuffing material, medicine
39	*Brachycorythis obcordata*	gamdol	80	O	WCE	MH	1000-2000m	Tu	medicine
40	*Calamus tenuis*	pani bet	5	Cl	WC	T	100-1000m	St	woods & crafts
41	*Calamus laptospadix*	dangre bet	5	Cl	WCE	TM	100-1500m	St	woods & crafts
42	*Calamus latifolius*	phekre bet	5	Cl	E	T	100-600m	St	woods & crafts
43	*Calamus acanthospathus*	gauri bet	5	Cl	WE	TM	400-1500m	St	woods & crafts
44	*Calotropis gigantea*	ank	150	S	C	T	170-600m	Fl,Rt,B,L	medicine
45	*Cannabis sativa*	bhang, ganja	300	H	WCE	MH	1200-2200m	St,L	food, medicine
46	*Cassia fistula*	rajbriksha	30	T	WCE	TM	150-1400m	L,Rt,Fr	medicine
47	*Cedrus deodara*	deodar	20	T	WC	MH	1900-2700m	L,Sd	medicine, essential oil

S.N.	Botanical Name	Vernacular Name	Price (NRs/kg) 2003	Life Form	Distribution			Parts Used	Commercial Use
					Regional	Alt . zone	Altitude		
48	*Celosia argentea*	sahastrajari		H	WCE	TM	100-1520m	Sd	medicine
49	*Centella asiatica*	ghod tapre	2	H	WCE	TM	500-2100m	Wp	medicine
50	*Choerospondias axillaris*	lapsi	65	T	WE	MH	950-1900m	Fr	food, medicine
51	*Cinnamomum camphora*	kapur	40	T	C	M	1300-2000m	L,Sd,W	medicine, essential oil
52	*Cinnamomum glaucescens*	sugandhakokila	900	T	W	M	1000-1500m	Sd,Fr	essential oil, medicine
53	*Cinnamomum tamala*	dalchini	45	T	WC	TM	450-2100m	B	spices & flavours
54	*Cinnamomum zeylanicum*	tejpat	25	T	WC	TM	450-2100m	L	spices & flavours, essential oil
55	*Citrullus colocythis*	indreni	5	Cl	CE	TM	200-2300m	Fr,Rt	medicine
56	*Cordia dichotoma*	bohari		T	CE	TM	200-1400m	B,L,Fr	medicine
57	*Cordyceps sinensis**	yarsagumba	125000	F	WE	H	3000-4500m	Wp	tonic, medicine
58	*Curculigo orchioides*	musli	25	H	CE	T	100-600m	Rt	food, medicine
59	*Curcuma angustifolia*	besar	60	H	C	TM	200-1900m	Rz	food, medicine, dye

S.N.	Botanical Name	Vernacular Name	Price (NRs/kg) 2003	Life Form	Distribution			Parts Used	Commercial Use
					Regional	Alt . zone	Altitude		
60	*Cymbopogon citratus*	lemongrass	50	H	WCE	T	150-1000m	Wp	essential oil, medicine
61	*Cymbopogon jwarancusa*	soti ghans		H	WE	MH	1600-3000m	Wp	essential oil
62	*Cymbopogon winterianus*	citronella		H	WCE	TM	180-1500m	Wp	essential oil
63	*Dactylorhiza hatagirea***	panchaunle		H	WCE	H	2800-4000m	Tu	medicine
64	*Daphne bholua*	lokta	80	S	CE	M	1500-2100m	B	plant fibre
65	*Daphne papyracea*	lokta	80	S	CE	M	1500-2100m	B	plant fibre
66	*Datura metel*	dhaturo		H	WCE	TM	300-1200m	Wp	medicine
67	*Delphinium denudatum*	nirbikhi, nirmansi	250	H	W	MH	1500-2700m	Rt	medicine
68	*Delphinium himalayai*	atis	300	H	WC	H	3000-4500m	Rt	medicine, food, tonic
69	*Dendrocalamus hamiltonii*	tama bans		S	E	T	100-1070m	Sh,St,Rz	food, medicine
70	*Dendrocalamus strictus*	bans		S	CE	TM	100-1500m	St	plant fibre
71	*Desmotichum fimbriatum*	jibanti		T	C	T	100-500m	B	medicine, tonic

S.N.	Botanical Name	Vernacular Name	Price (NRs/kg) 2003	Life Form	Distribution			Parts Used	Commercial Use
					Regional	Alt . zone	Altitude		
72	*Didymocarpus villosus*	kumkum		H	E	MH	1500-2500m	Fr,St	medicine
73	*Dioscorea bulbifera*	ban tarul		Cl	WCE	TM	150-2100m	Tu	medicine, food
74	*Dioscorea deltoidea*	vyakur		H	WC	TM H	900-3000m	Rt,Fr	food, detergent
75	*Diospyros melanoxylon*	bindipat, tendu	10	T	CE	TM	100-1500m	L	wrapper for bidi
76	*Diospyros malabarica*	tendu, teju		T	CE	TM	100-1500m	Fr	food, medicine
77	*Drosera peltata*	jhingejalo, kitas		H	W	H	2500-3400m	Wp	medicine,
78	*Edgeworthia gardnerii*	argeli	150	S	CE	MH	1500-3000m	B	plant fibre
79	*Elaeocarpus sphaericus*	rudraksha		T	W	TM	800-1500m	Fr	medicine
80	*Emblica officinalis*	amala	45	T	CE	T	200-1200m	Fr	food, medicine
81	*Entada phaseoloides*	pangra		Cl	E	TM	300-1600m	Fr	medicine
82	*Ephedra gerardiana*	somlata	60	S	W	H	3700-5200m	Tg	medicine
83	*Eulaliopsis binata*	babiyo, sawai grass	1	H	WC	TM	150-2600m	Wp	plant fibre

S.N.	Botanical Name	Vernacular Name	Price (NRs/kg) 2003	Life Form	Distribution			Parts Used	Commercial Use
					Regional	Alt . zone	Altitude		
84	*Eulophia dabia*	kaladana		H	W	MH	2000-3100	Tu	food, medicine
85	*Gaultheria fragrantissimia*	dhasingare	900	T	W	MH	1500-2700m	L	essential oil, medicine
86	*Gentiana kurro*	karru		H	C	MH	1800-4000m	Rt	medicine, tonic
87	*Girardinia diversifolia*	allo	300	S	WC	M	1500-1800	St,L	plant fibre, food, vegetable
88	*Grewia optiva*	bhimal		T	WCE	TM	150-1800m	B	plant fibre, woods & crafts
89	*Hippophae salicifolia*	Dalechuck (chichi)	40	S	WC	MH	1500-3800m	Fr	food, Juice
90	*Hippophae tibetana*	Dalechuck (tora)	40	S	CE	H	3000-4500m	Fr	food, Juice
91	*Juglans regia L. var kaghazi*	dante okhar	100	T	W	MH	2000-2900m	B,Fr	food, dye
92	*Juglans regia L. var. kamaonica*	hade okhar	100	T	W	MH	2000-2900m	B,Fr	food, dye
93	*Juniperus indica*	dhup, dhupi	15	T	W	MH	1800-4100m	W,Fr	medicine, essential oil
94	*Jurinea dolomiaea*	kalthaple, dhupjadi	125	H	W	H	2500-3600m	Rt	incense
95	*Leucas cephalotes*	dronapuspi	40	H	WE	TM	150-2400m	Wp	medicine

S.N.	Botanical Name	Vernacular Name	Price (NRs/kg) 2003	Life Form	Distribution			Parts Used	Commercial Use
					Regional	Alt . zone	Altitude		
96	*Litsea cubeba*	siltimur		T	WE	MH	1000-2700m	Rt,B,Fr	medicine
97	*Lobelia pyrimidalis*	eklevir		H	WC	MH	1100-2300m	L,Fl	medicine
98	*Lycopodium clavatum*	nagbeli	200	Cl	WCE	MH	1200-3500m	Sp	medicine
99	*Madhuca latifolia*	mahuwa		T	CE	TM	300-1200m	Fl,Fr,Sd,B	medicine, food
100	*Maesa chisia*	bilaune		S	WCE	MH	1200-2600m	Rb	medicine
101	*Mallotus philippinensis*	sindure	250	T	WE	TM	150-1800m	B,L,Fr	medicine
102	*Mentha arvensis*	pudina	60	H	WC	MH	1800-2700m	Wp	food, medicine, essential oil
103	*Mesua ferrea*	nageshwar	30	T	CE	T	400-900m	Fl,Sd	medicine
104	*Mimosa pudica*	lajjawati		H	CE	TM	200-1200m	Rt,L	medicine
105	*Momordica charantia*	karela	25	Cl	CE	TM	300-2100m	Rt,L,Fr	medicine
106	*Morchella conica*	guchhi chayau	5500	F	WCE	MH	2000-3500m	Wp	food, tonic, vegetable
107	*Morchella elata*	guchhi chayau	5500	F	WCE	MH	2000-3500m	Wp	food, tonic, vegetable

S.N.	Botanical Name	Vernacular Name	Price (NRs/kg) 2003	Life Form	Distribution			Parts Used	Commercial Use
					Regional	Alt . zone	Altitude		
108	*Morchella esculenta*	guchhi chayau	5500	F	WCE	MH	2000-3500m	Wp	food, tonic, vegetable
109	*Myrica esculenta*	kafal		S	WCE	MH	1200-2300m	B,Fr	food, dye
110	*Nardostachys grandiflora*	jatamansi, bhulte	140	H	W	H	3600-4800m	Rz	essential oil
111	*Neopicrorhiza scrophulariiflora*	kutki	144	H	W	H	3000-4200m	Rt	medicine
112	*Ocimum sanctum*	Tulsi	3800	H	CE	T	400-900m	Rt,L,Sd,Sh	medicine, essential oil
113	*Osyris wightiana*	nundhiki		S	CE	MH	1100-2600m	L,Hw	food, dye, beverage
114	*Paris polyphylla*	satuwa	150	H	CE	H	2000-3100m	Rz	medicine
115	*Parmelia nepalensis*	jhayu		H	WCE	MH	1000-3000m	Wp	medicine, food
116	*Pinus roxburghii*	rani salla	18	T	WE	TM	900-2100m	W,La,Tg	gums & resins, essential oil
117	*Piper chaba*	chabo	80	Cl	WCE	TM	100-1500m	Fr	medicine
118	*Piper longum*	pipla	85	Cl	WCE	T	200-1000m	Fr,Rt	medicine
119	*Pistacia integerima*	kakarsinghi	170	T	W	TM	300-1500m	P	medicine, food

S.N.	Botanical Name	Vernacular Name	Price (NRs/kg) 2003	Life Form	Distribution			Parts Used	Commercial Use
					Regional	Alt . zone	Altitude		
120	*Prinsepia utilis*	dhatelo		T	W	MH	2000-2700m	Fr	edible oil & fat
121	*Pyrus pashia*	mayal		T	WCE	TMH	750-2700m	Fr,L	food, dye
122	*Rauvolfia serpentina*	sarpagandha	150	S	CE	TM	100-1100m	Rt	medicine
123	*Rheum australe*	padamchal	40	H	W	H	3000-4200m	Rt,St	medicine
124	*Rhododendron anthopogon*	sunpati		S	W	H	3000-4800m	Sd,L	essential oil, incense
125	*Rhododendron arboreum*	lali gurans	40	S	WCE	MH	1500-3300m	L,Fl	food, incense, medicine, Juice
126	*Rhododendron lepidotum*	gurans	40	S	WCE	MH	2400-4600m	Fl,L	biopesticide, incense
127	*Rhododendron barbatum*	Rato guras	40	S	WCE	H	2700-3600m	Fl	food, incense, medicine, Juice
128	*Ricinus communis*	ander	15	S	WCE	TM	150-2400m	Rb,L,Fl,Sd	medicine
129	*Rubia cordifolia*	majitho	35	H	CE	MH	1200-3200m	St,Rt	dye, tonic
130	*Rubus ellipticus*	ainselu		S	WC	MH	1800-2500m	Fr,Rt	food, medicine
131	*Sapindus mukorossi*	rittha	18	T	WE	M	1000-1500m	Fr	detergent

S.N.	Botanical Name	Vernacular Name	Price (NRs/kg) 2003	Life Form	Distribution			Parts Used	Commercial Use
					Regional	Alt . zone	Altitude		
132	*Saussurea lappa*	kuth	60	H	W	H	2000-3300m	Rt	medicine
133	*Schleichera oleosa*	kusum	2	T	W	T	100-800m	Sd,B	medicine
134	*Selinum tenuifolium*	bhutkesh	80	H	WCE	H	2500-4000m	Wp	medicine, food
135	*Shorea robusta*	sal, Sakhuwa		T	WCE	TM	150-1500m	L,Sd,La	woods & crafts
136	*Sida cordifolia*	balu		S	WCE	TM	500-1100m	Rt,L	medicine, woods & crafts, essential oil
137	*Solanum xanthocarpum*	kantakari	20	H	WCE	T	300-900m	Fr,Sd	medicine
138	*Swertia chirayita*	chiraito, tite	160	H	CE	MH	1500-2500m	Wp	medicine
139	*Swertia ciliata*	chiraito	160	H	WCE	H	2800-4000m	Wp	medicine
140	*Swertia recemosa*	chiraito	160	H	WCE	H	3000-5000m	Wp	medicine
141	*Swertia aungustifolia*	chiraito	160	H	WCE	TM	600-2600m	Wp	medicine
142	*Swertia multicaulis*	chiraito	160	H	CE	H	4000-4900m	Wp	medicine
143	*Swertia tetragona*	chiraito	160	H	W	H	2400-3300m	Wp	medicine

S.N.	Botanical Name	Vernacular Name	Price (NRs/kg) 2003	Life Form	Distribution			Parts Used	Commercial Use
					Regional	Alt . zone	Altitude		
144	*Swertia nervosa*	chiraito	160	H	WCE	TM H	700-3000m	Wp	medicine
145	*Swertia dilatata*	chiraito	160	H	WCE	MH	1800-4000m	Wp	medicine
146	*Swertia alata*	chiraito	160	H	WC	MH	2000-3600m	Wp	medicine
147	*Syzygium cumini*	jamun		T	WCE	TM	100-1200	St,Sd,Fr	medicine, food
148	*Taxus baccata subsp.Wallichiana*	lauthsalla	55	T	WCE	H	2100-3400m	L,B	medicine, anticancer
149	*Terminalia arjuna*	arjun		T	CE	TM	200-1400m	B	medicine
150	*Terminalia bellirica*	barro	25	T	CE	TM	300-1100m	Fr	medicine
151	*Terminalia chebula*	harro		T	CE	TM	150-1100m	Fr	medicine
152	*Thysanolaena maxima*	amriso	25	H	C	TM	500-2000m	Fl,St	broom
153	*Tinospora sinensis*	gurjo	20	Cl	CE	T	300-500m	St	medicine, food, tea
154	*Toona ciliata*	tooni		T	WCE	TM	200-2500m	Fl,B,W,L	woods & crafts, food, tea
155	*Tridax procumbens*	kurkure jhaar		H	C	TM	1000-2500m	St	medicine

S.N.	Botanical Name	Vernacular Name	Price (NRs/kg) 2003	Life Form	Distribution			Parts Used	Commercial Use
					Regional	Alt . zone	Altitude		
156	*Valeriana hardwickei*	nakali sugandhawal		H	C	H	3500-4500m	Rt	medicine, tonic
157	*Valeriana jatamansi*	sugandhawal	105	H	WC	MH	2000-2700m	Rt	essential oil
158	*Viscum album*	hadchur		S	WCE	TM	1000-2500m	Fr,Rt	medicine
159	*Withania somnifera*	aswagandha	150	S	W	T	100-1000m	Rt,L	medicine
160	*Woodfordia fruticosa*	dhaairo	25	S	CE	TM	200-1800m	Fl,L	medicine
161	*Zanthoxylum armatum*	timur	105	S	W	M	1000-2500m	Fr	spices & flavours, essential oil

* Banned for export without processing

** Bannded for collection

Distribution: C=Central Nepal; E=East Nepal; W=West Nepal; H= High Mountains(2500-5000m);M=Midhills (1100-2500m); T=Terai (100-1000m)

Life Form: T= Tree; S= Shrub; H= Herb; Cl= Climber;Cr= Creeping herb, F=Fungi, O= Orchid

Parts Used: B=Bark, Bu=Bud, Fl=Flower, Fr=Fruits, L=Leaves, La=Latex, P=Pod, Rb=Root bark, Rs=Root stock, Rt=Root, Rz=Rhizomes, Sd=Seeds, Sh=Shoot, Sp=Spores/Sporangia, St=Stem, Sw=Sap wood, Tg=Twig, Tu=Tubers, W=Wood, Wp=Whole plant

Annex 4: Questionnaire and checklists used for data collection from CFUGs in participatory action research

Format 1-A: Conservation Variables

SN सि.नं.	CFUG Name Address सामुदायिक वनको नाम, ठेगाना	CF Area (ha) सा.व.क्षेत्रफल (हे.)		HH (No.) घरधूरी संख्या		विस्तृत रुपमा स्रोत सर्भेक्षण तथा व्यवस्थापन योजना (✓×)	CFUGs aware on biodiversity threats समूह खतरा प्रति सजग (✓×)	Threat assessment and identification खतरा पहिचान (✓×)	Threats mitigation planning खतरा घटाउने कार्यक्रमको योजना (✓×)	Threats mitigation practices and review खतरा घटाउने कार्यक्रमको समिक्षा (✓×)	Harvesting rules and regulation developed स्रोत संकलनको पद्धती र नियमहरुको विकास (✓×)	No. of species identified for Subsistence use घरयासी प्रयोगका लागी पहिचान गरिएका प्रजातीको संख्या	Species for which detailed resources assessment and planning undertaken विस्तृत रुपमा स्रोत सर्भेक्षण तथा यवस्थापन योजना गरिएका NTFP प्रजातीको नाम	Name. of red listed species included for management* व्यवस्थापनका लागी तोकिएका खतराको सूचीमा सूचीकृत प्रजातीको नाम
		Before पहिले	After पछि	Before पहिले	After पछि									

Code of species: 1 =Jatamansi; 2=Morel; 3 =Kutki; 4 =Attish; 5 =Sugandhawal; 6 =Padamchal; 7 =Panchaule; 8 =Juniper berry; 9 =Sunpati; 10 =Silajit; 11 =Bajadi, 12 =Yarsagumba; 13 =Lokta; 14 =Bikh; 15 =Dhatalo; 16 =Satuwa; 17 =Timur; 18 =Bojho; 19 =Okhr; 20 =Rittha; 21 =Chiraito; 22 =Nigalo. *(add more if required)*

Level (स्तर): Grade 0 refers "no" to 4 refers "sufficient"

Format 1-B: Conservation Variables

CFUG Name Address सामुदायिक वनको नाम, ठेगाना	Controlled grazing system नियन्त्रित चरिचरण पद्धति		Fire control mechanism आगलागी नियन्त्रण संयन्त्र		Tending operations वन सर्म्वधन कार्य		Regeneration management पूनरोत्पादन व्यवस्थापन		Harvesting rules in practice स्रोत संकलनको पद्धती र नियमहरुको कार्यान्वयन	
	Level स्तर	Description विस्तृत जानकारी	Level स्तर	Description विस्तृत जानकारी	Level स्तर	Description विस्तृत जानकारी	Level स्तर	Description विस्तृत जानकारी	Level स्तर	

Format 1-C: Conservation Variables

CFUG Name Address सामूदायिक वनको नाम, ठेगाना	Immature harvesting अपरिपक्व स्रोत संकलन		Provision of monitoring policies /strategies in OP कार्ययोजनामा अनूगमनको निती–तौर/तरिका सम्वन्धि प्रावधान		Monitoring system and practices in place अनूगमनको निती–तौर/तरिका सम्वन्धि प्रावधानको अभ्यासहरु/कार्यान्वयनको अवस्था		Adaptive System in Practices		Change in resource use practices* स्रोत उपयोगीताको अभ्यासहरु/कार्यान्वयनको अवस्था	
	Level स्तर	Description विस्तृत जानकारी	Level स्तर	Description विस्तृत जानकारी	Level स्तर	Description विस्तृत जानकारी	Level स्तर	Description विस्तृत जानकारी	Level स्तर	Description विस्तृत जानकारी

Format 2: Livelihood and incomes Variables

CFUG Name Address सामूदायिक वनको नाम, ठेगाना	Legal access to forest products वन पैदावारहरुमा कानूनी पहूंच	Availability of fuel wood दाउराको उपलब्धता	Availability of fodder डालेघांसको उपलब्धता	Availability of timber काठको उपलब्धता	Number of participating HH in economic activities कूल घरधूरी मध्ये व्यवशायीक क्रियाकलापमा संलग्न घरधूरी संख्या		Increased number of participants per household प्रति घरधूरी व्यवशायीक क्रियाकलापमा संलग्न सहभागीको संख्या		Average incomes per HH (in NRs.) प्रति घरधूरी औसत आम्दानी (रु.)		FUG fund (2003) २०६० सम्म सा.व.को कोष (रु.)
					Before पहिले	After पछि	Before पहिले	After पछि	Before पहिले	After पछि	

Format 3-A: Social equity and governance Variables

CFUG Name Address सामूदायिक वनको नाम, ठेगाना	No. on FUG committee उपभोत्ता समितीमा संख्या													Access of FUG members to subsistence products आधारभुत वन पैदावारमा समूह सदस्यहरुको पहुँच									
	DAG दलित						Women महिला				Total जम्मा		Poor गरिब		Middle मध्यम		Rich धनि		DAG दलित		Women महिला	
	Before पहिले			After पछि			Before पहिले		After पछि		Before पहिले	After पछि										
	tal Household जम्मा घरधुरी	In committee समितीमा	In major 4 positions मूख्य ४ पदमा	Total Household जम्मा घरधुरी	In committee समितीमा	In major 4 positions मूख्य ४ पदमा	In committee समितीमा	In major 4 positions मूख्य ४ पदमा	In committee समितीमा	In major 4 positions मूख्य ४ पदमा			Level स्तर	Description विस्तृत जानकारी	Level स्तर	Description विस्तृत जानकारी	Level स्तर	Description विस्तृत जानकारी	Level स्तर	Description विस्तृत जानकारी	Level स्तर	Description विस्तृत जानकारी

Major 4 positions includes Chairperson, Vice-Chairperson, Secretary and Treasurer मूख्य ४ पद भन्नाले अध्यक्ष, उपाध्यक्ष, सचिव र कोषाध्यक्षलाई जनाउछ ।.

Format 3-B: Social equity and governance Variables

CFUG Name Address सामूदायिक वनको नाम, ठेगाना	Case of Benefit Distribution फाईदा वितरणका विवरण/घटनाहरु

Format 3-C: Social equity and governance Variables

CFUG Name Address सामूदायिक वनको नाम, ठेगाना	Case of Benefit Distribution फाईदा वितरणका विवरण/घटनाहरु

Level 0 (No system and practice) to Level 4 (adequate system developed and in practice)

Format 3-D: Social equity and governance Variables

सामूदायिक वनको नाम, ठेगाना	संस्थागत प्रणालीहरुको विवरण/घटनाहरु								Remarks कैफियत
	Account keeping लेखा		Decision making निर्णय प्रकीया		Fund management कोष परिचालन		Monitoring अनूगमन		
	Level स्तर	Description विस्तृत जानकारी	Level स्तर	Description विस्तृत जानकारी	Level स्तर	Description विस्तृत जानकारी	Level स्तर	Description विस्तृत जानकारी	

Annex 5. A checklist for collecting information from community-based forest enterprises

A. Outcomes

1. Enterprise profit (break even)
2. Number of local people earning at least Rs.1000 per year
3. Employment: full time male female total
4. Employment: part time male female total
5. Sourcing of raw materials
6. Forest management plan
7. Forest management practices
8. Monitoring system/practice
9. Adaptive management

B. Factors

1. Marketing outlets:
    - market demand,
    - marketing information,
    - marketing channels and
    - marketing infrastructure.
2. External inputs:
    - awareness raising,
    - technical assistance (resource management, enterprise development, technology, operation)
    - financial support
    - marketing support
3. Community characteristics:
    - Leadership quality,
    - Indigenous expertise,
    - local institutions,
    - entrepreneurship culture,
    - transaction costs and economies of scale
    - economic objectives of the entrepreneurs and opportunity costs,
4. Natural resource base:
    - Resource type,
    - condition and abundance of the resource,
    - property rights
5. Technology:
    - Degrees of technological sophistication,
    - Appropriateness of technology
    - assessment and selection of improved technologies technology built on traditional knowledge or expertise
    - maintenance
    - energy (source, consumption, costs)
6. Policy factors:
    - Raw material acquisition,
    - Registration,
    - Financing,
    - Marketing,

C. General Description

- General statement describing the area in which the enterprise exists.
- The product(s) sold, its traditional uses, the season when it's available, the activities needed for collecting the product.
- The source of the raw materials.
- The activities of the enterprise or of the enterprise male and female participants (collection, drying, grading, processing, packaging) and the roles of the enterprise to support these activities.

Annex 6. List of variables and indexes used in participatory action research

Code No.	Variable code	Variables
1	FUGNAME	CFUG Name
9	HHNOB	Total Number of Household - Before
10	HHNOA	Total Number of Household - After
11	CFAREAB	CF Area Before (ha.)
12	CFAREAA	CF Area After (ha.)
13	CFAREHHB	CFArea Per HH Before (ha.)
14	CFAREHHA	CFArea Per HH After (ha.)
15	AREHHCNG	Change in CF area/HH
17	DASSESS	Detail management-assessment (Y/N)
18	THRTAW	Community aware on Threats (Y/N)
19	THRTIDEN	Threat identification (Y/N)
20	THRTMITI	Threat migitation practices (Y/N)
21	THRTREV	Review of threat migitation practices (Y/N)
22	HARRUDV	Harvesting rules and regulation (Y/N)
23	GRAZING	Grazing Management (1 to 4 rating)
24	FIRE	Fire Control (1 to 4 rating)
25	TENDSILV	Tending and Silvicultural Operations (1 to 4 rating)
26	REGMGT	Regeneration Management (1 to 4 rating)
27	HARRUPRA	Harvesting Rules in Practice (1 to 4 rating)
28	IMMHARV	Immature Harvesting Control (1 to 4 rating)
29	MONPOL	Monitoring Policy (1 to 4 rating)
30	MONPRA	Monitoring Practices (1 to 4 rating)
31	ADPTPRA	Adaptive Management Practices (1 to 4 rating)
32	RESUSPRA	Resources Use Practices (1 to 4 rating)
33	LGACCESS	Legal Access Rating (1 to 4 rating)
34	FWOODAV	Availibility of Fuel Wood (1 to 4 rating)
35	FODDERAV	Availibility of Fodder (1 to 4 rating)
36	TIMBERAV	Availibility of Timber (1 to 4 rating)
38	ECOPTPGB	Percentage of Economic Participants Before
39	ECOPTPGA	Percentage of Economic Participants After
40	ECOPTNOB	Economic Participants Before
41	ECOPTNOA	Economic Participants After
42	TINCB	Total Income Before
43	TINCA	Total Income After
44	AINCHHB	Average HH Income Before
45	AINCHHA	Average HH Income After
46	CHANGINC	Change in income
47	PCHANGE	Percentage of change in Income
48	FUGFUN03	FUG Funds in 2003
49	DGTHHB	Total Number of Dalit HHs Before
50	DGFUCB	Dalits in FUGC Before
51	DGFUC4B	Dalits in Key Positions of FUGC Before
52	DGHHPGB	Percentage of Dalit HHs Before
53	DAGFUPGB	Percentage of Dalits In FUGC Before
57	DGFUCPG	Percentage of Dalits In FUGC After
58	DGHHPG	Percentage of Dalit HHs After
59	DGTHHA	Total Number of Dalit HHs After
60	DGFUCA	Dalits in FUGC After
61	DAGFUC4A	Dalits in Key Positions of FUGC After
62	WOFUCPGB	Women % in CFUGC in proportion to their pop. Before
63	WOMFUCB	Women in FUGC Before
64	WOMFUC4B	Women in Key Positions of FUGC Before
65	WOMFUCPG	Women % in CFUGC in proportion to their pop. After
68	WOMNFUC	Women in FUGC After
69	WOMFUC4A	Women in Key Positions of FUGC After
70	FUCNOB	Total Members in FUGC Before
71	FUCNOA	Total Members in FUGC After
73	ACCSUBPR	Access of Poor to Subsistence Products (1 to 4 rating)
74	ACCSUBMD	Access of Middle to Subsistence Products (1 to 4 rating)
75	ACCSUBRH	Access of Rich to Subsistence Products (1 to 4 rating)
76	ACCSUBDG	Access of Dalits to Subsistence Products (1 to 4 rating)

77	ACCSUBWM	Access of Women to Subsistence Products (1 to 4 rating)
79	INTSYAC	Accounting System (1 to 4 rating)
80	INTSYDM	Decision Making System (1 to 4 rating)
81	INTSYFM	Fund Mobilization System (1 to 4 rating)
82	INTSYMON	Monitoring System (1 to 4 rating)
83	CFARHCAT	CF Area Per HH (ha.)
84	NOSPSPDM	No of Specise in OP for detail management
85	NOSPSLIS	No of Specise listed in OP

Code No.	Index code	Indexes	Detail
2	ALTCAT	Altitudinal Category	1=around 2500m, 2=around 3000m and 3=around3500m
3	YEARCAT	Year of Start	1=<3year, 2=3 to 6 year, and 3=>6year in 2003
4	ECOCIDX	Economic Index	INCRT x 0.6 + SUBBEIDX x 0.4
5	INCRT	Income category (Rs.)	1=AINCHHA below 2000, 2=1=AINCHHA >= 2000 and <4000, 3=AINCHHA >= 4000 and <7500 and 4=AINCHHA>=7500
6	SUBBEIDX	Subsistence Benefit Index	Average of variables 37, 54 and 72
7	CONCIDX	Conservation Index	Average of variables 16-32
8	SOCCIDX	Social Index	Average of variables 36,48,57,63,66,69-72
16	CHANGERT	Rating of change in CF area/HH	1=AREAHHCNG<2, 2=AND(AREAHHCNG>=2 and AREAHHCNG<5, 3=AREAHHCNG>=5 and AREAHHCNG<10, 4=AREAHHCNG>=10
37	ECOPTRT	Economic Participation Rating After	1=ECOPTPGA<=25%, 2=ECOPTPGA>25% and ECOPTPGA<50%, 3=ECOPTPGA>50% and ECOPTPGA<75%, 4=ECOPTPGA>=75%
54	WDGFUCRT	Women and Dalits rep. in CFUGC in proportion to their pop. After	Average of variables 56 and 67
55	DGFUCRTB	Dalits rep. in CFUGC in proportion to their pop. Before	1=(DAGFUPGB/DGHHPGB)<40%, 2=(DAGFUPGB/DGHHPGB)>=40% and (DAGFUPGB/DGHHPGB)<80%, 3=(DAGFUPGB/DGHHPGB)>=80% and (DAGFUPGB/DGHHPGB)<120% and 4=(DAGFUPGB/DGHHPGB)>120%
56	DGFUCRT	Dalits rep. in CFUGC in proportion to their pop. After	1=(DGFUCPG/DGHHPG)<40%, 2=(DGFUCPG/DGHHPG)>=40% and (DGFUCPG/DGHHPG)<80%, 3=(DGFUCPG/DGHHPG)>=80% and (DGFUCPG/DGHHPG)<120% and 4=(DGFUCPG/DGHHPG)>120%
66	WOFUCRTB	Women in FUGC Before	1=WOFUCPGB<40%, 2=WOFUCPGB>=40% and WOFUCPGB<80%, 3=WOFUCPGB>=80% and WOFUCPGB<120% and 4=WOFUCPGB>120%
67	WOMFUCRT	Women in FUGC After	1=WOFUCPGA<40%, 2=WOFUCPGA>=40% and WOFUCPGA<80%, 3=WOFUCPGA>=80% and WOFUCPGA<120% and 4=WOFUCPGA>120%
72	SFPDGIDX	Index for Access of Poor, Dalit and women to Subsistence Products	Average of variables 73,76 and 77
78	INTSYIDX	Institutional System Index (1 to 4 rating)	Average of variables 79-82

SUMMARY

1. In developing countries, generally two approaches of biodiversity conservation are adopted. The traditional approach is to make protected areas, in which all kinds of regulatory measures are taken. The other approach emphasizes effective role of local communities in biodiversity conservation. This research, based on the second approach of conservation, focuses on biodiversity-linked enterprises that generate meaningful income for improving the livelihood of local communities. Apart from this, an analysis of potential of non-timber forest products (NTFPs) at country level was made.

2. In the study on enterprise-oriented community forest management (EOCFM), the major question addressed was whether it can improve the livelihood of local communities as well as biodiversity conservation. The factors required to achieve this goal were also analyzed.

3. Spread over an area of 147,181 km^2, Nepal is primarily a mountainous country with a wide ecological range from tropical to alpine. One of the global biodiversity hotspots is located in Nepal. Harboring about 7000 species of flowering plants, Nepal is exceptionally rich in biodiversity and NTFPs of commercial use (more than 160 species already in NTFPs trade). However, the anthropogenic pressure on rich biodiversity is high. To indicate the scale of NTFPs used following observations may be cited: according to an estimate 10-15 thousand tons of NTFPs are harvested from high mountain areas of Nepal alone; NTFPs worth US $8.6 million end-up in Indian market annually; the total sales is estimated to be US $26 million annually; in total about 1000 species are used economically.

4. In spite of enormous biological wealth, Nepal is one of the poorest countries (per capita GDP estimated at US $269). Agriculture is the

mainstay of the economy providing livelihood for 80% of the population and accounting for 50% of national GDP. However, in mountains agriculture accounts for less than 10% of geographical area, it is primarily rain-fed and is able to meet foodgrain requirements of local people for less than 6 months. People derive fodder, firewood, and litter (for maintaining cropfield soil fertility) from the forest.

5. The country level analysis of NTFPs in this work was primarily based on secondary sources, while research on EOCFM was based on sampling of 37 CFUGs of districts, Humla, Jumla, Dolpa, Darchula, Bajhang and Dolakha. These high mountain districts are characterized by inaccessibility, remoteness, poverty of people, but rich biodiversity of forests and meadows. Identification of specific issues and their relationship in the 37 CFUGs were made following participatory action research. The major variables studied were biodiversity (amount, distribution of species populations, conservation measures, threats and ecosystem health), enterprises (types, distribution, technology, sales, income, employment, etc.), communities (institutional capabilities, technological knowledge, interest and dependency), and benefit sharing and community participation in biodiversity management. Efforts were made to examine the various aspects of interplays between biodiversity, enterprise and community, the three components which constitute the EOCFM system.

6. Vegetation of the area where the study CFUGs occurred consisted of both forests and meadows. The major forest species included *Quercus semecarpifolia* (an evergreen oak), *Rhododendron spp, Abies spectabilis* (silver fir), *Pinus wallichiana* (blue pine), *Taxus spp, Accer spp* (maples), *Picea smithiana* (spruce), *Betula utilis* (birch), and *Juniperus spp* (junipers). The major NTFP species in the region were *Daphne spp* (lokta), *Nardostachys grandiflora* (jatamansi), *Neopicrorhiza schrophulariflora* (kutki), *Valeriana jatamansi* (sugandhwal), *Swertia chirayita* (chiraito), *Rhododendron anthopogan* (sunpati), *Morchella spp* (morels), *Podophyllum hexandrum* (laghupatra), *Cordyceps sinensis* (yarshagumba), *Berberis aristata* (chutro), and *Dactylorhiza hatagirea* (panchaunle).

7. The main proximate threats to biodiversity are man-made fires, unmanaged harvesting, overgrazing, and conversation of forest into cropland. Though poaching of wild animal is common, people think that it is manageable. However, the underlying causes of threats

include acute poverty, immediate cash need and lack of alternative income generating opportunities, uncertainly about property rights, lack of economic incentives for conservation, and lack of knowledge and training in management. Apart from these, external market demands often become a major threat in certain areas.

8. The NTFPs trade is based on a long marketing chain, starting from local harvesters to retailers both inside and outside the country. The local harvesters are primarily the village people who have limited knowledge of and exposure to marketing and entrepreneurship. They harvest NTFPs from wild, and clean, dry, store and transport them (business ranges between Rs. 10,000 and 50,000). The other groups in market chain are village traders, who play an important role in distribution of NTFPs to market places; local processors, who process NTFPs employing simple techniques; roadhead/airport traders, who are relatively wealthy rural people; regional traders, who export but remain well connected with rural trade system; big processors and manufacturers, which include national level companies with a legal backing; and retailers, who make heterogeneous group ranging from small shopkeepers exclusively dealing in herbal medicines or spices to large business houses handling finished goods in large cities. The scale of business increases along with this chain. For example, village traders do business of Rs. 50,000 to Rs. 100,000, roadhead traders up to Rs. 500,000, and regional traders upto Rs. 20 million. Though village collectors get only about their labor cost or bit more, this seasonal employment generates about 30-50% of their income.

9. In recent years government has taken initiatives to involve poor communities in resource management. Initiated in 1978, community forest user groups (CFUGs) have become a major institution in participatory natural resource management. Currently, there are more than 13,000 CFUGs, involving nearly one-third of the total population and managing about one-fourth of the total forest area of the country. A CFUG represents a group of people who use a particular forest land. It may consist of all villagers or part of them or also some individuals from other villages. A CFUG is legally recognized autonomous entities with ongoing succession. Its governance is defined by its constitution registered in District Forest Office (DFO), and the provisions for management and use of forests are specified in community forest management operational plan. To some extent, the CFUGs have freedom to modify their constitution, therefore constitutions across CFUGs may differ in certain details.

10. In our analysis of the study of the 37 CFUGs of 6 mountain areas the following criteria were used to examine whether EOCFM is able to contribute to both livelihood and conservation: economic – increase in cash income to households, subsistence benefits, such as availability of fodder and firewood, and the amount of group fund generated; social – involvement of dalits and women, participation of household in economic activities, access of dalits, women and other poor people to forest resources, group fund mobilization and capacity building; conservation – increase in the area of forests and meadows under CFUG management, quality of management plan, improvement in harvesting practices, assistance to regeneration, and threat mitigation. For each of the criteria used, ratings were given on performance. For each of the components, economic, social and conservation, composite indexes were developed. This exercise was done for the study CFUGs, and correlations in different parameters were examined. Some of the major findings of this analysis are given below.

11. Interventions related to EOCFM brought significant increases in the participation of households in forest enterprise activities (from 1733 to 3254 households) and their income (on average by about Rs. 4000 per household). The two parameters showed significant positive correlation ($r = 0.394$, $p<0.05$), indicating that the CFUGs with higher income also had higher household participation. Some of the factors that contributed to increase in household income were: 1) increased availability of NTFPs with the improvement of forest management, 2) increased selling prices of NTFPs with improved marketing information, and 3) use of processing which added value to NTFPs. The price of jatamansi rose from Rs. 15 to Rs. 45, as an example.

12. Since the management also improved the subsistence benefits, there was a positive correlation between increase in cash income and subsistence benefits across the CFUGs.

13. The above improvements were achieved through increased interest of people in conservation. With the realization of the cash value of NTFPs, people were observed to apply improved harvesting practices and impose regulations on themselves. In part, these changes were possible also because of the increased feeling of ownership of both resources and enterprises.

14. The enterprise-oriented CFUGs took care to provide employment to dalits, women and other disadvantaged people. The CFUGs provided cash and access to forest resources to dalits and other poor people for enterprise activities and raised group funds. Furthermore, the representation of women and dalits increased after the EOCFM interventions.

15. On the conservation front, the EOCFM brought about the following improvements: increased use of thinned and pruned branches for firewood to reduce whole tree cutting; initiation of nurseries and plantations; application of less wasteful methods while collecting lichens; reduced burning in meadows to save NTFP species, such as jatamansi; people undertook steps to secure natural regeneration; adoption of rotational/block-wise harvesting; employment of watchers; and introduction of monitoring of harvesting impacts. Though many of these measures are still in initial stage, it is important that conservation has been integrated in EOCFM.

16. This study clearly showed that it is possible to create synergy between improvement in livelihood and conservation ($r = 0.48$ between indexes of economic performance and conservation performance; $p< 0.01$). We suggest that some economic incentives or amelioration of economic hardship is necessary to make people suffering from acute poverty interested in conservation. EOCF empowers local people to choose an action that they think will be more rewarding in the long-run. The study provides support to this on the basis of a fairly large number of sample, studied over an extended period. However, even the period of 4 to 8 years, as in this study, is not enough to transform the whole society in the direction of conservation, as conservation requires people to be educated and made aware of many related aspects demanding greater manpower, funding and other efforts. Several facilitating steps may be required in this context: necessary policy changes to ensure certainty with regard to land tenure and resource use; technical assistance in enterprise development and management; capacity building in processing and marketing of NTFPs; improved knowledge about the ecology and the sustainable use of the species.

INDEX